# NEW STRATEGIES IN COLLEGE TEACHING

## Succeeding in Today's Academic World

**ALLYN AND BACON**

Boston ■ London ■ Toronto ■ Sydney ■ Tokyo ■ Singapore

**Executive Editor and Publisher:** *Stephen D. Dragin*
**Editorial Assistant:** *Barbara Strickland*
**Marketing Manager:** *Kathleen Morgan*
**Manufacturing Buyer:** *Chris Marson*
**Cover Administrator:** *Kristina Mose-Libon*
**Electronic Composition:** *Omegatype Typography, Inc.*

Internet: www.ablongman.com

Between the time Website information is gathered and published, some sites may have closed. Also, the transcription of URLs can result in typographical errors. The publisher would appreciate notification where these occur so that they may be corrected in subsequent editions.

**ISBN: 0-205-35024-0**

Printed in the United States of America

10  9  8  7  6  5  4  3  2  1     06  05  04  03  02  01

# CONTENTS

132934

# INTRODUCTION

Most of us can remember a time when higher education was seemingly insulated from the pressures of our larger society. Professors taught their course loads during daytime hours, and their institutions were governed through academic freedom and collegial decision-making exclusively. Undergraduates completed their degrees in four years by attending full time and invested evening hours in study and social pursuits that complemented the "college experience." In recent years however, a number of significant external forces have increasingly intruded into colleges and universities, significantly impacting the way higher education is perceived and delivered, and the criteria upon which decisions are made.

With the passage of a series of legislative acts, the student population began to change dramatically. Beyond ethnicity and economic class, the average age of students, the life experiences they brought to college, and learning styles fostered in a broader environment began to impact the culture of most of our institutions. A growing number of working students entered colleges and universities, requiring class scheduling more convenient to their availability and additional academic support services. The growing consumer mindset within society took root in higher education, resulting in ubiquitous adoptions of student ratings systems—now accessible online—and subsequent demands from students, parents, and trustees to enhance the overall quality of instruction. As most other products and services became available 24 hours a day, demand for instruction that could be delivered to time- and place-bound students increased, resulting in the rapid growth of distance education.

The business community, increasingly mindful of the importance of a more educated workforce, became more active in the environment of higher education. Willing to invest vast resources, employers expected learning outcomes that would directly benefit their organizational success and scheduling of courses more convenient to, or even within, their facilities. Having embraced technology to increase efficiency of their operations, the business community expected colleges and universities to do the same, and to provide up-to-date training on the use of these tools for their employee/students.

Most recently, through the lobbying of economic development entities, taxpayer groups and others, legislatures have mandated increased accountability for student outcomes, and linked them to institutional funding levels. "Institutional effectiveness" (typically defined as improved student recruitment, retention, program/degree completion, and placement of graduates) has become the mantra of institutional administrators in a growing number of states, as well as of national political leaders. This movement will no doubt continue to grow in today's political environment, increasing pressure for improved teaching practices and measurable learning outcomes.

The changing student population, the increased significance of consumerism within higher education, the infusion of technology into today's society, and calls for increased accountability for learning outcomes have changed higher education and the teaching and learning process forever. While some traditionalists will resist this emerging fact of life and will wait as long as possible before reacting, others will see it as an opportunity to improve the overall quality of higher education and to bring promise to the lives of increasingly empowered students around the globe.

*New Strategies in College Teaching* is designed to increase awareness of the impact of these factors in today's teaching and learning environment, while demonstrating Allyn and Bacon's acumen for providing solutions. By providing selected chapters from several of our leading current titles, it addresses the ramifications of the issues addressed above and provides grounded insights and strategies that successful professors at all levels of higher education are employing. Since the chapters included were written within their own specialized context, each will be introduced briefly to enhance linkage with the larger scope of this book.

For their help in developing *New Strategies in College Teaching,* we want to thank each of the authors whose work is included. Their insights and commitment to the professional development of their colleagues have been consistently exemplary. We hope *New Strategies in College Teaching* proves to be a valuable resource in your professional library and that it fosters your interest in the Allyn and Bacon titles whose chapters are included.

Richard E. Lyons

# CHAPTER 1

# TODAY'S UNDERGRADUATE STUDENTS

Although grounded in their varied disciplines, the most successful of today's college and university professors focus their strategies on the student first. The most effective course plans are predicated upon where their students actually are academically, experientially, and psychologically—then proceed to build a syllabus and course strategy upon those factors. Through that process, increasingly informed students will seek out professors known to best meet their needs, will be retained in courses in which their expectations are fulfilled, and will be more likely to complete their entire degree program.

While Richard Lyons, Marcella Kysilka and George Pawlas researched and wrote this first chapter for the perspective of part-time instructors, its insights and suggestions are valid for all professors. It emphasizes more sensitized attention to the increasing diversity of students, providing richer instruction that addresses multiple learning styles, and the anticipation of potentially significant issues that professors will increasingly face as current trends evolve.

# TODAY'S UNDERGRADUATE STUDENTS

Chapter 4 from *Adjunct Professor's Guide to Success*
Richard E. Lyons, Marcella L. Kysilka, & George E. Pawlas
Allyn & Bacon, © 1999

## FOCUS QUESTIONS

- What are the significant demographic changes occurring among college students?
- How have perceptions toward attending college changed in the last generation?
- How should instructors structure their teaching to maximize results?

New adjunct professors, most of whom attended college full-time directly after completing high school with cohorts largely similar to themselves, are often surprised when they enter the classroom of their first assignment. Over the past twenty-five years or so, the undergraduate student populations of most colleges and universities have become increasingly diverse—in age, gender, ethnicity, working status, and other significant factors. Before a new faculty member can become successful, this new student population must be significantly understood, not only in the unique characteristics engendered by its demographic makeup, but in terms of the societal conditioning to which it has been exposed. This chapter will help you understand the dimensions of the increased diversity of undergraduate students, but more than that, build your understanding of ways in which students vary in attitudes toward school and learning styles.

## THE BIG PICTURE

According to data provided by the National Center for Educational Statistics, total enrollment in all forms of higher education increased 66% between 1970 and 1994. Much of this increase was among part-time students, who now comprise over 70% of total college enrollment. In most teaching assignments, adjunct professors will deal overwhelmingly, if not exclusively, with

2

part-time students. Between 1984 and 1994, the number of men enrolled increased 9%, while female enrollment increased 24%. Today, female undergraduate students outnumber males, and among part-time students, women students exceed men by 50%.

The number of "nontraditional" students, typically defined as 25 years of age or older, has been growing more rapidly than the number of younger students. Between 1980 and 1990, enrollment among younger (or "traditional-age") students increased 3%, while enrollment among nontraditional age students grew 34%. Enrollment increases, especially among older students, have been fueled by the growth of community colleges and extension programs by four-year institutions, as well as by changes in the economy that demand higher levels of academic skills from workers at all levels. Though there is a great deal of common ground between students of any age, it is very useful for the new adjunct professor to understand some of the key differences between younger and older students.

## TRADITIONAL STUDENTS

Students under 25 years of age comprise about 75% of the full-time undergraduate students in American college and universities, but considerably less than 50% of part-time students. Increasing numbers of traditional-age students are staying close to home to attend college while working full-time or in several part-time positions. Many have been at least partially supporting themselves for several years, often while accumulating significant debt through tuition costs, which have risen faster than the inflation rate, and/or the purchase of what were once considered luxury possessions for students.

Much more than in previous generations, these students are the product of dysfunctional families. Many younger students have parents who have divorced one or more times, sometimes remarrying other divorcees with children to form "blended families." Other students' parents have never been married. Such situations have contributed to the stifling of psychological and academic development during some students' most formative years, residually affecting their college-age performance. These students have often "discovered" that commitment to others hurts as much as it heals.

The parents of today's younger college students were more likely to have been employed under the unsettling circumstances of "downsizing" and corporate mergers and to have changed jobs and residences. As a result, their now college-age children have changed elementary and secondary schools far more often than was the custom only a few decades ago. Such students often exhibit socialization problems throughout their college years, isolating themselves, becoming medically depressed, and sometimes turning to unhealthy lifestyles. Many traditional-age students have been "latch-key kids," entertained too much by television programs and videos with violent and otherwise negative themes. Parents, exhausted when they arrived home after working long hours and sometimes an extended commute, have failed to read to them or to provide coaching for homework assignments during students' early years.

More likely to have worked part-time while in high school—often well past what most adults would consider reasonable hours—today's traditional-age college students have not been as focused on school success as those of two decades ago. Because of their employment, younger students are less likely to have played organized sports or to have been involved in other constructive school activities; consequently they may not have had the opportunity to learn the skills of cooperation and compromise. Barely old enough to drive an automobile, many have maintained their own households, frequently cohabitating with equally challenged peers. They have engaged in all sorts of other "adult" activities for which they were insufficiently prepared and have developed extensive coping mechanisms for dealing with the obstacles in their lives. Without structure and consistently communicated standards, many have not developed the self-discipline (some might call it "responsibility") that we typically associate with success in higher education.

From another perspective, traditional-age students have grown up in a society largely influenced by consumerism, materialism, increased demands for individual rights, and decreased time horizons for nearly everything. One fast-food chain has promised to deliver their products "your way"—a theme replicated in thousands of other advertising messages that have inundated young college students' minds. Traditional-age students have been conditioned by the aftermath of Watergate, Three Mile Island, "insider-trading," and other high-profile ethical scandals, contributing to a mindset of cynicism and lack of respect for all authority figures—including college professors. Speaking spontaneously and angrily of alleged misdeeds by others and lodging complaints—even lawsuits—have become common behaviors. Students of this generation are quick to proclaim their "rights." Many of today's students perceive professors as service providers, class attendance as a matter of individual choice, and grades as "pay" to which they are entitled for meeting standards they perceive as reasonable.

A litany of reasons, including (but certainly not limited to) depersonalized schools, public school teacher turnover, and overemphasis on standardized tests, have contributed to a less than effective primary and/or secondary education for many students. A large number begin college requiring remediation in reading, writing, and mathematics skills. Conditioned by their "surfing" through MTV and dozens of other cable channels, violent computer games, instantaneous access to the entire world through the Internet, and other widespread technology, traditional-age students often exhibit extremely short attention spans and an affinity for color and rapid movement—qualities difficult to recreate in many traditional classrooms. These students have heard themselves identified as members of "Generation X" ("Generation Y" or the

"Baby Boomlet" is just over the horizon) and perceive an outside world that dislikes and—perhaps even worse—is unwilling to invest the time to understand them. This self-image often drives a self-fulfilling prophecy of boredom, negativity, and lowered academic expectations that exhibits itself in the classroom.

Many college professors who remember a time when students were perceived as more "responsible" and "appreciative" seem to expect today's students to miraculously act the same way, and become frustrated when it doesn't happen. Investing quality effort only with students who display more conservative, traditional values is not a prescription for achieving the degree of learning success that instructional leaders expect. All educators have a responsibility to all students and to the profession to accept all students "where they are," and to guide them toward an outcome that our highest standards indicate are appropriate. In his blockbuster book *The Seven Habits of Highly Effective People*, Steven Covey, himself a professor, encourages us to "Seek first to understand, then to be understood"—a requirement for achieving success with today's students, especially the traditional-age.

## NONTRADITIONAL STUDENTS

"Nontraditional" students have seen their ranks grow dramatically in recent years, especially in the evening and weekend classes that adjunct professors are most likely to teach. Many of these students have lost their jobs to "the new economy," been displaced by technology, and/or been unable to sustain an income that would enable them to provide adequately for their families. Although a disproportionate number of evening students are single women, many are single men, often also with children. They often lack the support from family and long-time friends, who now live far away. Even though their employers may support their education financially, nontraditional students feel resented by their co-workers when leaving work early, or arriving late, to pursue their college education.

Many older students are attending college after a long layoff, frequently doubting their ability to succeed. The other time-consuming challenges in their lives—children and other family responsibilities, caring for aging parents, work, civic, and religious responsibilities—often prevent adequate preparation for class or contribute to frequent absences. Nontraditional students commonly display test anxiety, a lack of confidence in their writing and mathematics skills, and hesitance in using computers and other technology.

On the "up side," many nontraditional students make it all work somehow. Those who overcome the initial obstacles of attending college and achieve a measure of success frequently become quite self-directed—thirsty for the knowledge they didn't get when they "should have." They are motivated first to "pass," then to achieve high grades. Adult learners often become "overachievers" who will rewrite entire papers to gain an extra point or two. While traditional-age students demand their "right," many older students won't ask for the smallest extra consideration, e.g., to turn a project in a few days late.

As their success as students builds, older students often become highly motivated to serve as a role model for their children in school. They often proudly speak of posting their successful exams and assignments on the family refrigerator! While "Gen X'ers" often mask their disappointments behind a blank countenance, the devastation older students perceive from failure is often painfully displayed on their faces and heard in their voices. Older students are far more likely to stay after class to share their frustrations with an empathetic instructor or to discuss stimulating concepts from the course material. In the process, it is not uncommon for emotional reliances, even "crushes," to develop, which require careful attention to prevent possible hurtful ramifications.

Most older students learn best by doing, by applying the theory of textbooks to the rich set of experiences they have accumulated over the years and to the reality of tomorrow at work and home. They have a great deal they want to share, and in an informal environment they will do so, in the process making connections for themselves with the learning goals of the course. They tend to be problem-centered, rather than content-centered, and will often lose focus (and patience) with an instructor who is intent on "covering the material." Adult learners, recalling the classrooms of their childhood, tend to respond most effectively when the classroom environment is organized and relatively quiet and when they perceive they have ready access to the instructor, even though they might not frequently take advantage of it.

In recent years, much has been written and spoken of a "generational gulf"—an inability or unwillingness of those in one generation to understand, value, and adapt to the significant differences that shape the way those of markedly different ages perceive and react to the world. An ineffective professor accepts the gulf as a "given," contributing to the development of a fragmented classroom environment in which individuals work at cross purposes. The enlightened professor proactively manages the classroom so that, regardless of the course or discipline, diverse students learn to work cooperatively, in the process creating a synergy that intensifies the rewards both students and the professor receive from the class experience.

## EMERGING INFLUENCES

Besides the generation to which students belong, other factors significantly impact their perceptions of college and their learning styles. Today, a fourth of all undergraduate students are members of minority groups—doubling their enrollment in the last twenty years. While enrollment growth among African Americans has exceeded that of white students, the sharpest percentage growth in minority enrollment in recent years has occurred among Asian Americans, Hispanics, and Native Americans. In many metropolitan colleges and universities, recent immigrants represent an especially significant student population. Obviously, ethnicity, language, religion, culture, and sexual orientation are each significant issues to which an adjunct professor must be sensitive, for each shapes the paradigm toward learning that each student brings to the classroom. The successful professor sees these differences as an opportunity rather than a threat to learning.

Seek continuously to understand more fully the perspectives of the types of students represented in your classroom through reading and discussions with colleagues, but more interestingly by listening intently and nonjudgmentally to individual students themselves. Identify well in advance the differences among students in your classroom and manage the ramifications. Incorporate your growing knowledge base into the richer environment that is created in your classroom when diverse perspectives are expressed. Although your job is identified as teaching a particular course, you could more appropriately define your role as creating an environment and providing appropriate stimuli for students to master a particular set of concepts, skills or attitudes. As stated before, our long-term goal is to equip students to become their own lifelong teachers.

In the past several years, a steadily increasing number of students with physical and mental challenges have begun to pursue an undergraduate education. Often, additional resources are made available so that visually disabled students can enroll in a computer science class, for example, or hearing disabled students can complete courses that largely employ a lecture method of instruction. As have other "minority groups," students with disabilities (and their families) have become politically active and assertive in recent years, expecting the educational community to more fully address their specific needs. You are legally and professionally mandated to accommodate such reasonable requests.

While it is important that you identify and impose high standards for all students in your class, it is also critical that you seek to understand the backgrounds of all your students and adopt a degree of flexibility in your interactions with them. The willingness to first understand the special conditions that influence your students enables you to treat each as an individual. Research of recent years tells us that there is not a single form of "intelligence."

When only the traditional definition of "intelligence" is accepted, a competitive classroom culture is fostered which ensures that some students will fail. In recent years, the concept of "multiple intelligences" has emerged to create a contrasting paradigm. Seeking to broaden the scope of human potential beyond the traditional IQ score, Howard Gardner developed the best-known theory of multiple intelligences. He challenged the validity of determining people's intelligence by taking them out of their natural learning environment and asking them to complete isolated tasks they have never done before. Gardner said intelligence has more to do with solving problems and creating products in a context-rich environment. His research yielded seven comprehensive categories of "intelligences":

- Linguistic intelligence—the capacity to use words effectively
- Logical-mathematical intelligence—the capacity to employ numbers effectively and to reason
- Spatial intelligence—the ability to visualize the visual-spatial world accurately
- Bodily-kinesthetic intelligence—expertise in using the entire body to express ideas and feelings
- Musical intelligence—the capacity to perceive, discriminate, transform and express musical forms effectively
- Interpersonal intelligence—the ability to perceive and make distinctions in the moods, motivations, and feelings of other people
- Intrapersonal intelligence—self-knowledge and the ability to act adaptively on the basis of that knowledge

In the traditional paradigm, students were either intelligent or they weren't. In Gardner's paradigm, students have more or less of a wide variety of intelligences. Our intention is not to introduce you to a complex concept in a "quick and dirty" way, as much as it is to sensitize you to the fact that each student has a gift that is worthy of nurturing. In the process of helping each student in your class develop to his or her fullest potential, not by imposing a preconceived limitation but by proactively soliciting students' individual input into learning decisions impacting them, your part-time job and heightened role in the human development process will become far more rewarding.

## DEALING POSITIVELY WITH COMMON PROBLEM SITUATIONS

Regardless of their demographics, consistently encourage, in a positive and nonjudgmental manner, self-direction and responsibility in all students. In recent years, our society seems to have fostered in both overt and tacit ways a sense of victimization among those who face challenges. Many students have been affected and will judge your standards and procedures accordingly. Be intellectually prepared and emotionally willing to share quietly why it is in your students' best long-term interest to rise to your high expectation of quality in their assignments and examinations. While they will often dispute your words initially, most will finish the term thanking you for pushing them to turn out their best work.

Some students, especially those with low self-esteem or especially difficult histories, will challenge your best-intended words as discriminatory. At such times, you will be buoyed by following the suggestions in Chapter 5 for proactively building your understanding of your students early in the course. When preparing each class meeting, it is critical that you think through your words prior to addressing topics that have a gender, racial, political, or related sensitivity, so that if challenged, you can accurately share exactly what was said.

Given the nature of your students' lifestyles, you can assume some common problems will inevitably affect your classroom: tardiness, absence, being ill-prepared for some examinations, occasional lack of focus, and perhaps others. Rather than becoming upset and taking punitive action, we suggest you plan for the situations and build a solution into your design of the course. For example, since students will occasionally be late from work or family obligations, we suggest you minimize the impact of their tardy entry into your classroom by reserving a section of the room for late-arrivers. Should you find, several weeks into the course, that the overwhelming majority of the class is a few minutes late, you might delay the beginning of the class ten minutes and reduce the length of your break by a commensurate amount of time. Be creative, yet conservative, and seek feedback from your discipline leader in advance whenever you have questions.

We have always believed that if an effective learning environment were established in each classroom, absences and other student motivation problems would largely take care of themselves. While there will always be a minority whose behavior is inconsistent with your acceptable standards, it is critical not to punish the entire group of students for the actions of the few. The key is timely, unemotional, and frank confrontation of the problem. Ignoring the problem, hoping it will "fix itself," will (as in most other arenas of life) lead to unsatisfactory results. In Chapter 7 we highlight a technique called "transactional analysis" that many college professors have employed to promote positive results in such situations. Beginning with the first class meeting, it is critical to demonstrate structure, establish your standards, reinforce them through consistent behavior, and take action promptly when warranted.

## LEARNING STYLES

In recent years, mountains of data have been gathered to help educators more conclusively understand how students learn. Presenting a great deal of that information at this stage in your development as an instructor would probably be counterproductive, but a sample might provide insight to aid you in your initial teaching assignment.

One of the most interesting efforts, commonly referred to as "brain-based" research, seeks to understand learning from the perspective of where and how certain types of information are processed. It suggests there are two major types of learners—those in whom the "right brain" is dominant, and those with a dominant "left brain." Right-brain learners tend to be intuitive, imaginative, and impulsive; they prefer to start with a broad idea and then pursue supporting information. They learn best by seeing and doing in an informal, busy, and somewhat unstructured environment. On the other hand, left-brain learners tend to be analytical, rational, and objective; they prefer putting together many facts to arrive at a general understanding.

Right-brain learners prefer group discussion, simulations, panels, and other activity-based learning, whereas left-brain learners prefer traditional lectures, demonstrations, and assigned readings. Although there are many exceptions, females tend to be right-brain dominant, while males tend to be left-brain dominant. The traditional lecture/demonstration approach is typically more effective with male learners rather than female students. At the same time, research indicates females are more effective in utilizing left-brain approaches than men are in utilizing right-brain approaches, and that females are more successful in transitioning from left-brain to right-brain approaches, and vice versa, than males are.

Another view of learning styles categorizes learners by the types of activities from which they derive the greatest payoff. It yields "tactile learners," who respond to physical objects that can be handled while studied; "visual learners," who facilitate their learning through use of charts, maps, and graphs; "auditory learners," who respond more effectively to the spoken rather than the written word, and others.

In this and other discussions related to teaching styles, the enlightened instructor probably will ask which of two major strategies is most effective. That is, should the professor initially adapt to the preferred learning styles of students or expect students to first adapt to his or her preferred methods? It is a highly complex issue with no instant answers. Each situation requires some study and individualized decisions to arrive at the "best" approach. Some professors can flex themselves quite effectively to the learning styles of students, while others would lose so much confidence in themselves in trying to do so that they might become totally ineffective in the classroom.

Having said all of this, remember that each student in front of you is in many ways unique. While it is useful to make yourself aware of the wide variety of issues impacting students today, there is risk in ever assuming you have heard or seen enough. Get to know each one of your students as well as you can, first by speaking with each one in the initial class, then asking each to complete the "Student Profile" form, located in Appendix 6-1. Later, build an ongoing dialogue with diverse students that will markedly increase your insights and create an accessibility to you in the students' minds that will markedly improve their motivation, attention levels, and understanding of your perspective. One of the greatest rewards of teaching is allowing yourself to be sufficiently vulnerable that you empower students to share more of themselves with you and their peers than might at times be comfortable. It is critical that you regularly assess your values and predispositions, talk with veteran instructors from whose experiences you can learn, and reflect upon your teaching experiences.

## WHAT STUDENTS WANT FROM COLLEGE INSTRUCTORS

While each student subgroup has particular characteristics that affect the dynamics of a college learning environment, students consistently need the following from their college instructors:

- Expectations of student performance that are reasonable in quantity and quality and are consistently communicated
- Sensitivity to the diverse demands on students and reasonable flexibility in accommodating them
- Effective use of class time
- A classroom environment that values students' input and protects their dignity
- A classroom demeanor that includes humor and spontaneity
- Examinations that address issues properly covered in class, are appropriate to the level of the majority of students in the class, are punctually scored and returned, and are used fairly to determine final class grades
- Consistently positive treatment of individual students, including a willingness to spend extra time before or after class meetings to provide additional support

While these needs may represent a marked shift from the college environment of several decades ago, they approximate those which most contemporary employees have of their employers, taxpayers have of government, or customers have of businesses they frequent. While many of the trappings of higher education will no doubt remain, this new paradigm of "colleges and universities as service providers to consumer-oriented students" is now firmly entrenched. The successful adjunct professor will do well to embrace it.

## THROUGH THE ADJUNCTS' EYES

### MARGARET:

As I prepare myself to teach, I've reflected back on my past few years of working and some of the values and habits of the younger employees. I recall sensing a reduced loyalty to the company, a reduced attention span, an unwillingness to come in a little early or stay a little late to complete a big assignment, and an inability or unwillingness to invest time in building relationships with their co-workers. Since those employees and many of my students will be in the same generation, I expect to see some of the same. There are reasons I don't fully understand that explain why today's young people tend to be this way. I really need to understand rather than judge this behavior, or my time in the classroom will become misery.

**KAREN:**

Mr. Jackson and I were talking yesterday about changes he has seen among students in recent years. There are many more "nontraditional" students who are often reluctant to objectively evaluate their long-held beliefs. Since I will be focusing on political and legal issues which have been questioned extensively through some high-profile court cases of the last few years, and because I lack the age and perceived wisdom of Mr. Jackson, it may be especially challenging for me to get my students to look at issues analytically. While I'll probably be a little more understanding than Mr. Jackson with younger students, I am concerned that I will lack patience for those who come to class late or want extra consideration because of work or family demands. Getting through law school and establishing a career took a lot of focus and commitment on my part. Maybe it's as important for me to teach such values to students as it is to teach about the political system.

**JUAN:**

As a teaching assistant at the university, I seldom have a student question much of anything I say in a significant way. Oh, they'll challenge me on due dates for assignments and things like that, but those are rather easy to deal with by focusing on the course syllabus which the professor gave them. In the class I will teach for the community college at night, many of the older students will be much more willing and able to freely discuss things from a set of deeply-held values. Many have worked in some very responsible jobs, have served in the military, and had other significant life experiences. Baby Boomers tend to value genuineness and relevance, so I need to be sure to provide that. One of the other teaching assistants at the university who taught at the community college told me about being "eaten alive" one night by an older student who had read and experienced some things related to a topic for which my friend had not prepared very well. I realize things will not turn out very well for me unless I am able to establish my credibility to teach the course material early in the term.

Most community colleges students are somewhat older, and the percentage who are female and minority is typically higher than in universities. Some are "late bloomers" who, though bright, did not apply themselves well in high school. Others have been "re-engineered" out of their jobs and require more sophisticated academic skills. It apparently won't be uncommon for me to have students in my class who are older than I am! Since many have been out of school for a period of time, "nontraditional" students often lack confidence in their academic ability and need encouragement and information about tutoring resources. Nearly all community college students work full-time or close to it and have limited time to do reading and homework. Therefore, my assignments need to be perceived as relevant and practical so that students will be able and willing to complete them. Community college students are commuters, which requires me to be more sensitive to issues like childcare, family finances, and transportation problems. This will be very different from teaching at the university, where most students live on or near campus and have their tuition and other expenses paid by parents.

## TIPS FOR THRIVING

While we typically think in terms of teaching accounting, world religions, or another "course," or of teaching "night students," athletes, or some other "group," those adjunct professors who derive the greatest reward from their part-time teaching careers have adopted a different paradigm. They think in terms of the rich mosaic of individuals in their classrooms—each with a unique background of academic, occupational, family, social, economic, military, recreational, and other categories of experiences. Such teachers are energized by students who "don't get it," rather than judgmental of their shortcomings. These professors view differences of opinions as adding richness to the classroom, rather than challenging their authority. They view themselves as "facilitators of learning," rather than "sages on stage." Finally, they realize that, more than anything, their students thrive on feedback that is FAST—frequent, accurate, specific, and timely.

## REVIEW OF KEY POINTS

- Today's college and university students are far more likely to be older and part-time than those of previous times.

- For very understandable reasons, many traditional-age college students lack self-discipline and academic foundation.
- Older students typically have many lifestyle challenges to overcome in order to attend college.
- Once oriented to college and with some measure of success behind them, adult learners are typically highly motivated to succeed.
- Common student success problems should be anticipated prior to the class, with solutions designed into the course.

## SUGGESTED READINGS

Coulter, M. W. (1993, January–March). Modern teachers and postmodern students. *Community College Journal of Research and Practice, 17*(1), 51–58.

Howe, N., & Strauss, B. (1993). *13th gen: Abort, retry, ignore, fail?* New York: Vintage Books.

Knowles, M. S. (1980). *The modern practice of adult education: From pedagogy to andragogy.* Chicago: Follett.

Knowles, M. S. (1989). *The making of an adult educator.* San Francisco: Jossey-Bass.

Sheehy, G. (1995). *New passages.* New York: Random House.

Upcraft, M. S. (1996). Teaching and today's college student. In R. J. Menges & M. Weimer (Eds.), *Teaching on solid ground: Using scholarship to improve practice* (pp. 21–41). San Francisco: Jossey-Bass.

# FACULTY: THE FOCAL POINT

In the past few years, outside stakeholder groups have increasingly questioned the workload components of college and university faculties. Fueled by anecdotal stories of faculty members who keep few office hours to support student learning, who fail to return telephone calls and e-mails, and who allegedly practice similar habits that inhibit student learning, critics have sought to impose new policies and procedures to increase faculty productivity and, in the process, improve student success.

In this chapter, James Fairweather provides a well-researched perspective on the workload activities of faculty members at a cross section of U.S. institutions. Its findings are essential for all those who will increasingly be expected to explain faculty productivity issues to their ever-growing, more inquisitive constituencies and who will lead the future of higher education.

# FACULTY
## THE FOCAL POINT

Chapter 2 from *Faculty Work and Public Trust*
James S. Fairweather
Allyn & Bacon, © 1996

## THE FACULTY POSITION

When academic leaders pledge to involve their institutions in major research cooperatives with industry, promise to build research parks, encourage technology transfer through consulting, or even promote personnel exchanges between industry and higher education, the involvement of faculty is crucial. Even in major research universities where substantial technology transfer activities involve nonteaching research staff and take place outside of traditional departments, key faculty often play lead roles.[1] Similarly, promises to increase the value of teaching in the academy rely on having faculty pay greater attention to students and to curriculum reform. In sum, the faculty comprise the "raw material" for any academic effort requiring expertise, whether devoted to training students or carrying out research.

Current proposals for restoring the value of teaching and enhancing the role of public service, whether in the shape of a congressional report, a state budget, or the minutes of a college faculty senate meeting, make certain assumptions about the nature of faculty work. Understanding faculty roles and work patterns is fundamental to creating new policies, structures, and procedures designed to help academic institutions respond to changing needs. Before any state legislator or federal policymaker proposes legislation or regulations to codify faculty workloads, and before any academic leader invests time in helping reshape academic values to meet emerging societal needs, let us first examine what faculty actually do with their time.

Faculty have multiple roles. As Gmelch, Wilke, and Lovrich describe, "The plethora of roles (e.g., teacher, adviser, researcher, university citizen, and departmental colleague) and the existence of numerous factions demanding attention produce a multifaceted complex of strains on individuals in the academic role."[2] According to Bowen and Schuster, these roles include instruction, research, public service, and institutional governance and operation (i.e., administration).[3] Yuker argues for including professional development as a separate activity category.[4] Consulting is an accepted part of the academic profession, best studied as a separate activity rather than imbedded in a generic research or service category.[5] Furthermore, each generic activity category contains the distinct concepts of workload, time allocation, and productivity. Measures of instructional activity, for example, might include the number of hours per week spent on teaching (workload); the relative percentage of time spent on teaching activities to other tasks (time allocation); and the number of student contact hours generated (productivity).

The generic behavioral categories also contain a variety of distinct activities. *Instruction* is not limited to classroom teaching. It includes time spent on working with student organizations; formal classroom instruction; independent instruction; noncredit instruction; advising, counseling, and supervising students; and grading papers, preparing courses, and developing new curricula. *Research* includes measures of time spent on research *and* scholarship, including preparing for and conducting research, preparing or reviewing articles or books, attending professional meetings, giving performances in the fine or applied arts, and seeking outside funding for research.

To understand the potential of a variety of institutional activities to effect change, I focus in this chapter on faculty workload (e.g., hours assigned to teach in class), time allocation (e.g., percentage of time spent on teaching, research, and public service), and productivity (e.g., scholarly publications), and examine the profiles of faculty who spend the most time on teaching and research. Results are shown by type of 4-year institution. Based on the Carnegie Foundation for the Advancement of Teaching classification, the types of 4-year schools include: public and private *research universities*, whose faculty train the majority of doctorates in the United States and which house the majority of funded research; public and private *doctoral-granting universities*, whose faculty also train doctoral students and conduct research but whose production of doctorates and research dollars generated are less than found in research universities; public and private *comprehensive colleges and universities*, which focus on liberal arts and professional programs at the undergraduate and master's-degree levels; private *liberal arts colleges;* and *other 4-year institutions*, which in this study were predominately professional schools of engineering and medicine.[6]

## HOW BUSY ARE FACULTY?

Faculty in 4-year institutions averaged almost 55 hours worked per week in 1987–88 (Table 2.1).[7] Almost 49 of these hours were spent working at their institution; the remainder was about evenly split between other paid activities and unpaid service. Although hours worked per week varies slightly by type of institution, faculty in each type of 4-year institution averaged at least 52 hours per week on the job.

TABLE 2.1    Mean Hours Worked per Week, by Type of Institution

| TYPE OF INSTITUTION | ACTIVITIES AT THIS INSTITUTION | OTHER PAID ACTIVITIES | UNPAID SERVICE | TOTAL |
|---|---|---|---|---|
| All 4-Year | 48.84 | 3.20 | 2.64 | 54.68 |
| Research | 51.71 | 3.16 | 2.45 | 57.32 |
| Doctoral | 48.47 | 3.26 | 2.60 | 54.33 |
| Comprehensive | 46.02 | 3.37 | 3.09 | 52.48 |
| Liberal Arts | 48.17 | 2.45 | 2.33 | 52.95 |
| Other 4-Year | 48.77 | 3.39 | 1.82 | 53.98 |

Source: NSOPF 1988

These data are consistent with a review of more than 100 previous studies of faculty workload, which found an average of more than 50 hours per week across the various studies.[8] The NSOPF estimates are higher than those found in 1981 by the National Science Foundation (NSF). Looking only at faculty in the sciences, engineering, and the social sciences, which could account for the difference in estimates, the NSF found faculty across all 4-year institutions spent an average of 45.8 hours per week working at all activities. Faculty in doctoral-granting universities spent 48.2 hours working per week, while their peers in other 4-year schools averaged 42.7 hours per week.[9]

## HOW DO FACULTY SPEND THEIR TIME?

Faculty in 4-year institutions, on average, spent more than half of their time on instruction-related activities in 1987–88. About one-quarter of their time was spent on research, 14 percent on administration, and less than 5 percent each on service, consulting, and professional development (Table 2.2).

Teaching- and research-related activity patterns vary directly by type of 4-year institution. Faculty in research universities and in other 4-year institutions, which are predominantly engineering- and health-science-related in the NSOPF sample, spent the least time on instruction. Faculty in doctoral-granting institutions spent the next lowest amount of time on instruction, followed by their peers in comprehensive and liberal arts colleges, respectively. Faculty who spent less time on teaching invested the hours saved in research. The same pattern described above holds inversely by type of institution; that is, faculty in liberal arts colleges spent the least time on research, their peers in comprehensives the next lowest percentage, and so on.[10]

Time spent on administration and on professional development does not vary by type of 4-year institution. Similarly, although faculty in research

**TABLE 2.2  Time Allocation, by Type of Institution**

| | | | PERCENT OF TIME | | | |
|---|---|---|---|---|---|---|
| TYPE OF INSTITUTION | TEACHING | RESEARCH/ SCHOLARSHIP | ADMINISTRATION | SERVICE | CONSULTING | PROFESSIONAL DEVELOPMENT |
| All 4-year | 53.2 | 22.0 | 14.0 | 2.0 | 4.8 | 4.1 |
| SE | .36 | .30 | .23 | .06 | .17 | .11 |
| Research | 42.6 | 31.4 | 14.6 | 1.6 | 6.1 | 3.8 |
| SE | .55 | .54 | .40 | .10 | .35 | .20 |
| Doctoral | 53.7 | 23.6 | 13.4 | 2.2 | 3.4 | 3.8 |
| SE | .74 | .68 | .54 | .14 | .25 | .22 |
| Comprehensive | 63.8 | 12.6 | 13.4 | 2.4 | 3.6 | 4.2 |
| SE | .53 | .33 | .39 | .10 | .21 | .17 |
| Liberal Arts | 68.0 | 10.5 | 13.8 | 2.3 | 1.6 | 3.8 |
| SE | .96 | .63 | .72 | .19 | .23 | .31 |
| Other 4-year | 39.9 | 27.5 | 15.4 | 1.3 | 10.4 | 5.5 |
| SE | 2.28 | 1.97 | 1.20 | .33 | 1.44 | .93 |

*Source:* NSOPF 1988
SE = Standard Error

universities spent slightly less time on service than their peers in other institutions,[11] in general time spent on service does not vary by type of institution. Faculty in other 4-year institutions spent the most time consulting, followed by their peers in research universities. Faculty in liberal arts colleges spent the least time consulting.[12]

Considering that instruction-related activities are accorded the greatest percentage of time by all faculty, these results are consistent with previous research indicating that faculty felt teaching was their primary activity.[13] The time that faculty allocated to various activities in 1987–88 was remarkably similar to that of 1977–78, although faculty in doctoral-granting institutions spent a bit less time on teaching than they did ten years previously.[14] The finding that faculty in research universities spend less time teaching and more time on research than faculty in other types of institutions is consistent with other studies.[15] However, the finding that faculty in doctoral-granting institutions spend less time on teaching and more on research than their colleagues in comprehensive institutions, and that faculty in comprehensive colleges and universities spend less time on teaching and more on research than faculty in liberal arts colleges, is new.

## Program Area

The pattern of faculty activities varies by program area (Table 2.3). Faculty in agriculture/home economics and the health sciences spent below-average percentages of time on teaching in 1987–88; faculty in business, education, the humanities, the social sciences, and other fields spent above-average percentages of time on this task. Faculty in engineering, the fine arts, and the natural sciences spent average percentages of their time on teaching.[16] Faculty in agriculture/home economics and the natural sciences spent the most time on research and scholarship, whereas their colleagues in education, the humanities, and other fields spent the least time.[17] Faculty in the health sciences spent the most time on administration; faculty in business and in engineering spent the least time on institutional governance.[18]

Faculty in education and other fields were the most likely to spend time on public service in 1987–88, whereas their peers in the humanities and natural sciences were less likely to do so.[19] Consulting activity also varies by field: faculty in the health sciences spent above-average amounts of time consulting, whereas their peers in agriculture/home economics, education, the humanities, the natural sciences, the social sciences, and other fields consulted less frequently.[20] Faculty in the fine arts and health sciences spent the most time on professional development, whereas their colleagues in the humanities, natural sciences, social sciences, and other fields spent the least time.[21]

These results are consistent with previous research by Blau, Fulton and Trow, Orlans, and Smart and McLaughlin,[22] which showed that faculty in the natural sciences and social sciences spend more time on research than do

**TABLE 2.3  Time Allocation, by Program Area: 4-Year Institutions**

| PROGRAM AREA | TEACHING | RESEARCH/ SCHOLARSHIP | PERCENT OF TIME ADMINISTRATION | SERVICE | CONSULTING | PROFESSIONAL DEVELOPMENT |
|---|---|---|---|---|---|---|
| Agriculture/Home Economics | 47.6 | 31.6 | 13.6 | 1.8 | 1.6 | 3.9 |
| SE | 1.81 | 1.76 | 1.10 | .23 | .33 | .42 |
| Business | 58.0 | 19.4 | 11.2 | 2.5 | 4.8 | 4.0 |
| SE | 1.51 | 1.24 | .89 | .30 | .65 | .50 |
| Education | 59.6 | 13.6 | 15.9 | 3.4 | 3.6 | 4.0 |
| SE | 1.02 | .68 | .81 | .27 | .38 | .27 |
| Engineering | 56.5 | 22.5 | 11.4 | 1.7 | 4.1 | 3.8 |
| SE | 1.48 | 1.38 | .89 | .26 | .57 | .46 |
| Fine Arts | 55.2 | 19.8 | 12.6 | 2.1 | 4.4 | 5.9 |
| SE | 1.08 | .91 | .83 | .22 | .53 | .49 |
| Health Sciences | 36.1 | 24.5 | 17.3 | 1.7 | 13.3 | 7.0 |
| SE | 1.44 | 1.31 | 1.07 | .23 | 1.23 | .69 |
| Humanities | 63.0 | 17.4 | 14.0 | 1.7 | 1.4 | 2.5 |
| SE | .60 | .46 | .47 | .10 | .14 | .14 |
| Natural Sciences | 54.2 | 26.3 | 12.6 | 1.4 | 2.2 | 3.3 |
| SE | .99 | .97 | .58 | .14 | .24 | .28 |
| Social Sciences | 55.7 | 22.4 | 14.0 | 2.2 | 2.9 | 2.8 |
| SE | .80 | .69 | .56 | .16 | .24 | .19 |
| Other Fields | 59.2 | 18.1 | 13.9 | 2.7 | 3.0 | 3.0 |
| SE | 1.26 | 1.01 | .87 | .25 | .36 | .26 |

*Source:* NSOPF 1988

faculty in education and the humanities. As discussed in Chapters 3 and 4, however, the allocation of time to task is *not* synonymous with faculty reward structures; i.e., the amount of time spent on teaching is not indicative of its relative importance in the faculty reward structure.

## Academic Rank

Time allocation varies by academic rank (Table 2.4). In 4-year colleges and universities, teaching is inversely related to rank: professors were less likely to spend time teaching than associate professors in 1987–88, and associate professors were less likely to spend time teaching than assistant professors. Professors were the most likely to spend time on research and administration; associate professors spent more time on administration than their junior colleagues. Time spent on service and consulting does not vary by academic rank; professors spent less time on professional development than their junior colleagues.[23]

The results for faculty in 4-year institutions are consistent with work done by Hesseldenz and by Ladd and Lipset,[24] who found that percent of time spent on teaching declines with increases in rank. Hesseldenz also found that time spent on administration increases with rank.[25]

## HOW PRODUCTIVE ARE FACULTY?

Faculty in 4-year institutions averaged 9.4 hours in class per week in 1987–88, generating 322 student contact hours per semester. Most faculty in 4-year institutions taught both undergraduate and graduate students. In 1987–88, the average faculty member in 4-year colleges and universities had 25 career publications; about one-quarter were principal investigators of funded research projects in Fall term 1987 (Table 2.5).

Measures of teaching workload vary by type of 4-year institution, but teaching productivity does not vary substantially. Faculty in research and doctoral-granting universities and in liberal arts colleges were the most likely to teach only undergraduate students; faculty in other 4-year institutions were the least likely. Faculty in other 4-year institutions and in research universities were the most likely to be assigned solely to teaching graduate students. Hours spent in class per week varies directly by type of 4-year institution, with faculty in research universities spending the least time in class and faculty in comprehensives and liberal arts colleges spending the most time in class. Faculty in other 4-year institutions had the greatest number of average student contact hours in Fall term 1987, faculty in liberal arts colleges the least. The student contact hours generated per semester by faculty in research universities, doctoral-granting universities, and comprehensive institutions were virtually identical.[26]

**TABLE 2.4  Time Allocation, by Academic Rank**

| | | | PERCENT OF TIME | | | |
|---|---|---|---|---|---|---|
| RANK | TEACHING | RESEARCH/ SCHOLARSHIP | ADMINISTRATION | SERVICE | CONSULTING | PROFESSIONAL DEVELOPMENT |
| Professor | 49.8 | 23.0 | 16.8 | 2.1 | 4.7 | 3.6 |
| SE | .54 | .45 | .39 | .09 | .24 | .15 |
| Associate | 53.7 | 21.5 | 13.7 | 1.9 | 4.7 | 4.4 |
| SE | .64 | .54 | .38 | .10 | .30 | .23 |
| Assistant | 56.8 | 22.3 | 9.9 | 1.9 | 5.1 | 4.0 |
| SE | .72 | .62 | .34 | .13 | .40 | .21 |

*Source:* NSOPF 1988

**TABLE 2.5  Mean Workload and Productivity, by Type of Institution**

| TYPE OF INSTITUTION | TEACHING | | | | RESEARCH | |
| --- | --- | --- | --- | --- | --- | --- |
| | TAUGHT ONLY UNDERGRADUATES | TAUGHT ONLY GRADUATES | STUDENT CONTACT HOURS | HOURS IN CLASS (WEEK) | PUBLICATIONS, CAREER | PRINCIPAL INVESTIGATOR |
| All 4-Year | 8.4% | 11.7% | 322.3 | 9.4 | 25.1 | 24.7% |
| SE | .41 | .48 | 7.60 | .11 | .63 | .64 |
| Research | 11.3 | 20.1 | 322.9 | 7.7 | 38.4 | 40.2 |
| SE | .82 | 1.04 | 17.67 | .22 | 1.31 | 1.27 |
| Doctoral | 9.1 | 6.5 | 303.5 | 8.8 | 23.4 | 22.3 |
| SE | 1.03 | .88 | 14.08 | .18 | 1.35 | 1.49 |
| Comprehensive | 5.9 | 3.3 | 318.8 | 11.1 | 11.5 | 10.7 |
| SE | .58 | .44 | 7.99 | .15 | .67 | .76 |
| Liberal Arts | 8.3 | NA | 233.8 | 10.6 | 8.1 | 8.5 |
| SE | 1.35 | NA | 8.83 | .26 | .75 | 1.36 |
| Other 4-Year | 3.6 | 32.9 | 495.9 | 9.6 | 45.1 | 34.1 |
| SE | 1.57 | 3.94 | 59.77 | .67 | 4.36 | 3.98 |

Source: NSOPF 1988
NA = Not Applicable

Measures of research productivity vary substantially by type of 4-year institution. Total publications for a career varies directly by type of institution; faculty in research universities and other 4-year institutions (i.e., predominantly engineering and medical schools) have the greatest number of publications, faculty in liberal arts colleges the least. Faculty in research universities, other 4-year institutions, and doctoral-granting universities were the most likely to be a principal investigator on a funded research project in 1987–88.[27]

The 1987-88 findings confirm results in earlier studies, which showed that faculty in more prestigious institutions generate more publications and lead more research projects than faculty in non-doctoral-granting institutions.[28] However, the findings in previous research that teaching loads vary inversely by institutional prestige are only partially supported. According to previous studies, faculty in research universities have the lowest teaching loads, both in the hours spent in class and in student contact hours.[29] In 1987-88, faculty in research and doctoral-granting institutions did spend less time in class per week, but they generated as many student contact hours as their peers in master's-level institutions. This result is a function of the larger class sizes in doctoral-granting and research universities.

## Program Area

Teaching workload and productivity vary by program area (Table 2.6). Faculty in agriculture/home economics, engineering, and the natural sciences were more likely to teach only undergraduates in 1987–88; faculty in business and in the humanities were the least likely to teach only undergraduates.[30] Faculty in the health sciences were the most likely to teach only graduate students; faculty in business, education, engineering, fine arts, the humanities, the social sciences, and other fields had fewer faculty who taught only graduate students.[31] Health sciences faculty generated the most student contact hours; less than average student contact hours were generated by faculty in agriculture/home economics, education, engineering, fine arts, the humanities, and other fields.[32] Finally, faculty in the fine arts and health sciences spent the most time in class, faculty in agriculture/home economics, business, the natural sciences, and the social sciences the least.[33]

Research productivity varies by program area. Faculty in the natural sciences have greater than average number of publications for their careers, whereas faculty in business, education, fine arts, and the humanities publish less often.[34] Faculty in agriculture/home economics, engineering, the health sciences, and the natural sciences were the most likely to head funded research projects in 1987–88; their compatriots in business, education, fine arts, the humanities, the social sciences, and other fields were less likely to lead research projects.[35]

TABLE 2.6 Mean Workload and Productivity, by Program Area: 4-Year Institutions

| TYPE OF INSTITUTION | TEACHING | | | | RESEARCH | PRINCIPAL INVESTIGATOR |
| --- | --- | --- | --- | --- | --- | --- |
| | TAUGHT ONLY UNDERGRADUATES | TAUGHT ONLY GRADUATES | STUDENT CONTACT HOURS | HOURS IN CLASS (WEEK) | PUBLICATIONS, CAREER | |
| Agriculture/Home Economics | 24.9% | 9.7% | 230.2 | 7.7 | 29.3 | 58.7% |
| SE | 3.08 | 2.11 | 20.04 | .40 | 3.00 | 3.51 |
| Business | 4.4 | 4.0 | 295.0 | 8.5 | 10.6 | 4.5 |
| SE | 1.50 | 1.45 | 13.94 | .25 | .95 | 1.53 |
| Education | 5.6 | 6.4 | 227.2 | 9.2 | 17.5 | 14.6 |
| SE | 1.13 | 1.21 | 9.60 | .29 | 1.43 | 1.74 |
| Engineering | 15.8 | 6.4 | 266.8 | 8.5 | 20.2 | 37.6 |
| SE | 2.79 | 1.87 | 19.80 | .39 | 2.33 | 3.71 |
| Fine Arts | 6.5 | 2.9 | 259.7 | 11.6 | 9.0 | 6.1 |
| SE | 1.39 | .94 | 13.31 | .36 | .96 | 1.35 |
| Health Sciences | 7.1 | 30.1 | 488.5 | 12.7 | 30.2 | 38.5 |
| SE | 1.54 | 2.75 | 53.34 | .94 | 2.20 | 2.92 |
| Humanities | 4.0 | 2.8 | 234.5 | 9.5 | 21.1 | 6.5 |
| SE | .58 | .49 | 5.05 | .12 | 1.18 | .73 |
| Natural Sciences | 13.9 | 14.3 | 363.7 | 8.1 | 34.4 | 44.7 |
| SE | 1.49 | 1.51 | 33.45 | .22 | 2.45 | 2.14 |
| Social Sciences | 8.7 | 5.9 | 317.2 | 8.2 | 24.7 | 16.7 |
| SE | 1.01 | .85 | 12.21 | .15 | 1.29 | 1.34 |
| Other Fields | 5.7 | 5.8 | 251.2 | 9.2 | 21.7 | 15.1 |
| SE | 1.28 | 1.29 | 11.60 | .23 | 2.64 | 1.98 |

Source: NSOPF 1988
NA = Not Applicable

## Academic Rank

In 4-year institutions, number of publications varies directly by academic rank—professors published the most—and senior faculty were the most likely to be principal investigators on research projects (Table 2.7).[36] These results support Fulton and Trow's work, but contradict studies by Hesseldenz and Allison and Stewart which found no relationship between academic rank and number of publications.[37]

Professors were the most likely to teach only graduate students in 1987–88, although assistant professors were more likely than associate professors to do so. Student contact hours produced has a U-shaped distribution with professors generating the least amount on average, associate professors the most, and assistant professors in between the two. Finally, professors spent the lowest average hours in the classroom; assistant and associate professors do not differ significantly on this instruction-related indicator.[38]

## PROFILES: THE TEACHER AND THE RESEARCHER

What characteristics and behaviors distinguish faculty who spend the most time teaching and the most time on research and scholarship? I examine faculty in the top quartile of time spent on teaching and on research, respectively.[39] I compare these faculty with their colleagues, focusing on demographic characteristics, teaching-related activities and productivity, research-oriented workload and productivity, and other activities.

## Teaching Faculty

In all but other 4-year institutions, faculty who spend the most time on teaching are older and have spent more years at their current institutions (Table 2.8). In all but research universities and liberal arts colleges, the most teaching-oriented faculty are less likely to hold the doctorate. In doctoral-granting institutions only, teaching-oriented faculty are more likely to be women and less likely to be members of racial/ethnic minority groups.

Faculty who spend more than three-quarters of their time on instruction are less likely to teach only graduate students. They spend more hours in the classroom per week, on average. However, only in comprehensive and liberal arts colleges do these faculty generate more student contact hours.

In all 4-year institutions, faculty who spend the most time on instruction spend less time on research, administration, and service. At most institutions, they have fewer publications and were less likely to be a principal investigator on a funded research project in Fall term 1987.

TABLE 2.7  Mean Workload and Productivity, by Academic Rank

| | TEACHING | | | | RESEARCH | |
| RANK | TAUGHT ONLY UNDERGRADUATES | TAUGHT ONLY GRADUATES | STUDENT CONTACT HOURS | HOURS IN CLASS (WEEK) | PUBLICATIONS, CAREER | PRINCIPAL INVESTIGATOR |
|---|---|---|---|---|---|---|
| Professor | 8.8% | 14.8% | 303.7 | 8.8 | 42.9 | 29.2% |
| SE | .64 | .80 | 9.92 | .16 | 1.29 | 1.02 |
| Associate | 9.0 | 7.7 | 372.9 | 9.8 | 17.5 | 24.7 |
| SE | .78 | .72 | 18.75 | .20 | .56 | 1.17 |
| Assistant | 6.7 | 11.4 | 298.4 | 9.7 | 7.0 | 19.6 |
| SE | .78 | .99 | 11.17 | .21 | .31 | 1.24 |

Source: NSOPF 1988

**TABLE 2.8  Profile of Tenure-Track, Full-Time Faculty Who Spend the Most Time on Teaching**

| | RESEARCH UNIVERSITIES | | DOCTORALGRANTING UNIVERSITIES | | COMPREHENSIVE UNIVERSITIES | | LIBERAL ARTS COLLEGES | | OTHER 4-YEAR INSTITUTIONS | |
|---|---|---|---|---|---|---|---|---|---|---|
| | TOP QUARTILE, TIME SPENT ON TEACHING | ALL OTHER FACULTY (MEAN) | TOP QUARTILE, TIME SPENT ON TEACHING | ALL OTHER FACULTY (MEAN) | TOP QUARTILE, TIME SPENT ON TEACHING | ALL OTHER FACULTY (MEAN) | TOP QUARTILE, TIME SPENT ON TEACHING | ALL OTHER FACULTY (MEAN) | TOP QUARTILE, TIME SPENT ON TEACHING | ALL OTHER FACULTY (MEAN) |
| *Demographics* | | | | | | | | | | |
| Minority | 9.7% | 10.5% | 3.1% | 8.2%** | 13.1% | 10.7% | 7.2% | 13.5% | 18.2% | 10.0% |
| Male | 79.0% | 82.8% | 67.4% | 80.0%** | 72.8% | 76.7% | 79.4% | 72.1% | 90.2% | 89.4% |
| Age (years) | 50.4 | 47.2*** | 50.9 | 47.1*** | 49.5 | 47.3*** | 48.5 | 45.3*** | 49.3 | 48.9 |
| Years at Current Institution | 15.1 | 12.1*** | 13.2 | 11.6* | 13.7 | 12.2** | 13.3 | 10.8** | 10.3 | 11.9 |
| Highest Degree—Doctorate | 87.4% | 92.7% | 74.6% | 86.9%*** | 65.0% | 77.6%*** | 64.3% | 70.0% | 60.8% | 93.8%*** |
| *Teaching* | | | | | | | | | | |
| Student Contact Hours | 399.0 | 314.4 | 326.8 | 298.1 | 356.5 | 293.0*** | 270.4 | 194.8*** | 639.5 | 465.3 |
| Hours in Class/Week | 9.3 | 7.5** | 10.9 | 8.3*** | 12.1 | 10.3*** | 11.2 | 9.8* | 12.3 | 9.0* |
| Taught Only Undergraduate Students | 13.2% | 11.1% | 3.4% | 10.5%*** | 3.2% | 7.6%*** | 7.2% | 9.4%* | 3.2% | 3.7% |
| Taught Only Graduate Students | 7.0% | 21.4%*** | 1.1% | 7.8%*** | 0.8% | 4.9%*** | NA | NA | 18.3% | 35.8%*** |
| *Research* | | | | | | | | | | |
| Percent of Time Spent, Research | 8.4% | 33.8%*** | 6.7% | 27.7%* | 5.6% | 17.4%*** | 5.2% | 16.1%*** | 2.3% | 32.5%*** |
| Publications (career) | 25.1 | 39.8* | 11.7 | 26.2*** | 6.7 | 14.6*** | 7.1 | 9.1 | 25.7 | 48.9* |
| Principal Investigator | 20.1% | 42.2%*** | 11.0% | 25.0%*** | 5.9% | 14.0%*** | 4.7% | 12.5%** | 0% | 40.8%*** |

*(continued)*

29

**TABLE 2.8** Continued

| | RESEARCH UNIVERSITIES | | DOCTORAL-GRANTING UNIVERSITIES | | COMPREHENSIVE UNIVERSITIES | | LIBERAL ARTS COLLEGES | | OTHER 4-YEAR INSTITUTIONS | |
|---|---|---|---|---|---|---|---|---|---|---|
| | TOP QUARTILE, TIME SPENT ON TEACHING | ALL OTHER FACULTY (MEAN) | TOP QUARTILE, TIME SPENT ON TEACHING | ALL OTHER FACULTY (MEAN) | TOP QUARTILE, TIME SPENT ON TEACHING | ALL OTHER FACULTY (MEAN) | TOP QUARTILE, TIME SPENT ON TEACHING | ALL OTHER FACULTY (MEAN) | TOP QUARTILE, TIME SPENT ON TEACHING | ALL OTHER FACULTY (MEAN) |
| *Administration and Service* | | | | | | | | | | |
| Percent of Time Spent, Administration | 5.9% | 15.5%*** | 5.6% | 15.2%*** | 5.7% | 18.7%*** | 7.4% | 20.5%*** | 8.1% | 16.8%*** |
| Percent of Time Spent, Service | 0.9% | 1.6%*** | 1.0% | 2.5%*** | 1.4% | 3.1%*** | 1.3% | 3.3%*** | 1.6% | 1.2% |

Source: NSOPF 1988

*** = p < .001; ** = p < .01; * = p < .05.

## Research-oriented Faculty

In contrast to teaching-oriented faculty, faculty who spend the most time on research and scholarship are more likely to hold the doctorate (Table 2.9). At research, doctoral-granting, and comprehensive universities, these faculty are more likely to be male, younger, and to have spent fewer years at the institution.

At all 4-year institutions, research-oriented faculty spend less hours in the classroom per week and spend less time overall on teaching. Only in research universities and liberal arts colleges do these faculty generate fewer student contact hours, however. At the most graduate-oriented universities, research-oriented faculty are more likely to teach only graduate students.

Not surprisingly, research-oriented faculty are more likely to have published and to have been a principal investigator during Fall term 1987. At most institutions, these faculty spent less time on administration and service than their less research-oriented colleagues.

## SUMMARY

Faculty average more than 50 hours of work per week. For research, publishing, obtaining grants, and consulting, the NSOPF survey results confirm institutional diversity: faculty in research and doctoral-granting institutions spend more time on research, obtain more external funds, publish more, and consult more than their colleagues in master's- and bachelor's-level institutions. Faculty in the latter types of institutions spend more of their time on teaching, although teaching productivity does not vary substantially by type of institution. Time spent on administration, professional development, or public service does not vary substantially by type of institution. Few faculty, even those in institutions with professed public service missions, spend much of their time on service to the community.

For all institutions except research universities, these findings support Fulton and Trow,[40] who found that faculty who spent more time on research did less of other activities. However, these findings contradict Fulton and Trow's claim that faculty at research universities who spent the most time on research did as much teaching and administration as their less research-oriented colleagues. The NSOPF data reveal that in 1987–88 faculty in research universities who focused on research spent *less* time on teaching, administration, and service than their peers. The integrated picture described by Fulton and Trow for research university faculty no longer exists.

## NOTES

1. M. J. Dooris and J. S. Fairweather, "Structure and Culture in Faculty Work: Implications for Technology Transfer," *Review of Higher Education*, 17 (1994): 161–78.

2. W. Gmelch, P. Wilke, and N. Lovrich, "Dimensions of Stress among University Faculty Members: Scope and Depth of Involvement," *Research in Higher Education*, 24 (1986): 267.

**TABLE 2.9 Profile of Tenure-Track, Full-Time Faculty Who Spend the Most Time on Research**

| | RESEARCH UNIVERSITIES | | DOCTORAL GRANTING UNIVERSITIES | | COMPREHENSIVE UNIVERSITIES | | LIBERAL ARTS COLLEGES | | OTHER 4-YEAR INSTITUTIONS | |
|---|---|---|---|---|---|---|---|---|---|---|
| | TOP QUARTILE, TIME SPENT ON RESEARCH | ALL OTHER FACULTY (MEAN) | TOP QUARTILE, TIME SPENT ON RESEARCH | ALL OTHER FACULTY (MEAN) | TOP QUARTILE, TIME SPENT ON RESEARCH | ALL OTHER FACULTY (MEAN) | TOP QUARTILE, TIME SPENT ON RESEARCH | ALL OTHER FACULTY (MEAN) | TOP QUARTILE, TIME SPENT ON RESEARCH | ALL OTHER FACULTY (MEAN) |
| *Demographics* | | | | | | | | | | |
| Minority | 10.7% | 10.2% | 7.5% | 7.1% | 17.7% | 11.2% | 10.5% | 10.3% | 3.0% | 16.1%** |
| Male | 84.8% | 80.8%* | 86.4% | 74.4%** | 83.1% | 74.5%* | 69.6% | 76.1% | 89.0% | 89.8% |
| Age (years) | 45.7 | 48.8*** | 46.2 | 48.4** | 45.3 | 48.4*** | 43.3 | 47.1 | 49.4 | 48.8 |
| Years at Current Institution | 11.5 | 13.1*** | 10.6 | 12.3* | 10.7 | 13.0** | 10.9 | 12.2 | 10.4 | 12.4 |
| Highest Degree-Doctorate | 96.5% | 89.2%*** | 94.4% | 80.9%*** | 89.5% | 71.2%*** | 77.8% | 66.5% | 95.2% | 84.5%* |
| *Teaching* | | | | | | | | | | |
| Percent of Time Spent, Teaching | 31.8% | 50.6%*** | 36.8% | 60.0%*** | 41.6% | 65.6%*** | 40.9% | 69.5%*** | 21.3% | 50.8%*** |
| Student Contact Hours | 229.4 | 386.6*** | 285.2 | 309.9 | 329.9 | 318.0 | 150.3 | 237.8*** | 571.3 | 454.8 |
| Hours in Class/Week | 5.8 | 8.9*** | 7.0 | 9.5*** | 9.4 | 11.2*** | 7.9 | 10.7*** | 7.2 | 10.9** |
| Taught Only Undergraduate Students | 13.8% | 9.4%* | 14.6% | 7.1%** | 6.2% | 5.8% | 3.6% | 8.5% | 2.8% | 4.1% |
| Taught Only Graduate Students | 24.9% | 16.7%*** | 16.3% | 2.9%*** | 4.6% | 3.2% | NA | NA | 55.6% | 20.1%*** |

*Research*

| | | | | | | | | | |
|---|---|---|---|---|---|---|---|---|---|
| Publications (career) | 47.9 | 31.7*** | 35.8 | 18.9*** | 26.1 | 10.3*** | 17.4 | 7.6* | 68.2 | 32.0*** |
| Principal Investigator | 57.9% | 27.5%*** | 44.8% | 14.2%*** | 28.3% | 9.3%*** | 29.8% | 7.4%* | 60.0% | 19.4%*** |

*Administration and Service*

| | | | | | | | | | |
|---|---|---|---|---|---|---|---|---|---|
| Percent of Time Spent, Administration | 10.2% | 17.8%*** | 7.9% | 15.4%*** | 7.7% | 13.9%*** | 5.7% | 14.2%*** | 13.8% | 16.3% |
| Percent of Time Spent, Service | 0.9% | 2.1%*** | 1.0% | 2.6%*** | 0.9% | 2.6%*** | 0.6% | 2.4%*** | 0.6% | 1.7%* |

Source: NSOPF 1988

*** = $p < .001$; ** = $p < .01$; * = $p < .05$.

3. H. R. Bowen and J. H. Schuster, *American Professors: A National Resource Imperiled* (New York: Oxford University Press, 1986), 15.

4. H. E. Yuker, *Faculty Workload: Research, Theory, and Interpretation*, ASHE-ERIC Higher Education Research Report No. 10 (Washington, D.C.: Association for the Study of Higher Education, 1984), 22–3.

5. J. D. Marver and C. V. Patton, "The Correlates of Consultation: American Academics in the Real World," *Higher Education*, 5 (1976): 319–35.

6. Carnegie Foundation for the Advancement of Teaching, *A Classification of Institutions of Higher Education* (Princeton, N.J.: Carnegie Foundation for the Advancement of Teaching, 1987).

7. The data on estimated number of hours worked per week are self-reported and subject to bias. However, the estimates are consistent across many years of faculty surveys.

8. Interuniversity Council of Ohio, *Faculty Load Study* (Columbus, Ohio: Interuniversity Council of Ohio, 1970).

9. National Science Foundation, *Activities of Science and Engineering Faculty in Universities and 4 Year Colleges: 1978–79* (Washington, D.C.: National Science Foundation, 1981).

10. Percent of time spent on teaching: $t$(research/doctoral) = $-10.86^{***}$; $t$(doctoral/comprehensive) = $-11.01^{***}$; $t$(comprehensive/liberal) = $-3.54^{***}$ [where $^{***} = p < .001$; $^{**} = p < .01$; $^{*} = p < .05$]. Percent of time spent on research: $t$(res/doc) = $8.99^{***}$; $t$(doc/comp) = $14.59^{***}$; $t$(comp/lib) = $3.03^{**}$.

11. $t$(res/doc) = $-3.71^{***}$.

12. $t$(other/res) = $2.93^{**}$; $t$(res/doc) = $6.21^{***}$; $t$(comp/lib) = $5.97^{***}$. For a more extensive discussion of consulting activities, see Chapter 8.

13. Carnegie Foundation for the Advancement of Teaching, *The Condition of the Professoriate: Attitudes and Trends, 1989* (Princeton, N.J.: Carnegie Foundation for the Advancement of Teaching, 1989); E. C. Ladd, Jr. and S. M. Lipset, *Survey of the American Professoriate* (Storrs, Conn.: University of Connecticut, 1977).

14. J. V. Baldridge, D. Curtis, G. Ecker, and G. Riley, *Policy Making and Effective Leadership* (San Francisco: Jossey-Bass, 1978).

15. Baldridge, Curtis, Ecker, and Riley, *Policy Making and Effective Leadership*; A. E. Bayer, "Teaching Faculty in Academe: 1972–73," *ACE Research Reports*, 8 (1973): 1–68; E. C. Ladd, Jr., "The Work Experience of American College Professors: Some Data and an Argument," *Current Issues in Higher Education* (Washington, D.C.: American Association of Higher Education, 1979).

16. $t$(agriculture) = $-3.17^{*}$; $t$(business) = $3.23^{*}$; $t$(education) = $6.49^{***}$; $t$(health sciences) = $-12.29^{***}$; $t$(humanities) = $17.95^{***}$; $t$(social sciences) = $3.40^{**}$; $t$(other) = $4.94^{**}$.

17. $t$(agriculture) = $5.63^{**}$; $t$(education) = $-12.37^{***}$; $t$(humanities) = $-10.56^{***}$; $t$(natural sciences) = $4.81^{**}$; $t$(other) = $-3.98^{**}$.

18. $t$(business) = $-3.18^{*}$; $t$(engineering) = $-2.94^{*}$; $t$(health sciences) = $3.22^{*}$.

19. $t$(education) = $5.60^{**}$; $t$(humanities) = $-3.28^{*}$; $t$(nat sci) = $-4.42^{**}$; $t$(other) = $2.95^{*}$.

20. $t$(agriculture) = $-9.16^{***}$; $t$(education) = $-3.14^{*}$; $t$(health sciences) = $7.32^{***}$; $t$(humanities) = $-17.73^{***}$; $t$(nat sci) = $-9.67^{***}$; $t$(soc sci) = $-7.44^{***}$; $t$(other) = $-4.88^{**}$.

21. $t$(fine arts) = $3.86^{**}$; $t$(health sciences) = $4.43^{**}$; $t$(humanities) = $-27.94^{***}$; $t$(nat sci) = $-3.00^{*}$; $t$(soc sci) = $-6.94^{***}$; $t$(other) = $-7.10^{***}$.

22. P. M. Blau, *The Organization of Academic Work* (New York: John Wiley & Sons, 1973); O. Fulton and M. Trow, "Research Activity in American Higher Education," *Sociology of Education*, 47 (1974): 29–73; H. Orlans, *The Effects of Federal Programs on Higher Education* (Washington, D.C.: Brookings Institute, 1962); J. C. Smart and G. W. McLaughlin, "Reward Structures of Academic Disciplines," *Research in Higher Education*, 8 (1978): 39–55.

23. Percent of time spent on teaching: $t$(professor/associate) = $-4.91^{***}$; $t$(associate/assistant) = $-3.23^{***}$. Percent of time spent on research: $t$(prof/assoc) = $2.14^{*}$. Percent of time spent on administration: $t$(prof/assoc) = $5.64^{***}$; $t$(assoc/asst) = $7.31^{***}$. Percent of time spent on professional development: $t$(prof/assoc) = $-2.88^{**}$.

24. J. S. Hesseldenz, "Personality-based Faculty Workload Analysis," *Research in Higher Education*, 5 (1976): 321–34; Ladd and Lipset, *Survey of the American Professoriate*.

25. Hesseldenz, "Personality-based Faculty Workload Analysis."

26. Mean comparisons for teaching only undergraduate students: $t(\text{res}/\text{comp}) = 5.40^{***}$; $t(\text{doc}/\text{comp}) = 2.76^{**}$; $t(\text{lib}/\text{other}) = 2.27^{*}$; $t(\text{doc}/\text{other}) = 2.96^{**}$; $t(\text{res}/\text{other}) = 4.35^{***}$. Mean comparisons for teaching only graduate students: $t(\text{res}/\text{doc}) = 10.07^{***}$; $t(\text{doc}/\text{comp}) = 3.20^{**}$; $t(\text{res}/\text{other}) = -3.50^{***}$. Mean comparisons for student contact hours per semester: $t(\text{doc}/\text{lib}) = 4.19^{***}$; $t(\text{doc}/\text{other}) = -2.78^{**}$. Mean comparisons for hours spent in class per week: $t(\text{res}/\text{doc}) = -4.09^{***}$; $t(\text{doc}/\text{comp}) = -9.40^{***}$; $t(\text{comp}/\text{other}) = 2.15^{*}$; $t(\text{res}/\text{other}) = -2.71^{**}$.

27. Mean comparison for total publications (career): $t(\text{res}/\text{doc}) = 8.00^{***}$; $t(\text{doc}/\text{comp}) = 7.90^{***}$; $t(\text{comp}/\text{lib}) = 2.94^{**}$. Mean comparison for principal investigator status: $t(\text{res}/\text{doc}) = 9.06^{***}$; $t(\text{doc}/\text{comp}) = 6.90^{***}$.

28. Baldridge, Curtis, Ecker, and Riley, *Policy Making and Effective Leadership*; Fulton and Trow, "Research Activity in American Higher Education"; Orlans, *The Effects of Federal Programs*.

29. Baldridge, Curtis, Ecker, and Riley, *Policy Making and Effective Leadership*; Bayer, "Teaching Faculty in Academe"; Fulton and Trow, "Research Activity in American Higher Education"; T. Parsons and G. M. Platt, *The American Academic Profession: A Pilot Study* (Cambridge, Mass.: Harvard University Press, 1968).

30. $t(\text{agriculture}) = 5.56^{**}$; $t(\text{business}) = -2.68^{*}$; $t(\text{engineering}) = 2.73^{*}$; $t(\text{humanities}) = -7.68^{**}$; $t(\text{nat sci}) = 4.06^{**}$.

31. $t(\text{business}) = -5.41^{**}$; $t(\text{education}) = -4.46^{**}$; $t(\text{engineering}) = -2.85^{*}$; $t(\text{fine arts}) = -8.87^{***}$; $t(\text{health sciences}) = 7.05^{***}$; $t(\text{humanities}) = -15.15^{***}$; $t(\text{soc sci}) = -6.95^{**}$; $t(\text{other}) = -4.59^{**}$.

32. $t(\text{agriculture}) = -4.48^{**}$; $t(\text{education}) = -8.27^{***}$; $t(\text{engineering}) = -2.71^{*}$; $t(\text{fine arts}) = -4.22^{**}$; $t(\text{health sciences}) = 3.30^{*}$; $t(\text{humanities}) = -10.51^{***}$; $t(\text{other}) = -5.42^{**}$.

33. $t(\text{agriculture}) = -4.28^{**}$; $t(\text{business}) = -3.42^{**}$; $t(\text{fine arts}) = 6.24^{***}$; $t(\text{health sciences}) = 3.73^{**}$; $t(\text{nat sci}) = -5.87^{**}$; $t(\text{soc sci}) = -7.30^{***}$.

34. $t(\text{business}) = -13.13^{***}$; $t(\text{education}) = -5.32^{**}$; $t(\text{fine arts}) = -14.80^{***}$; $t(\text{humanities}) = -3.90^{**}$; $t(\text{nat sci}) = 4.20^{**}$.

35. $t(\text{agriculture}) = 9.97^{***}$; $t(\text{business}) = -12.52^{***}$; $t(\text{education}) = -5.97^{**}$; $t(\text{engineering}) = 3.77^{**}$; $t(\text{fine arts}) = -13.28^{***}$; $t(\text{health sciences}) = 4.93^{*}$; $t(\text{humanities}) = -22.34^{***}$; $t(\text{nat sci}) = 10.19^{***}$; $t(\text{soc sci}) = -5.85^{**}$; $t(\text{other}) = -4.98^{**}$.

36. Publications (career): $t(\text{prof}/\text{assoc}) = 18.07^{***}$; $t(\text{assoc}/\text{asst}) = 16.26^{***}$. Principal investigator status: $t(\text{prof}/\text{assoc}) = 2.88^{**}$; $t(\text{assoc}/\text{asst}) = 3.00^{**}$.

37. P. Allison and J. A. Stewart, "Productivity Differences Among Scientists: Evidence for Accumulative Advantage," *American Sociological Review,* 39 (1974): 596–606; Fulton and Trow, "Research Activity in American Higher Education"; Hesseldenz, "Personality-based Faculty Workload Analysis."

38. Taught only graduate students: $t(\text{prof}/\text{assoc}) = 6.57^{***}$; $t(\text{assoc}/\text{asst}) = -3.06^{**}$. Student contact hours: $t(\text{prof}/\text{assoc}) = -3.26^{**}$; $t(\text{assoc}/\text{asst}) = -3.23^{**}$. Hours in class per week: $t(\text{prof}/\text{assoc}) = -3.67^{***}$.

39. Top quartile, percent of time spent on teaching: More than 71 percent for faculty in 4-year institutions. Top quartile, percent of time spent on research: More than 33 percent for faculty in 4-year institutions.

40. Fulton and Trow, "Research Activity in American Higher Education."

# CHAPTER 3

# A PROBLEM-SOLVING THEORY OF TEACHING

Viewing the changes within higher education today as opportunities rather than threats, Sharon Baiocco and Jamie DeWaters provide a detailed perspective on strategies being employed by some of the nation's more distinguished professors to achieve more successful teaching and learning outcomes. Each employs relationship-building strategies with their increasingly diverse students and a continually improved teaching style to achieve more accountable results.

The following chapter specifically addresses the intuitive mechanism that all the distinguished professors they studied had honed. This "radar" continually scans the classrooms and laboratories to identify the learning problems students are experiencing and intervenes with tactics designed to eliminate barriers and facilitate grounded learning. By reviewing their work, any professor will be better grounded in the thinking processes and teaching behaviors that are essential to achieving more effective learning.

# A PROBLEM-SOLVING
# THEORY OF TEACHING

Chapter 9 from *Successful College Teaching*
Sharon A. Baiocco & Jamie N. DeWaters
Allyn & Bacon, © 1998

We have said that teaching excellence involves character, knowledge, actions, and outcomes. In previous chapters we presented case study narratives of observations and interviews with award-winning professors, and we analyzed the professorial character from the perspective of a set of acquired behaviors. These behaviors, which comprise emotional intelligence, are mapped on to genetic personality dispositions. Then we investigated the professors' beliefs, knowledge of pedagogy, planning, and methods. Finally we showed how the distinguished college teachers applied what they knew to solve instructional problems with individual students and groups.

Thus far we have clarified two elements in our theory of teaching excellence: the character of the professors (who they are) and knowledge (what they know and believe). What we have not yet done, and what we set as one of our chief purposes in writing this book, was to articulate a theory to explain our research findings about what excellent professors do in the classroom that distinguishes them from those who perform competently. Ultimately, theories have useful predictive features, applications, and implica-tions. These will be the focus of Chapters 10 and 11. In this chapter, we will draw upon our observations, interviews, and experience to support the problem-solving model within our theory of excellent teaching.

## THE "AHA!" EXPERIENCE: MUCKING AROUND
## IN THE DATA

Theories take the form of statements of truths about something. They are developed by gathering facts, making hypotheses, experimenting, and drawing conclusions. Most of us are trained in the scientific method of inquiry, which consists of these orderly and logical steps. However, without creative intuition, researchers who employed only the scientific method would never make a serious discovery. In this section we will describe our own "Aha!" experience—the intuitive discovery of our hypothesis that the actions of excellent teachers are indeed what Robert Gagné called the highest order of cognition, problem solving (1975), and what Gardner described as intelligence (1993, p. 7).

At the beginning of our research, our goal was to discover markers of excellence among professors who had won recognition for their distinguished teaching. Our problem was that there was a lot of data, but the system to organize and explain it seemed inadequate. Nevertheless, we immersed ourselves in the research, having a hunch as to what we would find regarding the importance of problem solving, but also hoping—even expecting—to have that moment of intuition that would enable us to tie everything together.

Early on in our examination of the data, we each began to glimpse the theory we were seeking. Baiocco's education was in problem-solving theory of composing processes and the arts, whereas DeWaters had a more scientific background and had developed expertise in behavior analysis and the preparation of teachers. Like the serendipitous combination of chocolate and peanut butter that inspired Reese's Peanut Butter Cups, these two ways of looking at the essence of excellent teaching suddenly merged into the model we are proposing. Baiocco approached the investigation of excellence in teaching from a cognitive perspective, looking at the way teachers *think,* whereas DeWaters, coming from a behaviorist angle, focused on what teachers *do.* Both of us agreed upon the term of "radar" to describe the intuitive aspect demonstrated by all of the distinguished professors we observed. We saw this monitoring ability as a kind of "radar" which is always turned on, responding to cues in the instructional environment. We believed instinctively that our theory was both accurate and powerful. Our experiences told us that teachers at every level—from pre-kindergarten to graduate school—planned, acted, and evaluated routinely and frequently and that they drew upon their experiences to guide their decision making. As we observed similarities between our theory and our data, our hunch that the process of excellent teaching is a form of problem solving was further confirmed. Thus, in a sense, the manner in which we developed the answer to our research question, "What is distinguished teaching?" exemplifies the very thing we are trying to explain—the high level cognitive skills of problem solving. As we continued our research, we expanded and refined our original hypothesis into a set of postulates about excellent teaching which derived from our observations and experience as well as from previous theoretical models of problem solving and communication.

## THE ECLECTIC FIELD OF PROBLEM SOLVING

Currently, the field of problem solving is vast and eclectic. However, a more unified theory of problem solving is emerging as the result of interdisciplinary conferences and collaboration between experts in intersecting fields such as mathematics, philosophy, cognitive psychology, education, creative studies, artificial intelligence, and psycholinguistics.

Focusing on the literature on teaching as problem solving, Schön (1983) viewed "professional action" as involving the problem-solving processes of framing or naming the problem, taking action, and responding to the consequences of the actions. Sherman et al. (1987) looked at the cognitive components in terms of strategies for attacking a teaching problem and called for a theory of teaching excellence. Ramsden (1992) supported the notion that teaching is a problem-solving activity and pointed toward a reconceptualization of teaching centering around student learning problems. Menges and Rando (1996) produced a problem-solving model of the process of seeking and using feedback to improve teaching and learning that includes four phases of a cycle: (1) seeing and gathering, (2) interpreting and valuing, (3) planning and building, and (4) doing and checking. They also presented a taxonomy of instructional problems (p. 241).

As in our initial analogy of the blind man and the elephant (p. 94), researchers in problem solving all touch on different aspects of how the mind works. Most of the research supports the concept that problems have certain characteristics: givens, goals, and obstacles. Researchers further agree that problem solving is a complex set of processes that are recursive and, unlike machines, human beings are capable of going outside the problem to find novel solutions.

## TEACHING AS COGNITIVE PROCESSING

When it comes to theory development, we believe in the law of parsimony: Simple and elegant is preferable to complex and flashy. We set as our goal the development of a theory that, though comprehensive enough to explain our findings, would also be simple enough to be user-friendly. After considering many existing theories of problem solving as potential models, we eliminated (a) those that used unfamiliar terminology, (b) those that used empirical data derived from observations remote from educational settings, and (c) those that seemed unnecessarily complex. Particularly appealing in one model, a cognitive process theory of writing (Hayes & Flower, 1980; Flower & Hayes, 1981), was the reference to "flexibility and creativity," both being characteristics of the distinguished professors we studied. Although Flower and Hayes investigated the impact of flexibility and creativity in writing processes, we examined how these characteristics were demonstrated in the teaching processes.

Our theory suggests that teaching revolves around the ability (partially innate, partially learned) of some people to identify, analyze, and solve all types of problems. We believe that the brain functions like an airport terminal, with many activities occurring simultaneously while the main business of the terminal is directed and monitored from the control tower. Through a radar-like system that scans and interprets the learning environment, distinguished teachers make instructional decisions that guide students toward the overall goal of becoming independent learners. Sherman et al. (1987) described this "radar" as *metacognition.*

Standing in front of a class, the teacher sends and receives signals. All prior experience is called upon to interpret these signals as a professor makes judgments as to what the return signal will be. The ever-changing environment (including students, the physical space, and so on) demands flexibility and creativity in order that the professor meet the challenges of a diverse population. This dynamic system is not fixed or linear. Like a radar scope, the teacher is tracking multiple, and sometimes contradictory, signals. Some signals appear in isolation and others in a squadron, and some move at different speeds, appearing in differing intensities and directions. In what appears to be a chaotic environment, there are many opportunities for misreading these signals. For example, one day as Professor N. was leading a class discussion, students began firing questions at him from all directions. In a moment of insight, he described how he could see the questions (representing the students' varying levels of comprehension) stacked like aircraft in a holding pattern, one above the other in developmental order. His "radar" told him that reorganization of the questions was essential to the students' comprehension. Although others may have misinterpreted the questions as being random, Professor N. was able to make sense of them. In the remainder of this chapter we will expand on a concept of teaching as detecting, interpreting, and reacting to signals from students. We will frame this discussion by analyzing excellent instruction in terms of problem-solving theory.

## THREE COMPONENTS TO THE PROCESS

Problem-solving theorists disagree about how to classify the major problem-solving processes. For our purposes, we have chosen to describe three processes—(a) assessment and identification, (b) planning and implementation and (c) evaluation—while acknowledging that these categories are artificial, since inherent in the notion of process is the concept of something ongoing and continuous.

### Problem Identification and Assessment

During the first process, problem identification and assessment, problem solvers detect something in the environment that needs to be changed in order for them to reach a goal. In the instructional environment, this might be a student's negative attitude or a textbook which is unnecessarily complex. Typically, problem solvers will try to get a handle on the problem by attempting to find and examine causes for the problem and then divide the problem into parts, a process that problem-solving theorists call *problem analysis.*

## Planning and Implementation

The next process in the problem-solving model is planning and implementing the solution. For example, an excellent teacher's plan to find a new textbook might begin with ordering examination copies from publishers. During this process the teacher might seek recommendations from colleagues and show prospective texts to selected students. These are examples of how problem solvers use divergent thinking and then convergent thinking, as they assess the merits of a particular solution. In problem-solving lingo, these activities would be called *strategies* or *subgoals.*

Somewhere during this search for solutions, the problem solver—here, our instructor in search of a better textbook—will probably decide to "give it a rest" and leave the problem for a time. This deliberate postponement of decision making is what problem-solving researchers call *incubation.*

Creative studies research shows that such time off-task is often essential to the choice of a good solution. This allows our professor the time to reconsider course objectives or even go outside the traditional avenues to find a good textbook. During this downtime, one professor we know, for example, discovered on-line information sources, downloaded them, and had them compiled into a class reader. Another could decide to write his own textbook. The moment when the choice of a new textbook is made thus can be rather routine or can involve inspiration, that intuitive leap we described earlier.

Once a likely solution is found, problem solvers begin to act. One professor might decide to adopt a new text the next time the course is offered. Another might begin to collect readings or play with the notion of writing his own text. To be sure, when they all begin using a new text, they are likely to be tentative, conducting a classroom test of how successfully the new text meets their instructional goals of clarity and emphasis.

## Evaluation

The final problem-solving process, evaluation, is very like the assessment feature in the initial process of problem identification. Throughout the course when our instructor tests the utility of her new text, she will seek to evaluate whether the solution, the chosen textbook, is effective. Thus we see that teaching well requires an experimental frame of mind.

Throughout the test run with the new textbook, an excellent teacher will be monitoring whether students are learning better. The new text has been the "intervention" in a classroom experiment. If the class learns no better than it did previously, the professor may decide to revert to a former textbook, or, since real life classrooms are not laboratories, he may conclude that other variables influenced the outcome of his experiment and decide to give the text a longer trial period.

This ability to step back and take a global view of the instructional environment in total, including one's own teaching role, is a kind of metacognitive assessment that our case study professors reported during our interviews with them. They told us that they were always asking themselves, "How's this going?" and "Is this working?" If the answer was "Not well," then they shifted gears.

But rather than do as so many faculty do and blame the students for the learning problems, they first held themselves responsible for making improvements. They asked themselves, "What am I doing that should change?" Wise professors also understand that teaching experiments often fail, but they are willing to take calculated risks in hopes that better learning will result. When an instructional experiment flops, they are able to be philosophical and to learn from their mistakes.

Here is where the optimism that we wrote of as a key characteristic of outstanding teachers is crucial. Rather than becoming depressed by poor outcomes, distinguished teachers are spurred to keep trying. Problem-solving theorists would say that they have overcome "set rigidity," that is, they have not become fixated on the problem to the extent that they cannot see alternative solutions.

## THE THEORY IN ACTION

Now let us see the theory in action by taking a look at how these problem-solving processes are reflected in two problem scenarios. In Chapters 7 and 8 we provided a catalog of instructional problems and illustrated how award-winning professors addressed individual learning problems and problems with groups of students. The Problem-Solving Matrix (Table 9.1) is a useful framework for organizing our analyses, though we do not claim that it is comprehensive.

**TABLE 9.1  Instructional Problem-Solving Matrix**

|  | IDENTIFICATION & ASSESSMENT | PLANNING & IMPLEMENTATION | EVALUATION |
|---|---|---|---|
| Individual Problems |  |  |  |
| Group Problems |  |  |  |
| Content Problems |  |  |  |
| Environment Problems |  |  |  |
| Instructor Problems |  |  |  |

The problem-solving analyses in this chapter will highlight instructional problems related to content material and instructional environments.

## Scenario One: An Environmental Problem

Let's put Professor H.'s teaching under our microscope. An experienced professor of biology who has taught a course in gross anatomy for several years, he is becoming increasingly dissatisfied with his initial solution to a logistical problem. Professor H.'s laboratories do not have the television equipment he needs to enable groups of students to view close-ups of dissections. Initially, he decided to have students stand on lab stools in the back rows so they could see the procedure, but this solution proved unsatisfactory. His colleague in physics suggests that he look for interactive computer software to simulate the dissections; finding none, they decide to create one themselves—a daunting task, but one that absorbs them over a period of years.

During the first years of teaching the course, Dr. H. also has observed how students respond to their first encounters with cadavers and decides, after consulting his colleague in religious studies, that he would like to promote a respectful and appreciative attitude among his students toward the bodies. He gets the idea to initiate a new routine: the "blessing" of the bodies at the beginning of each semester. What we have witnessed here is the manner in which Professor H. continues to refine and improve the way in which he teaches a single course.

## Scenario Two: A Content Problem

In another illustration, Dr. E., an English professor, has successfully used students' reading response journals as a springboard to writing in her communications course for first-year students. She notices that students usually choose topics related directly to their own experience (personal narratives) or else write about the short stories or news articles they are reading for class discussion. She believes that the notion of community might be an excellent way to move her traditional 18-year-old students away from their egocentric stage of development toward the social involvement of a young adult. Drawing on what she knows about the novice writer, she designs an assignment that will force the students to focus on the outside worlds of the campus and the larger community.

She also wants to help students overcome their initial shyness and begin to make acquaintances in the classroom community, so she decides to pair up residents and commuters and ask them to collaborate on an observation of a campus site and report to the class for a prospective paper. The students eagerly choose sites. Curious to see how the experiment is going, Dr. E. directs each pair to report to the class during the next meeting and to turn in a jointly authored informal report. She hopes that the experience of co-authoring will be new for the students and will give them a taste of real world writing.

All but two students complete the assignment—an excellent success rate—and several pairs also report having benefited from collaborating in their writing. This leads Dr. E. to the question of how she will award grades to co-authored papers. Perhaps this seems contrary to what we have found about excellent teachers with respect to clarity. One would think that grading policy should be decided upon before the assignment is given. In this case, because this assignment is an experiment, she decides to negotiate the grading policies with the students. The real test of the assignment's success, she believes, will be whether any students choose to develop the assignment into a quality paper and submit it for a grade.

When the students' folders are submitted, 25% of the students have written about their venture into their new campus community, with the average grade of B on the six papers. Dr. E. assesses her new assignment as meeting her goals, but still needing refinement (an illustration of monitoring).

In both of these scenarios, we have observed how excellent teachers use a set of processes to meet instructional goals. The first scenario demonstrated the development and improvement of an existing course by the professor's creation of new strategies to improve the class setting. The second narrative described how a professor created a new assignment within an old course plan.

As we have said in other chapters, outstanding college teachers are excellent planners. When they sense problems or opportunities for learning, they are experts at setting objectives, inventing new solutions, creating new plans, employing new methods, evaluating the results, and making refinements.

## Phase One: Problem Identification and Assessment

Now let's examine the two scenarios in terms of the professors' problem identification and assessment.

*Scenario One, Phase One:* Dr. H. identified the instructional problem as an environmental interference. Students could not see the dissections.

*Scenario Two, Phase One:* Dr. E. was unhappy with the fact that students usually limited their choices for writing to personal narratives.

Dr. H.'s problem analysis most likely began with a sense of a logistical problem. There were simply too many students and too few cadavers to enable students to view the dissections clearly. The givens of his problem were the number of cadavers (they are very expensive) and the numbers of students in his lab sections. One solution—television equipment—was not available to him due to its expense. Yet Professor H. knew that the value of the lab experience was in the tactile and visual learning—the psychomotor dimension—that occurred during the dissections. How would he solve this logistical problem?

Dr. E.'s problem analysis most likely began with her awareness of the limitations of the personal narratives that students usually submitted as their first papers in this first-year English course. She could assign topics as many of her peers did, but she had a higher objective of making students responsible for their writing topics to assure that they were both interested and committed to their writing. Her decision to provide the community writing stimulus came out of the reading she had been doing in higher education, as well as the value she placed on collaboration.

## Phase Two: Planning and Implementation

*Scenario One, Phase Two:* Professor H. considers the alternatives and decides to allow students to stand on stools to observe dissections.

*Scenario Two, Phase Two:* Dr. E. designs a community writing assignment and pairs students to visit campus sites.

In this phase of planning and implementation, Dr. H. and Dr. E.'s actions are deceptively simple. Because excellent teachers are efficient, they manage more than one goal simultaneously. This concept of multiple goal processing explains how excellent teachers can successfully conduct groups and individuals simultaneously. For example, Dr. H. was in the process of solving one instructional problem—the logistics of viewing dissections—at the same time as he was becoming aware of another problem—an irreverent attitude by students towards the cadavers.

Dr. E.'s community assignment incorporated several layers of goals and objectives, although she only articulated the superficial goal of extending their concept of community (a cognitive objective). For example, pairing residence students and commuters was a strategy designed to build friendships among first-year students (an affective objective), and the site observations were an extension of that. However, she never informed students of her overriding goal, to move students away from an egocentric writing style to an expository one, believing that goal was too abstract for them to understand until the later developmental stages of writing.

In general, we have found that teachers frequently have far-reaching goals that go beyond the immediate objectives. Gradually, as the criteria for success are met, the students gain insight and are ready to understand more sophisticated goals. Thus, teachers frequently must present what are interpreted as stringent guidelines for the students to follow in attempt to guide them toward an understanding of the larger picture. For example, professors find themselves repeating certain foundation information again and again in order to form the basis for a conceptual framework.

## Phase Three: Evaluation

Now consider how these two professors approached the evaluation phase of problem solving.

*Scenario One, Phase Three:* Dr. H. is concerned that the "solution" he first arrives at is dangerous. He talks to a colleague, who suggests that they develop an interactive computer simulation of dissections, an anatomy almanac that students can preview prior to the dissection.

*Scenario Two, Phase Three:* Dr. E. assesses the assignment as successful because students eagerly present reports in class (affective objective) and an increased percentage of the class submits papers developed from the observation, rather than solely from their personal experience (cognitive objective).

In both of these scenarios, we see that the professor evaluated the effects of the strategy (solution) they had developed. Dr. H. was dissatisfied with the only solution he and his class could find at the time, and thus he began to search for a long-term solution. Meanwhile, he lived uncomfortably with the temporary solution. Dr. E. decided that the community assignment has been modestly successful and was worthy of continuing, but she would refine it further the next time. Thus we see that the problem-solving processes have come full circle: They move from assessment to assessment, and then the cycle begins again.

## TEACHING AND LEARNING AS DISCOURSE

We soon discovered a significant shortcoming of Flower and Hayes' (1981) composing process theory as a model for explaining teaching behavior: Its scope is too narrow. It was developed to explain one kind of communication problem—writing. We have said that instruction is not a single act of communication but an ongoing discourse in which teachers and students use a variety of language options, not simply writing. In fact, learning and instruction mostly involve spoken communication and nonverbal communication, with writing reserved for the more formal aspects of the teacher–student relationship.

To fill this gap in the cognitive process model of writing, we have incorporated into our theoretical framework some additional concepts derived from a psycholinguistic theory of discourse (Clark & Clark, 1977; MacWhinney, 1983), because they allow us to explain the more complex and ongoing natures of the communications between students and teachers.

During a semester, students in effect carry on a conversation with the professor as they interpret what linguists call "points," and generate responses in the form of papers, contributions to class discussions, and answers on tests. Teaching and learning are cooperative acts, just as our distinguished teachers so eloquently described them as a "shared responsibility" in their philosophies of teaching in Chapter 6.

In order to begin the instructional discourse, the professor must establish the students' baseline level of comprehension. The emphasis our participants placed on preliminary status assessment, identifying the entering knowledge and skills of students, shows that they are aware of how crucial that preassessment is to successful instruction. And, because students' responses are almost always presented in some linguistic form for evaluation—either speech or writing—the outstanding teacher is also remarkably sensitive to the fact that knowledge of prerequisite terms and behaviors are essential to the understanding of certain concepts and skills. Consequently, they continually seek to give students the language and terminology they will need to learn a particular subject.

This analysis of the social contexts for discourse are salient if we apply them to instructional failures as well as successes. Within the instructional dialogue that occurs between teachers and students, outstanding teachers know that there are many opportunities for communication errors: Sometimes students incorrectly anticipate what is expected in the course; sometimes teachers' intentions are misunderstood; and other times, conventions of academe—such as the time allotted for a student to learn a particular skill or concept—interfere with instruction.

An important fact to remember is that people only solve the problems that they find. Professors who fail to recognize anything more than superficial problems in their classes, who think that because they are lecturing, students are learning, will never become excellent teachers unless they are taught to see differently.

In our study, we found that one of the ways in which distinguished teachers differed from other teachers was their ability to identify a vast array of learning problems. Like the musician who has learned to hear the subtleties of sound, or the artist who can distinguish between a hundred shades of green, the excellent teacher is expert at finding and analyzing a wider variety of instructional problems, perhaps even a different kind of problem. Our data clearly showed that novice teachers identified a more basic level of problems than did our excellent, experienced teachers. For example, novices were concerned about lecturing in an interesting way or about selecting course readings, often viewing elements in the instructional environment as the problem, unlike our expert teachers, who more often focused their attention instead on the behaviors of individuals and groups—including themselves—as the problem.

Our findings suggest that there may be a hierarchy of instructional problems, and that faculty see the classroom environment differently depending on their level of experience. Beginning teachers' instructional problem solving may be hampered by their inability to accurately locate the learning problems. Their need to survive in the academy dictates that they focus on aspects of the instructional environment that have become second nature to experienced professors, who are intimately familiar with their fields, instructional materials, presentation techniques, and the evaluation process.

## PUTTING THE THEORY TO USE

In this chapter, we traced the genealogy of our problem-solving theory of teaching from cognitive science, education research, and discourse theory, and we suggested that the distinguished professors we observed appeared to posses a superior ability to scan and interpret the learning environment. From our case study analysis, we presented and illustrated three problem-solving processes: (a) assessment and identification, (b) planning and implementation, and (c) evaluation. Then, in our "Problem-Solving Matrix" (See Table 9.1), we showed how these processes might be applied across the domain of instructional problems, which we viewed as having five strands: individual learning problems, problems of aggregates of students, content problems, instructional environment problems, and instructor problems. We also suggested that the distinguished teaching professors we observed understood the cooperative nature of learning and made fine distinctions about students' learning problems.

In the next chapter, we will show how our problem-solving approach might be used to assist new professors with their teaching. We will discuss the lack of preparation of graduate students for college teaching, contrast the concerns of teaching assistants and experienced faculty, and finally present an array of solutions to common problems proposed by new professors.

## REFERENCES

Clark, H., & Clark, E. (1977). *Psychology and language: An introduction to psycholinguistics.* New York: Harcourt Brace Jovanovich.

Flower, L. S., & Hayes, J. R. (1981). A cognitive process theory of writing. *College Composition and Communication, 32,* 365–387.

Gagné, R. M. (1975). Human problem solving: Internal and external events. In B. Kleinmuntz (Ed.), *Problem solving: Research, method and theory* (pp. 127–148). Huntington, NY: Robert E. Krieger.

Gardner, H. (1993). *Multiple intelligences: The theory in practice.* New York: Basic.

Hayes, J. R., & Flower, L. S. (1980). Identifying the organization of writing processes. In L. W. Gregg and E. R. Steinberg (Eds.), *Cognitive processes in writing* (pp. 3–30). Hillsdale, NJ: Lawrence Erlbaum.m

MacWhinney, B. (1983). Motives for sharing points. (National Science Foundation Linguistics Program Grant #BN57905755). Pittsburgh: Carnegie Mellon University.

Menges, R. J., & Rando, W. C. (1996). Feedback for enhanced teaching and learning. In R. J. Menges, M. Weimer, & Associates (Eds.). *Teaching on solid ground: Using scholarship to improve practice.* (pp. 233–255). San Francisco: Jossey-Bass.

Ramsden, P. (1992). *Learning to teach in higher education.* London: Rutledge.

Rice, R. E. (1991). The new American scholar: Scholarship and the purposes of the university. *Metropolitan universities: An international forum,* 1(4), 7–18.

Schön, D. (1983). *The reflective practitioner,* New York: Basic Books.

Sherman, T. M., Armistead, L. P., Fowler, F., Barksdale, M. A., & Reif, G. (1987). The quest for excellence in university teaching. *Journal of Higher Education, 58,* 66–84.

# CHAPTER 4

# UNDERSTANDING HALLMARKS OF LEARNER-CENTERED TEACHING AND ASSESSMENT

Among the leaders of the movement to foster a shift from a teacher-centered to a learner-centered paradigm, Mary E. Huba and Jann E. Freed present in this chapter the foundational elements and useful examples of their approach. Their eight hallmarks of learner-centered teaching guide the self-assessing professor to insights that are sure to foster a more contemporary approach to their profession and a more civil and effective learning environment for students.

Among the more important elements of this chapter is the series of scenarios taken from the classrooms of leading facilitators of learning, in disciplines as diverse as forestry and mathematics. This tactic engenders a creative enthusiasm among readers that is sure to trigger immediate insights into their regular teaching practices, fostering changes that could very quickly improve the quality of student learning in their classrooms.

# UNDERSTANDING HALLMARKS OF LEARNER-CENTERED TEACHING AND ASSESSMENT

Chapter 2 from *Learner-Centered Assessment on College Campuses*
**Mary E. Huba & Jann E. Freed**
**Allyn & Bacon, © 2000**

There is a slow, but growing trend for practicing quality concepts in teaching ...classes have become more learner-centered, classes are more focused on learning than teaching, and faculty members have found ways to involve students so that students take more ownership for their learning. In addition, faculty members are systematically collecting feedback from students so that they can make incremental improvement for the students during the course rather than waiting until the course is over (Freed & Klugman, 1997).

While teacher evaluation focuses on teachers and teaching, Classroom Assessment focuses on learners and learning (Angelo, 1994, p. 10).

---

**MAKING CONNECTIONS**

*As you begin to read the chapter, think about ideas and experiences you've already had that are related to learner-centered teaching and assessment...*

- With what aspects of your *teaching* do you feel satisfied? Dissatisfied?
- With what aspects of *assessment* do you feel satisfied? Dissatisfied?
- How and to what extent do your students take ownership of their learning?

- What changes would you like to make in your teaching and assessing?
- How might these changes best be made?

*What else do you know about learner-centered teaching and assessment?*

*What questions do you have about learner-centered teaching and assessment?*

In this chapter, we will examine eight hallmarks of learner-centered teaching that derive from the field of continuous improvement and from the research of cognitive psychologists and educational researchers. We will see how they are related to some of the propositions for learning developed by the Joint Task Force on Student Learning appointed by the American Association for Higher Education (AAHE), the American College Personnel Association (ACPA), and the National Association of Student Personnel Administrators (Joint Task Force, 1998a, 1998b).

For each hallmark, we will review one or more examples, as well as some questions you can use to reflect on your own teaching. In the remainder of the book, the principles presented here will be translated into specific techniques to help make teaching more learner-centered.

Figure 2.1 summarizes the hallmarks of learner-centered teaching. Several hallmarks focus on learners, describing how they spend their time in ways that promote learning in a learner-centered environment. Other hallmarks focus on the professor, pointing out the viewpoints and activities that professors can employ in order to maximize student learning. The final hallmark indicates that, in learner-centered teaching, learning is viewed as an interpersonal activity. As theorists would put it, learning is "socially constructed." In learner-centered environments, all learners—students and professors—are respected and valued.

## LEARNERS ARE ACTIVELY INVOLVED AND RECEIVE FEEDBACK

> Learning is an *active search for meaning* by the learner—constructing knowledge rather than passively receiving it, shaping as well as being shaped by experiences (Joint Task Force on Student Learning, 1998a, p. 2).

**FIGURE 2.1   Hallmarks of Learner-Centered Teaching**

- Learners are actively involved and receive feedback.
- Learners apply knowledge to enduring and emerging issues and problems.
- Learners integrate discipline-based knowledge and general skills.
- Learners understand the characteristics of excellent work.
- Learners become increasingly sophisticated learners and knowers.
- Professors coach and facilitate, intertwining teaching and assessing.
- Professors reveal that they are learners, too.
- Learning is interpersonal, and all learners—students and professors—are respected and valued.

Over the past 20 years, psychological researchers have documented that the human mind actively creates what it knows. Cognitive psychologists tell us that from the very first moments of life humans begin to interact with and explore the world, actively searching for meaning, constructing and reconstructing mental representations of what it's all about (Copple, Sigel, & Saunders, 1984; Gardner, 1991). Humans seem insatiable for new information and driven to make sense of it. This theory of learning is called constructivism (Bransford, Brown, & Cocking, 1999; Brooks & Brooks, 1993; Duffy & Cunningham, 1996; Fosnot, 1996).

Children, of course, who have less experience than adults and different ways of processing information, develop different perspectives as they grow. But their urge to make their own kind of sense out of what they experience is never ending. As shown in the following examples, cartoonists have made careers out of this characteristic, making us laugh at the unexpected statements of the children in their cartoons, statements that from an adult's perspective are "misconceptions."

- Dennis the Menace, dressed up and sitting in his booster seat at a fancy restaurant, looks at the large menu and says to his parents, "Is this one of those *slow-food* places with carrots on the menu?" (Ketcham, 1997a)
- Dennis the Menace looks up at the lifeguard on the beach and says, "I say, what flavor are the jellyfish today?" (Ketcham, 1997b)
- The little girl in The Family Circus stands by the flowers in the garden and patiently explains to her younger brother, "Butterflies are quiet, but bumblebees have motors" (Keane, 1997).
- The little girl in The Family Circus looks up as she eats her hamburger and says, "If I planted sesame seeds, would I grow hamburger buns?" (Keane, 1998)

All of these are unmistakable examples of children's attempts to construct an understanding of the world that incorporates what they see, hear, and experience. For example, in the first cartoon, Dennis the Menace is using his existing knowledge of fast-food restaurants—their typical environment, menu, and dress—to reason that the current restaurant, which seems different in every way, must be a "slow-food" place. In the words of the Joint Task Force on Learning quoted at the beginning of this section, his existing knowledge about restaurants "is shaping" his current experience. On the other hand, his existing knowledge about restaurants is in turn being shaped by his experience of a formal dining environment. His understanding of the concept "restaurant" is being forever altered.

Experts know now that this process of creating understanding continues throughout a lifetime. This may come as no surprise to modern day followers of Socrates, but to those who approach teaching as though students' minds are blank slates waiting for inscription, it has far-reaching consequences.

For example, it has profound implications for those of us who teach in colleges and universities. Rather than focusing on learners, our traditional approach to teaching has focused on the professor. How organized is the lecture? How accurate and up-to-date is the information in it? Is it well-paced and timed to maintain the needed level of student interest? Teachers "pour in" knowledge, and students are expected to give it back as received. This is the traditional paradigm of teaching: teachers with all the answers performing to passive students.

Those among us who espouse traditional approaches to teaching feel responsible for imparting to students the most current information in our fields. We typically use the lecture method of instruction that requires the professor to seek out new information, integrate it with existing knowledge, organize it for presentation to students, and explain it orally to the class. Students are expected to listen carefully, perhaps asking an occasional question, but basically receiving the information of the lecture in a passive fashion for later regurgitation in a subsequent assessment, probably a test.

From a constructivist perspective, the individuals learning the most in this classroom are the professors. They have reserved for themselves the very conditions that promote learning: actively seeking new information, integrating it with what is known, organizing it in a meaningful way, and having the chance to explain it to others. In fact, all of us who have taught a class more than once know that each time we teach it, our understanding of the material deepens.

Interestingly, the traditional approach to teaching intellectual skills and concepts is not used in performance-oriented areas like the arts or sports. No one would ever think of teaching violin or basketball by having students watch and memorize, whether they watched the teacher or memorized rules. Watching and memorizing simply aren't enough to support learning. Students must be actively involved to learn the concepts and practice the skills.

One more key ingredient of effective learning is present in performance-oriented areas. Students receive constant feedback on their performance. Sending students out on the basketball court to try to shoot baskets or to explore the game doesn't ensure mastery. Students will undoubtedly have fun, and they will surely learn something. But they'll never master the many interrelated skills of the game unless they get feedback about how they are doing. Providing that feedback is what coaching—teaching and assessing—is all about.

Therefore, students in learner-centered environments learn course material in a way that promotes deep understanding. They are told the intended learning outcomes of their course or program (see Chapter 4), and they are encouraged to formulate their own learning goals (see Chapter 8). As will be discussed in Chapter 7, they complete assignments (assessments) that require them to seek out, organize, describe, and use new information as these activities are carried out in their disciplines. They explore, research, make choices, and explain, and this helps them develop an understanding of the discipline that matches that of experts in the field. In addition, they receive continuous feedback that keeps them on track to make continuous improvements in performance (see Chapter 6).

The learner-centered examples in Figures 2.2 through 2.6 illustrate this hallmark. In each example, the active involvement of the learners helps them make sense of the course material and develop a deeper understanding than they would if they passively listened to a lecture. Feedback to learners is provided through discussion with peers and the professor, through the use of criteria describing excellent work, or through summaries of student responses to in-class surveys.

---

**REFLECTIONS**

*As you create your own meaning from the ideas in this section, begin to think about…*

- How do I typically think about the students I teach? How would I describe them?
- At what times do I think of them as an audience to whom I play?
- At what times do I think of them as a collection of inquiring minds, each actively engaged in constructing understanding?

- In what ways do I expect my students to defer to me as an expert and an authority?
- In what ways do I work with students as partners in learning?
- When preparing for class, how much emphasis do I give to accurate and well-delivered lectures?
- How much emphasis do I place on activities in which students must *use* course material?

---

## LEARNERS APPLY KNOWLEDGE TO ENDURING AND EMERGING ISSUES AND PROBLEMS

---

Learning is enhanced by *taking place* in the context of *a compelling situation* that balances challenge and opportunity, stimulating and utilizing the brain's ability to conceptualize quickly and its capacity and need for contemplation and reflection upon experiences (Joint Task Force on Student Learning, 1998a, p. 1).

---

In learner-centered teaching, students are asked to do important things worth doing. They don't just acquire knowledge for knowledge's sake. They complete assessments designed around real-world problems (see Chapter 7), and in this way, they experience the compelling challenges typically faced by professionals in their disciplines. The problems they address are ill-defined, that is, they have no right answer and their structure is not always apparent. Some ill-defined problems are enduring (e.g., how to ameliorate world hunger) while others are emerging (how to use the capabilities of technology in an ethical manner). These enduring and emerging issues and problems are fraught with the complicating factors of real life (e.g., politics, value clashes, ambiguity, etc.).

Assessments in which students address ill-defined problems—authentic assessments—are engaging to college students who are making the transition from adolescence to adulthood. Most students enroll in college voluntarily, and they seek to develop an adult identity through the majors they have chosen. Real-world assessments reinforce students' desire to learn and achieve, and they help students develop the direction and identity they seek.

Completing ill-defined problems leads to the understanding that adults are judged on their ability to grapple with the unknown, using the known. As a professor of agriculture pointed out after returning from several years working in industry, "In my undergraduate and graduate education, I was taught using a black and white approach. When I went to work in industry, everything was gray. I know now that my task is to teach 'gray' when working with my own students" (T. Polito, personal communication, 1996).

In traditional educational environments, students typically encounter "black and white" problems that we refer to as "well defined." Well-defined problems are found at the end of most textbook chapters, and they have right answers that are keyed in the back of the book. These problems have been carefully constructed so that some problem elements are present and other problem elements are missing. In other words, the "messiness" of real life is removed so that students will be guided to apply a particular structured algorithm leading to a correct answer.

Well-defined problems are helpful for developing skills that involve many steps. When students complete them, they repeat the steps over and over so that they eventually become habits that can be used when needed. However, just solving well-defined problems doesn't help students know *when and how* the habits and skills should be *used*—and knowing *when and how to use* knowledge is critical to success in adult life. In other words, solving only well-defined problems in college does not prepare students to address the ill-defined problems that adults face daily in their personal and professional lives. Thus, the more we use authentic assessments in our teaching, the more we prepare students to use their knowledge effectively in the future.

Using authentic assessments has other advantages as well. For example, when students complete ill-defined problems, they have an opportunity to reveal their uniqueness as learners. Students bring different talents and learning styles to college, and learner-centered teaching and assessing honors them. Well-defined problems or traditional tests like multiple-choice tests require all students to respond in a uniform way. However, assessments that involve ill-defined problems allow each student to approach, solve, and communicate about the problem in his or her own way.

In addition, involving students in addressing real-world problems frequently leads to opportunities for students to work in teams. Learning is enhanced when it takes place in an environment in which cooperation instead of competition is cultivated. The process of working with others allows students to develop their own ideas through sharing them with others and listening to their feedback. It develops collaborative skills that will benefit them throughout life.

In the first three learner-centered examples (Figures 2.2 through 2.4) students are actively involved with complex issues and problems that are of current concern to practitioners in their discipline: processes for developing effective long-range strategic plans (Business Management), preparing successful bids for contracts (Construction Engineering), and understanding the implications of land management decisions (Forestry). Their ill-defined nature allows students to make errors and learn from them, developing a deeper understanding of their discipline as it is practiced in the real world.

**FIGURE 2.2    A Learner-Centered Example from Business Management**

Professor Sanchez teaches a capstone course for Business Management students. She assigns a long-term project for students to work on during the second half of the semester. The project describes a company whose profits have been steadily declining over recent years and requires students to design a process that management can use to develop a long-range, strategic plan. Students are expected to complete the project in teams.

Professor Sanchez outlines her expectations for the type of work students are to produce, and her expectations are based on criteria used in the business world. The purpose of the project is to design a process for developing a long-range, strategic plan that is feasible, defensible, and responsive to the particular company described. In order to do so, students must gather information about relevant legislation, common practice, company needs, and basic management protocol. In teams of three, students assign tasks to each other, discuss findings, brainstorm recommendations, and react to each other's ideas. Through the processes of inquiry, idea generation, and discussion, each student develops a deeper understanding of various aspects of the field of Management.

Feedback is provided when students react to each other's ideas in structured feedback sessions set up by the professor and in the final evaluation of the project. In the feedback sessions, two teams of students present their proposed process and its rationale to each other with one team defending and the other questioning their recommendations. The professor plays devil's advocate or prompts thoughtful reflection by questioning the team's proposals. When students find out, for example, that a certain proposal violates business standards, their understanding of good business practice increases. When each group completes their final project, it is presented to the professor and teaching assistants at which time further questioning takes place, and additional feedback is provided.

(Adapted from Ulrichson, 1998)

**FIGURE 2.3   A Learner-Centered Example from Construction Engineering**

For several years, Professor Jahren has been teaching his Construction Engineering students how to prepare bids for construction projects like building a bridge or grading a highway. For most of his career, he lectured about the cost estimating process and assigned homework problems and labs that were meant to help students develop necessary skills. His exams included problems and essay questions to test students' understanding of the basic knowledge and skills involved in preparing bids that meet specifications and are feasible, cost-effective, and technically sound. In recent years, however, he followed the lead of his senior colleagues and developed a simulated bid opening for his final lab in which students incorporated a myriad of subcontractor and supplier quotes into their bids and tendered their completed bids to him.

Professor Jahren was pleased by his students' enthusiasm for the simulated bid opening. He received many compliments on student evaluations as well as requests to make the simulation more realistic. Therefore, when local construction industry leaders suggested that his students submit mock bids at an actual state transportation bid-letting, he quickly agreed. The industry people had seen students participating in a similar activity in a neighboring state. They pointed out that the activity helps students learn to work in groups under stress and correctly make last minute modifications to a complicated analysis. In addition, it allows engineers in industry to share an important part of their job that is little understood by the general public.

Professor Jahren developed the activity into a special project course. In the course, students get credit for preparing bids for actual construction projects (e.g., replacing bridges, grading, paving) designed by state, county, and municipal transportation agencies around the state. Students present their bids to transportation officials as mock bids at the same time that local contractors submit their actual bids. The students' mock bids are examined and evaluated along with the real ones, and students receive feedback on their work.

In executing this project, sophomore through senior students work in teams of three or four with seniors serving as team leaders. They design the construction process on paper, using the same information that is available to other professionals in the community. Next, students estimate the cost of implementing their design. In this phase of the project, they have access to a local company whose staff have been assigned to act as mentors. Interacting with the mentors provides an opportunity to develop skills in professional interaction. Finally, students submit their project to the transportation officials according to the same deadline and standards followed by local contractors.

Professor Jahren and his practitioner colleagues have developed criteria for judging the students' work (e.g., timeliness of the proposal, quality of materials used, adequacy of structural design, ability to respond to changing conditions, effectiveness of written and oral communication). They share these criteria with students when the project is assigned, and each semester the students themselves help improve the criteria.

Over time, students have begun to use the criteria as guidelines for developing their project. Professor Jahren meets with students periodically for progress reports about their project. He and the students use the criteria to assess what they are doing well and where they need to improve. In the future, Professor Jahren plans to have students rate the final version of their project using the criteria and hand in their ratings with the project. Both students and professors in the program have come to a clearer understanding of how to prepare effectively for bid-letting competitions in the real world of engineering.

(Jahren & Kipp, 1999)

**FIGURE 2.4   A Learner-Centered Example from Forestry**

The faculty in a Forestry program organize their sophomore students into cohorts, and each cohort takes a five-course sequence of courses together. The courses in the sequence are taught by Forestry professors and are designed to integrate general education skills and disciplinary knowledge in Forestry. In each course professors teach and evaluate knowledge and skills related to inquiry, teamwork, application of mathematics, and oral and written communication, as well as standard course content.

Students complete a team project that gets them actively involved in addressing the political, environmental, economic, and social implications of land management decisions. Students gather data in the field, analyze it, and communicate their findings through oral and written reports. They confer regularly with the professor and participate in feedback discussions about their progress. At the conclusion of the project, students reflect about how well the team functioned as a whole and about how well they contributed individually to the team's success. They discuss together how they might do a better job working together in the future.

(Department of Forestry Faculty, 1998)

**REFLECTIONS**

*As you create your own meaning from the ideas in this section, begin to think about…*

- What *enduring* issues and problems do students address in my course? How do they address them?
- What *emerging* issues and problems do students address in my course? How do they address them?
- Where and how do students have opportunities to solve *well-defined* problems in my courses?
- Where and how do students have opportunities to solve *ill*-defined problems in my courses?
- How do my students see the connection between what they learn in my courses and how that information is used in real-world applications?

# LEARNERS INTEGRATE DISCIPLINE-BASED KNOWLEDGE AND GENERAL SKILLS

Learning is fundamentally about *making and maintaining connections*: biologically through neural networks; mentally among concepts, ideas, and meanings; experientially through interaction between the mind and the environment, self and other, generality and context, deliberation and action (Joint Task Force on Student Learning, 1998a, p. 1).

Assessments designed around ill-defined problems typically take the form of projects, papers, performances, portfolios, or exhibitions. Students completing them have to call upon and develop their disciplinary knowledge, as well as their skills in the areas of inquiry, reasoning, problem solving, communication, and perhaps teamwork. In other words, authentic assessments require that students make connections between the abilities and skills they have developed in the general education curriculum and the discipline-based knowledge and skills they have acquired in the major. When authentic assessments are used, the evaluation issue changes from, "Are students getting the right answers?" to:

- Can students demonstrate the qualities we value in educated persons, the qualities we expect of college graduates?
- Can they gather and evaluate new information, think critically, reason effectively, and solve problems?
- Can they communicate clearly, drawing upon evidence to provide a basis for argumentation?
- Do their decisions and judgments reflect understanding of universal truths revealed in the humanities and the arts?
- Can they work respectfully and productively with others?
- Do they have self-regulating qualities like persistence and time management that will help them reach long-term goals?

In sum, can students use the skills and abilities that the general education curriculum has been designed to develop?

Even more important, authentic assessments allow us to ask, "Can students demonstrate the characteristics we expect from professionals in our disciplines? Can students think and behave like biologists, statisticians, landscape architects, teachers, and so on?"

At this point, assessment questions become more refined. Rather than the general question, "Can students communicate clearly?" we ask the more specific question, "Can students communicate like professionals in their fields?" Clearly, communication and problem-solving skills, as well as others like the application of ethical principles, change from discipline to discipline. To some extent, the communication skills required of engineers are different from those required of journalists. To some extent, the ethical questions facing geneticists are different from those facing teachers. Authentic assessments provide excellent opportunities to tailor students' learning to the fields in which they will work.

Obviously, learner-centered teaching gives greater prominence to "process" abilities and skills like communication and reasoning than traditional teaching practices may have done. However, learner-centered teaching does not de-emphasize basic knowledge in the discipline. As Resnick and Resnick (1992) point out, students who have greater command of the knowledge of their discipline can reason and communicate more effectively than those with less knowledge. Professors who take a learner-centered approach do not shortchange students in basic knowledge—they help them *use* it.

The projects in the first three examples (Figures 2.2 through 2.4) require the integration of disciplinary knowledge and numerous skills and abilities from the general education curriculum in the areas of inquiry, communication, problem solving, and teamwork. They provide the means through which students can actually *use* the knowledge of their discipline.

---

**REFLECTIONS**

*As you create your own meaning from the ideas in this section, begin to think about...*

- How do I emphasize critical thinking and problem solving in my courses?
- How do I help students integrate the skills and perspectives they learn in general education with the content of my discipline?
- How do I help students make connections between my course and other courses they have had or will have in the curriculum?

- How do I help students think and behave like members of the discipline?
- How comfortable or uncomfortable am I with this idea?
- What do I think about focusing on communication, critical thinking, teamwork, and so forth, with students as they learn the content of my discipline? How will these skills help them learn content more effectively?

---

## PAUSE FOR AN EXAMPLE: DIFFERENCES BETWEEN TYPICAL TEACHING PRACTICE AND THE FIRST THREE HALLMARKS

Thus far, we have emphasized the active involvement of learners in activities and assessments that integrate discrete skills and abilities. We have also focused on the importance of helping students make connections between existing knowledge and new information and between what they learn in college and what takes place in the world of practice in their disciplines. How do these suggestions differ from the typical student experience? The following is an example.

Professors in most statistics departments probably expect their graduates to be able to explain statistical findings clearly to an educated audience that is not trained in statistics. This requires knowledge of statistical theory and practice, ability to use modern computing techniques, writing ability, and oral presentation skills (Department of Statistics, 1996).

Recognizing this, statistics faculty at most institutions have designed the curriculum so that students acquire the needed skills and understandings. Students take several courses in both parametric and nonparametric statistical theory. Some courses include computer applications that make use of modern computing technology. Built into the program is the general education requirement of a freshman writing course, and some students take a speech communication course as an elective. Does this ensure that the faculty's goal for graduates will be achieved? Probably not.

As it turns out, three difficulties occur with this approach. First, the important intended outcome of having graduates "explain statistical findings clearly to an educated audience that is not trained in statistics" is approached in the curriculum by having students take separate courses in statistics, computing, writing, and speaking. The writing and speech communications courses are probably outside their department. When important activities are divided up in this way, students learn the parts in isolation, but they receive no practice integrating the parts into a new, more complex "whole" (Resnick & Resnick, 1992). In this example, students are never asked to write and speak about statistics in their undergraduate program.

Second, the components tend to be taught outside the real-world context in which the performance typically takes place (Resnick & Resnick, 1992). Students lose the opportunity to see the real-world application for what they are studying; that is, they miss the forest for the trees. Motivation and a sense of direction are lost. In the example given, it probably never occurs to students in statistics classes that someday they will be asked to use their expertise to explain real-life data to "lay" audiences. They probably focus more on getting the right answers on tests than on integrating their statistical knowledge and communication abilities into a valued professional skill.

Third, the basic assumption that students will automatically apply knowledge when needed has turned out to be false. Research has shown that students can learn facts, theories, or individual tasks, but without the opportunity to use the knowledge or skill to achieve a goal, it is recalled only in the context in which it was learned (Bransford & Vye, 1989). In other words, the knowledge is "inert" (Whitehead, 1929).

This phenomenon helps explain why students who acquire knowledge and/or skills in one course seem unable to effectively use them in the next course. It may account for the extensive amount of on-the-job learning that college graduates typically need. They probably acquired the theory or some skills relevant to their job, but they need experienced co-workers to help them make the theory-to-practice connection. The public is becoming increasingly impatient with the training employers are required to provide for college graduates. Taxpayers today have higher expectations for higher education institutions, and they are demanding accountability.

A learner-centered solution to the statistics problem would retain the intended learning outcome of the statistics faculty ("Students should be able to explain statistical findings clearly to an educated audience that is not trained in statistics") because it focuses on student learning and reflects an important achievement valued by practicing statisticians. An additional step would be to reveal this intended learning outcome to students themselves in the college catalog and in course syllabi. (See Chapter 4 for a discussion of intended learning outcomes.)

The next step would be to provide opportunities for students to integrate the components of the outcome (statistical knowledge, computing, writing, and speaking) as students are learning about them. For example, as students learn about new statistical techniques in their statistics courses, they should not only solve numerical statistical problems, but they should also complete writing or speaking assignments interpreting the results. When this is done in beginning statistics courses, students will be relatively unsophisticated in integrating statistical knowledge, computing, writing, and speaking. The components will seem somewhat separate (Loacker, Cromwell, & O'Brien, 1986). However, by the time students have completed several courses, they will have developed rather sophisticated and well-coordinated abilities to "explain statistical findings clearly to an audience that is educated but not trained in statistics."

A related step for statistics faculty would be to teach students how to identify opportunities to apply their newfound skill in real-life applications and how to carry it out appropriately in different settings. In other words, statistics professors who want graduates to communicate effectively about statistics should ask students to do so while they are enrolled in their statistics courses.

We will now return to a consideration of additional hallmarks of learner-centered teaching and assessing.

---

**REFLECTIONS**

*As you create your own meaning from the ideas in this section, begin to think about...*

- What practices in my program reflect a learner-centered approach to teaching?

- What practices in my program interfere with a learner-centered approach to teaching?
- How could these practices be changed to reflect the hallmarks of learner-centered teaching and assessment?

---

## LEARNERS UNDERSTAND THE CHARACTERISTICS OF EXCELLENT WORK

---

Learning requires *frequent feedback* if it is to be sustained, *practice* if it is to be nourished, and *opportunities to use* what has been learned (Joint Task Force on Student Learning, 1998a, p. 3).

In a learner-centered culture in which students seek to address enduring and emerging issues and problems, we must develop a focus on the quality of work expected and allow students to make errors as they seek to achieve it. Solving ill-defined problems rather than problems with one right answer means that students *will* make errors. In learner-centered teaching, however, mistakes are opportunities on which to capitalize, rather than events to avoid.

> Errors are part of the process of problem solving, which implies that both teachers and learners need to be more tolerant of them. If no mistakes are made, then almost certainly no problem solving is taking place. Unfortunately, one tradition of schooling is that perfect performance is often exalted as the ideal. Errors are seen as failures, as signs that the highest marks are not quite merited…. Perfect performance may be a reasonable criterion for evaluating algorithmic performance (though I doubt it), but it is incompatible with problem solving (Martinez, 1998, p. 609).

Thus, a key ingredient in learner-centered teaching is allowing students to make mistakes and learn from them. In order for students to learn from their errors, we must create an environment of honesty without fear (Deming, 1986). We must provide students with a clear vision of what excellent work is like and help them use feedback to continually improve their own work and performance. We must develop clearly stated, public criteria in the form of scoring rubrics that describe excellent work and that can be used as the basis for feedback. Having clear standards of performance—that is, being able to describe the defining features of excellent work—is essential for improvement (Loacker, Cromwell, & O'Brien, 1986; Wiggins, 1993).

As will be discussed in Chapter 6, criteria in the form of rubrics can be developed by the professor or by the professor and students together. When public criteria are available and discussions about the quality of work are common, students don't have to wait for the first test to figure out what aspects of learning the professor considers important. They know right from the beginning. Using available criteria, students can assess and judge their own work, even in the early stages of formulation, and they are thus more motivated to take ownership of their own learning. Furthermore, students can work with each other to critique their work, judging it not simply by their own idiosyncratic standards, but also by the standards the professor has shared or developed with the class.

Most importantly, students can use the criteria to self-correct, because improvement in learning is what assessment is all about.

> We've heard a lot during the past ten or fifteen years in both the higher education and K–12 settings about the importance of student self-assessment. Despite the importance of the idea, it is a misleading phrase. Self-assessment is not the goal. Self-adjustment is the goal (Wiggins, 1997, p. 35).

The opportunity to self-correct and try again is essential to self-improvement and the development of lifelong learning skills; this is the underlying premise of continuous improvement. With rapid changes in the workplace due to the technology explosion, employers expect graduates to be able to learn independently. They must be flexible, skilled at making adjustments, and willing to take responsibility for making improvements.

In our role as professors, we can also use scoring criteria to give feedback about student work as it evolves. Furthermore, we can use the criteria to evaluate the final product. Assessing with clearly described criteria that have been publicly revealed is very different from assessing using an answer key that specifies "right" answers. We are able to evaluate qualities such as organization, communication, creativity, and ability to apply a known body of knowledge. We can allow students to approach assignments in unique ways, but we judge all work by the same criteria. By revealing standards of excellence, we remove barriers to learning. Of course, for many reasons, not all students will perform at the level of excellence, but revealing the standards held by educated people and by practicing professionals enhances students' chances of success.

Does this make assessments more subjective than tests that can be objectively scored by machines? Of course. But students will be judged subjectively throughout their adult lives. The important task is to let them know the standards shared by educated people and by individuals in their profession. In other words, assessment that is *subjective but public* may be more important than assessment that is *objective but private.*

In a learner-centered course, all students know the standards for excellence and therefore have a chance to produce excellent work. The instructor is not the only, or even perhaps the most important, evaluator. All engaged in the learning process have a stake in serving as assessors. Having public standards creates an environment that is fundamentally fair, downplaying the current need to figure out the system. This benefits all students, but it may be particularly helpful to nontraditional students who are faced with the need to "learn the ropes" on many fronts at college, creating barriers to learning. Learner-centered teaching helps circumvent those barriers. As the student population becomes increasingly more diverse, public standards of excellence ensure fairness for all.

The clearest example of this hallmark is found in Figure 2.3. In this Construction Engineering example, students and professors initially develop criteria for judging students' completed work. However, they soon find that the criteria are useful tools for students to use as they develop their work. The criteria are also a good basis for discussion when students talk about their progress with the professor. The professor in this example eventually decides to structure students' own assessment of their achievement into the project requirements.

**REFLECTIONS**

*As you create your own meaning from the ideas in this section, begin to think about...*

- How do my students and I view student errors? Are they something to avoid or are they learning opportunities?
- Do I expect excellent performance from all my students? How do I help them reach this level?

- How do I reveal to students the qualities that make an assignment excellent?
- Do I ever ask students what they think excellent work is like? Do we work together to develop the grading criteria on which their work will be judged?
- How can I encourage students to evaluate their own work, developing ideas about what they do well and where they could improve?

## LEARNERS BECOME INCREASINGLY SOPHISTICATED LEARNERS AND KNOWERS

Learning involves the *ability of individuals to monitor their own learning*, to understand how knowledge is acquired, to develop strategies for learning based on discerning their capacities and limitations, and to be aware of their own ways of knowing in approaching new bodies of knowledge and disciplinary frameworks (Joint Task Force on Student Learning, 1998a, p. 3).

Learning is *developmental*, a cumulative process *involving the whole person*, relating past and present, integrating the new with the old, starting from and transcending personal concerns and interests (Joint Task Force on Student Learning, 1998a, p. 2).

Much learning takes place *informally and incidentally*, beyond explicit teaching or the classroom, in casual contacts with faculty and staff, peers, campus life, active social and community involvements, and unplanned but fertile and complex situations (Joint Task Force on Student Learning, 1998a, p. 3).

Learning is *grounded in particular contexts and individual experiences*, requiring effort to transfer specific knowledge and skills to other circumstances or to more general understandings and to unlearn personal views and approaches when confronted with new information (Joint Task Force on Student Learning, 1998a, p. 3).

In learner-centered teaching, students reflect upon what they learn and how they learn. Reflection is a powerful activity for helping professors and students understand the present learning environment and think of ways to improve it. Research has shown that students who reflect on their learning are better learners than those who do not (Cornesky & Lazarus, 1995; Cross, 1996). In a learner-centered environment, reflections may take the form of journals or learning logs. They may also be included when portfolios are used in assessment (see Chapter 8).

As students reflect upon their knowledge, they—and we—begin to realize that learning about the topic of a course doesn't begin on the first day of a course. Students have either encountered course topics before or have developed related or prerequisite skills and abilities through their life experiences or in earlier stages of their education. We also come to realize that student learning isn't confined to course settings. Students may be learning about and applying course content in a variety of settings on and off campus (Kuh, 1997).

When we take a learner-centered approach, we are sensitive to the fact that, through these previous and current experiences, students may have developed understandings of concepts that will serve as an effective springboard for new learning, or they may have developed understandings that are superficial or inaccurate (Wandersee, Mintzes, & Novak, 1994). They may have acquired skills that can support increasingly sophisticated performance, or their skills may be poorly developed or incompatible with highly-skilled performance. These prior learnings must be addressed in teaching, because students will construct new understanding and skills by integrating new information with existing structures.

Therefore, in learner-centered teaching, it is important when we introduce new material or applications that we have students discuss what they already know about a topic, as well as the experiences that led to their knowledge. It may also be helpful in some situations to have students discuss how they feel about a topic.

> When certain topics or educational strategies are emotionally challenging for particular students, this situation should be acknowledged. For example, learning about atrocities conducted in a war in which a student's own relatives fought may make her wonder if her grandfather had been involved in such reprehensible conduct; studying about campus violence has made some men wonder if they have committed a rape.... To expect students to write detached, objective analyses of situations for which they have unresolved or emerging personal issues is to deny that students are multifaceted individuals, not just "talking heads," and that emotionally powerful questions may serve as barriers to reflective thinking on particular issues (King & Kitchener, 1994, p. 246).

Such discussion helps students become aware of their knowledge and feelings. When current concepts, skills, and attitudes are compatible with or supportive of new learning, discussion assists students as they attempt to make sense of new information.

When current concepts and habits are incompatible with progress in the discipline, we can engage students in inquiry (Kurfiss, 1988), providing opportunities for them to confront new information that challenges their existing view. We can guide students to new understandings that are in harmony with the best knowledge in the field. As Resnick and Klopfer (1989) point out, "Before knowledge becomes truly generative—knowledge that can be used to interpret new situations, to solve problems, to think and reason, and to learn—students must elaborate and question what they are told, examine new information in relation to other information, and build new knowledge structures" (p. 5).

Both before and after instruction, we may wish to anticipate common misunderstandings that students develop. For example, Wiggins and McTighe (1998) include "Misconception Alert" boxes throughout the chapters of their book. In these boxes, they expand upon what they meant in certain sections and point out what they didn't mean. We can use similar strategies to detect common misunderstandings when we interact directly with students. "Teaching for understanding requires time, a deep understanding of the subject on the part of the instructor, and a perceptiveness in diagnosing students' problems in understanding" (Kurfiss, 1988, p. 36).

In addition to issues associated with students' prior learning, there is another critical aspect of learning that we should attend to in learner-centered teaching. It derives from the fact that, over time, students change not only in terms of *what* they know, but also in terms of *how* they know (Baxter Magolda, 1992, 1996; King & Kitchener, 1994). An important role for professors is to provoke more sophisticated ways of knowing on the part of students.

To elaborate, Baxter Magolda (1992, 1996) identified several types of knowers in her research with college students. For example, she found that most college freshmen believe that knowledge is certain and that there are absolute or right answers in all areas of knowledge. For them, learning is a process of obtaining knowledge from a teacher, and evaluation is an opportunity to show the teacher what they know. This way of knowing reflects and undoubtedly develops from the role students experience in the traditional paradigm.

In contrast, the most sophisticated knowers in Baxter Magolda's (1996) study "believe that knowledge is uncertain and that one decides what to believe by evaluating the evidence in the context in question" (p. 284). They believe that both learning and evaluation should consist of interactions between students and professors in which students can think "through problems, integrating knowledge, and applying knowledge in context" (p. 284). In Baxter Magolda's study, only two percent of undergraduates had reached this viewpoint as they neared graduation.

Individuals tend to reach this level of knowing in graduate schools and professional schools or in the workplace (Baxter Magolda, 1996). Faculty in graduate and professional schools foster this development by helping students relate course material to their own experiences, providing challenging situations in which students can extend their knowledge, and encouraging students to analyze and justify their beliefs. In the workplace, individuals are "expected to function independently, make subjective decisions, take on the role of authority, and work collaboratively with coworkers" (p. 286). If we bring many of these positive features into the undergraduate environment through adopting a more learner-centered approach, we may help students learn how to learn in a more sophisticated manner.

Another implication of Baxter Magolda's research is that the success of student learning in a course may depend on students' paradigms about learning as much as it depends on professors' paradigms (Warren, 1997). This suggestion was raised in Chapter 1. Students who believe that knowing is accumulating certain and true information (Baxter Magolda, 1996) will be more comfortable in the traditional situation in which the professor imparts such information to them. This type of environment confirms their beliefs about the nature of knowledge and how it is acquired, and they will undoubtedly feel that they learn best in this environment.

Such students will initially feel confused and threatened in a learner-centered situation in which we coach and guide them to construct their own knowledge. This type of learning environment is based on an epistemology that is different from the one they currently endorse, and they will probably resist our attempts to engage them in new roles. Thus, when we shift from the traditional teacher-centered paradigm to a learner-centered paradigm, it is important that we discuss the process and the reasons for it with students. For learning to be maximized, we and our students must shift paradigms together.

In learner-centered environments then, we seek to understand not only what students know, but also how they know it. We help students develop insight into the nature of their current understanding of a field. We also help them understand their beliefs about knowledge and how it is acquired. Learner-centered professors use teaching techniques that help students develop into more sophisticated knowers. As students develop epistemologically, they become increasingly able to think and reason in ways that correspond to society's expectations for college graduates.

The professors in the Business Management and Construction Engineering examples in Figures 2.2 and 2.3 provide ample opportunities for students to address ill-defined problems, to reason, and to share their reasoning with others. Students develop ideas and discuss them with their peers and with the professors themselves. Constant questioning and dialogue expose students to the ideas and ways of thinking of others, helping them develop insights about the uncertain nature of knowledge. Questioning and dialogue also challenge students to defend their own ideas more rigorously.

The Mathematics and Sociology examples in Figures 2.5 and 2.6 illustrate respect for students' knowledge and ways of knowing. When Professor Jackson (Figure 2.5) senses that calculus courses are ineffective, he takes a risk and adopts a new strategy for helping students take ownership of their own learning. When Professor Okere (Figure 2.6) tries out a new teaching

**FIGURE 2.5    A Learner-Centered Example from Mathematics**

Faculty in the Mathematics Department are concerned about the low retention of students in introductory calculus classes, and they have been discussing ways to address the problem. Professor Jackson has heard about the base group technique of improving student involvement, and he decides to give it a try.

Professor Jackson divides his calculus students into teams of four—each is a base group—and tells them that the members of their base group *are expected* to work together on assigned out-of-class problems. Professor Jackson gives them some training on group effectiveness, covering topics like how to call a meeting, how to facilitate a meeting, and how to keep on task. The group is expected to turn in one completed assignment for the group, and all members are required to "sign off" that they participated and that they endorse the solutions submitted. When the group cannot come to consensus on a solution, they are expected to contact and work with another base group. They may also come to class and indicate that they are unable to move on to new material without more help. Some class time is occasionally devoted to having students work in base groups.

Over time, Professor Jackson observes a change in the course climate. Rather than feeling that he shoulders the burden for the achievement of the entire class, he begins to feel that the course is becoming the students' course. Students are spending more time on calculus, and they are partnering with him to determine the direction and pacing of the course. In-class participation has increased because students now know their peers personally and feel comfortable asking questions in front of them. Retention of knowledge improves, and grades on the final are dramatically better than those on the midterm.

(Adapted from the work of Keller, Russell, & Thompson, 1999)

technique, she relies on students to help her understand if the technique really improves student learning. These approaches honor students' insights into their learning and convey trust and respect for students as learners.

---

**REFLECTIONS**

*As you create your own meaning from the ideas in this section, begin to think about...*

- What do I do to find out what students already know about the topics of my courses? How do I use this information?
- How can I learn more about students' beliefs about knowledge and the way it is acquired?

- How do I help my students reflect on what they know and how they know?
- How can I help students with traditional teacher-centered views of learning shift to a more learner-centered paradigm?
- How can I identify students' misconceptions about my discipline and help modify them?

**FIGURE 2.6    A Learner-Centered Example from Sociology**

Professor Okere received her Ph.D. in Sociology twenty years ago and has been teaching undergraduate students since then, even though during her graduate program she received no formal training in teaching. Last year, Professor Okere joined a faculty development program on campus in order to learn some new techniques to make her teaching more effective.

Of all the techniques she learned about, Cooperative Learning was the most appealing, and Professor Okere decided to use it in her course entitled Sex and Gender in Society. Following the principles she learned in the faculty development program, she organized the class into cooperative groups that met for part of each class session. At the end of every other week, she used an anonymous questionnaire to survey her students about the effectiveness of the groups and their satisfaction with learning using this new approach. Professor Okere summarized the students' responses and shared them with the students themselves, asking for their help in interpreting some of the reactions she observed. Based on student feedback, she made continual modifications throughout the semester in the organization and implementation of the groups, and she observed that student satisfaction with the cooperative approach increased steadily.

Professor Okere also observed that students became increasingly comfortable with their role as classroom assessors. Students began to contact her on their own with occasional suggestions for course improvement. Often, they felt comfortable enough to identify themselves when they left or sent their messages. Through comments that students included on course evaluation forms, Professor Okere learned that students appreciated her flexibility in incorporating their suggestions into the course format.

(Okere, 1997)

## PROFESSORS COACH AND FACILITATE, INTERTWINING TEACHING AND ASSESSING

> Learning is strongly *affected by the educational climate* in which it takes place, the settings and surroundings, the influences of others, and the values accorded to the life of the mind and to learning achievements (Joint Task Force on Student Learning, 1998a, p. 2).

Previous sections of this chapter described new roles for students in learner-centered environments. When students are given new roles, professors have new roles as well. When teaching within the traditional model, we may be comfortable being the primary information givers and primary evaluators. However, shifting to a learner-centered approach challenges us to take risks and share these roles with students. Modifying traditional roles can be temporarily unsettling for us, but it does not mean that we "lose control" or lower our standards. Rather, by involving students in activities that enhance their learning, we more effectively control the direction and pace of learning in our courses. From a continuous improvement perspective, professors who are learner-centered:

> view themselves as supporters rather than judges, as mentors and coaches rather than lecturers, as partners with students, administrators, teachers, businesses, and communities rather than isolated workers within the walls of the classrooms. We now understand that the only way to ensure our own growth is by helping others to grow; the only way to maximize our own potential is by helping others to improve little by little, day by day (Bonstingl, 1996, p. 5).

When we take a learner-centered approach, we may also be considered leaders who facilitate and guide our students into new areas of understanding (Cornesky & Lazarus, 1995). Rather than simply imparting information, we make sure students understand and can *use* it. We provide a variety of opportunities for students to discuss and use new information.

For example, rather than lecturing for 30 minutes, a learner-centered professor may stop after several minutes to pose a question related to the material under consideration. The professor may then ask students to think for a minute about their own answers and to turn to another student to discuss their ideas and prepare an answer together. The professor can then call upon different students to share their answers with the class. The processes of sharing and of listening to and discussing the answers of others may reinforce students' own ideas, or they may provide an opportunity to modify them. In addition when students share their answers, professors can informally assess the depth of students' understanding.

When we participate in learner-centered teaching, we also guide students as they seek out information on their own. We teach students research skills and help them evaluate information and sources critically. As students share their findings, either orally or in writing, we can give feedback that students can use to improve their work. Other students can participate in giving feedback as well. Feedback is based on known standards for high quality work that we may have developed with students at the beginning of the course or project.

In this way, assessment in college courses changes from a process of occasionally monitoring student knowledge to one of providing continuous, meaningful feedback on important, valued characteristics. In the traditional paradigm, teaching and assessing are considered separate activities, with one following the other. Tests, the primary form of assessment, are scheduled at predictable times like midterm and finals week following several weeks of instruction. Their results give students a report about where they stand at any given point in time. However, "if assessment is viewed as a final judgment instead of a means to improvement, it can be a barrier to learning" (Griffith, McLure, & Weitzel, 1995, p. 1). Students not only fail to receive direction for improvement, but they also come to expect that learning can take place without it.

In a learner-centered environment, however, teaching and assessing are not separate, episodic events, but rather, they are ongoing, interrelated activities focused on providing guidance for improvement. If students are to develop important abilities and skills, they need to practice what they are learning and receive continuous feedback they can use to evaluate and regulate their performance. Students attempting to emulate practicing agronomists in the profession they aspire to join need feedback before midterm to know if they're on the right track. Both teaching and assessment must become ongoing activities that provide direction for learners.

When this happens, learning will be enhanced, but the learning environment will look and feel different than it has before. To individuals operating in the traditional teaching paradigm, it may seem unfamiliar.

> A biology instructor was experimenting with collaborative methods of instruction in his beginning biology classes. One day his dean came for a site visit, slipping into the back of the room. The room was a hubbub of activity. Students were discussing material enthusiastically in small groups spread out across the room; the instructor would observe each group for a few minutes, sometimes making a comment, sometimes just nodding approval. After 15 minutes or so the dean approached the instructor and said, "I came today to do your evaluation. I'll come back another time when you're teaching" (Barr & Tagg, 1995, p. 17).

As the example illustrates, a learner-centered approach requires faculty, students, and administrators to shift their paradigms to an understanding that teaching is engaging students in the creation of meaning.

The Management and Construction Engineering examples in Figures 2.2 and 2.3 illustrate this hallmark. In each case, the professor departs from the traditional role of lecturer to meet with small groups of students, react to their ideas, play devil's advocate, and prompt student reflection through questioning. Feedback is given continually, and in one case, clear and publicly stated criteria of good work form the basis of feedback. In these unconventional roles, the professors continually teach and continually assess learning.

---

**REFLECTIONS**

*As you create your own meaning from the ideas in this section, begin to think about...*

- For how long do I lecture without interruption?
- When I give students an opportunity to talk to each other about what I have presented, how do I structure their discussions?
- What aspects of my teaching could be considered "coaching and facil-

itating" rather than "selling and telling?"

- What are students doing when I am coaching and facilitating?
- To what extent do I consider assessment to be a periodic event that is *separate from* teaching?
- To what extent do I consider assessment to be a continual activity that is *part of* teaching?

## PROFESSORS REVEAL THAT THEY
## ARE LEARNERS, TOO

College instructors who have assumed that their students were learning what they were trying to teach them are regularly faced with disappointing evidence to the contrary when they grade tests and term papers. Too often, students have not learned as much or as well as was expected. There are gaps, sometimes considerable ones, between what was taught and what has been learned. By the time faculty notice these gaps in knowledge or understanding, it is frequently too late to remedy the problems (Angelo & Cross, 1993, p. 3).

Just as students need feedback to improve, so do the professors who provide the direction and guidance. We need to know what students understand and don't understand so that we can modify our own performance as teachers, if necessary. We also need to identify barriers to learning that students may be experiencing—even barriers that we may have inadvertently created. In other words, we need to adapt the definition of assessment presented in Chapter 1 to ourselves as teachers. We must use information from multiple and diverse sources to analyze, discuss, and judge our own performance in order to improve student learning.

Thus, when we take a learner-centered approach, we design assessments to gather opinions from students on a regular basis about how well they are learning and about how the course format helps or hinders their efforts (see Chapter 5). The information helps us "analyze, discuss, and judge" our own performance in order to remove obstacles in students' paths and enhance their ability to learn. This information is typically collected from students anonymously and the results are shared with the whole class. By revealing to students that we are willing to use their input to improve the course, we create an atmosphere of partnership and trust. We use assessment to reveal that we are learners, too.

There are also other ways in which we are learners in learner-centered courses, and we can reveal them to students as well. We mentioned earlier that each time we teach our courses, our understanding of the course content deepens. In addition, we learn new information as we keep up with developments in our fields and share new information with students. We also learn from guest presenters whom we may invite to class, and we learn from students themselves. The questions students ask and the insights they share provoke our own learning. We can also learn from nontraditional students who may have had more practical experience in our discipline than we have had.

There are several benefits of revealing to students that we view ourselves as learners. It helps students develop an appreciation and understanding of the importance of lifelong learning. It can also deepen their sense that professors and students are partners in learning, thus helping them shift from the traditional paradigm of teaching to a learner-centered paradigm. Finally, students appreciate and respect professors who attempt to become better teachers.

In one sense, all the examples in Figures 2.2 through 2.6 illustrate the fact that professors are learners, too. In each, the professor uses an approach to teaching that actively involves learners in creating their own knowledge and sharing their ideas with others. Through dialogue with students, professors continually learn more about how their students learn and about the ways their discipline is understood by others. In addition, three of the examples (Construction Engineering, Mathematics, and Sociology) describe professors who are learning new approaches to teaching. Not only have they revealed that fact to students, they have also asked students to help them know what works and what does not work.

---

**REFLECTIONS**

*As you create your own meaning from the ideas in this section, begin to think about...*

- How do I reveal to my students that I need their help in order to improve my teaching or make the course more useful for them?
- How could I improve this process?

- How do I reveal to students that I am continually learning more about my discipline?
- How can I help my students view me as a partner in learning?

---

## LEARNING IS INTERPERSONAL, AND ALL LEARNERS—STUDENTS AND PROFESSORS—ARE RESPECTED AND VALUED

---

Learning is done by *individuals* who are intrinsically *tied to others as social beings*, interacting as competitors or collaborators, constraining or supporting the learning process, and able to enhance learning through cooperation and sharing (Joint Task Force on Student Learning, 1998a, p. 2).

---

We referred earlier to Baxter Magolda's (1996) research with students in graduate and professional schools in which they discussed factors that helped them learn. Two important themes emerged, reflecting the contention of Seymour and Chaffee (1992) that "both the process and love of learning are fundamentally social phenomena" (p. 28).

One factor that helped students learn was mutual respect between students and teachers. Students reported that effective professors treated them like adults and involved them in making decisions regarding the class direction and activities. Students felt central to the class environment. In this atmosphere, they "were freer to explore their thinking, connect knowledge to self, and use their experience in settings characterized by mutual teacher–student respect" (Baxter Magolda, 1996, p. 298).

Another factor that facilitated learning was collaboration among peers in exchanging perspectives. Students came to learn that experience is part of knowing, and this realization increased their interest in hearing about the diverse experiences of others. Sharing their own experiences with others helped students clarify their own perspectives—"what to believe, why they believed something, and how to act on their beliefs" (Baxter Magolda, 1996, p. 300). As trust among students grew, students "were able to take greater risks in exploring their beliefs and take advantage of diverse perspectives in knowledge construction" (Baxter Magolda, 1996, p. 300).

The importance of mutual respect between us and our students and among students themselves is reflected in W. Edwards Deming's (1986) Fourteen Points of Quality. As discussed in Chapter 1, these points were originally developed for business settings. However, they apply to educational settings as well (Greenwood & Gaunt, 1994), and Deming's eighth point, "Drive out fear," is especially relevant to a discussion of the interpersonal nature of learning. Deming believed that people cannot perform up to their potential unless they feel free to act without fear, free to express ideas, and free to ask questions. For improved quality and productivity, individuals must feel secure. When fear is used artificially to improve performance, performance is not improved. Instead, much effort goes into dealing with the fear at the expense of performance.

Fear prevents people from thinking. "It robs them of pride and joy in their work and kills all forms of intrinsic motivation…Fear is a motivator—but it does not motivate toward constructive action" (Aguayo, 1990, pp. 184–5). Reporting on recent brain research, Marchese (1997) says that "when humans confront a situation they perceive as threatening, their brain 'downshifts'… higher-order cortical functioning is supplanted by the more elemental limbic …the emotions come to rule" (p. 85). What educators need to think about is the norm of relying on "sticks and carrots" (p. 85) in the learning process. An environment that promotes competition and few rewards is commonplace and yet is not a healthy environment for learning. "High challenge, yes,… high anxiety, no" (p. 85).

In an environment in which our approach to assessment is focused primarily on grades, fear increases rather than decreases (Milton, Pollio, & Eison, 1986). Furthermore, "grading does not provide the necessary information required for improvement" (Tribus, 1994, p. 7). Instead of emphasizing grades in assessment, the focus should be on descriptive feedback for improvement. Feedback that focuses on self-assessment and self-improvement is a form of intrinsic motivation. According to Tribus (1994), we should promote joy in learning and cooperation; we should discourage competition among students.

Our goal should be to develop student self-awareness and self-knowledge for improvement, and to achieve this goal we must cultivate an environment based on trust. Trust is built with each and every interaction. By modeling honesty in our actions over a period of time, we can lay the foundation for helping students to trust or mistrust each other.

> A teacher who takes students seriously and treats them as adults shows that she can be trusted. A teacher who emphasizes peer learning shows that it's important to trust other students. A teacher who encourages students to point out to her anything about her actions that is oppressive and who seeks to change what she does in response to their concerns is a model of critical reflection. Such a teacher is one who truly is trustworthy (Brookfield, 1995, p. 26).

Removing fear should not be interpreted to mean diluting learning and lowering standards. Our efforts should be directed to creating an environment in which students are free to learn the skills they need for success in higher education and beyond. At times, this will mean allowing students to make mistakes so that they may learn from their errors. Trust, rather than fear, helps create this environment. In fact, standards should increase in a learner-centered environment because criteria that define excellence are known to all.

With this approach, college courses become settings in which personal and professional relationships develop between us and our students and among the students themselves (see Chapter 8). Students are treated as active partners, and their advice and input are sought. They become adept at giving feedback to others, and they learn to show respect for their fellow students and for professors by reacting to their work honestly and tactfully. The sense of mutuality that characterizes these relationships leads to enhanced learning (Baxter Magolda, 1995). Courses become communities of learners, and the institution is freed from the popular criticism that college courses are impersonal "sink or swim" challenges. "Frequent student–faculty contact in and out of classes is the most important factor in student motivation and involvement" (Chickering & Gamson, 1987, p. 4). Learner-centered environments promote retention by transforming institutions into welcoming places in which intellectual and personal growth takes place.

All of the examples in Figures 2.2 through 2.6 are designed to illustrate courses in which learning is interpersonal and all learners—professors and students—are respected and valued. What are the elements in each example that reflect this hallmark?

---

**REFLECTIONS**

*As you create your own meaning from the ideas in this section, begin to think about...*

- How often do I schedule time to talk with my students individu-

ally about what they know and how they know?

- How do I get to know my students as people and as learners?

*(continued)*

REFLECTIONS  CONTINUED

- How can I determine if students feel fearful with some aspects of my courses?
- How do I help my students get to know each other? When and how do I provide time for them to talk to each other about what and how they are learning?
- How do I provide opportunities for students to work together?
- What activities can I incorporate into my courses so that students feel a sense of pride in their work and accomplishments?
- What changes could I make in the learning environment to decrease or minimize student fears?
- How can I give feedback to students in a way that reduces their level of anxiety?
- What do I do that leads students to feel that I respect them as people and as learners?

## LOOKING AHEAD

As we shift paradigms, it is critical that we examine our own practice as teachers and learn more about how students learn. Also important is the need to examine the role of the teaching professor in the entire educational system that flows from the teaching mission of the institution. A current aspect of that system that has important implications for learning is the assessment movement that began in higher education in the 1980s. Chapter 3 discusses principles of good practice in learner-centered assessment.

## TRY SOMETHING NEW

Completing the activities below will help identify aspects of your teaching you would like to change and the chapters in this book that are most relevant to your needs. You do not have to read the chapters in the order in which they are written. However, we would suggest that any efforts to change should start with Chapter 4, " Setting Direction with Intended Learning Outcomes." As the saying goes, if you don't know where you are going, you may never get there.

1. Review the hallmarks presented in this chapter, your responses to the Reflections questions, as well as Figures 1–1 and 1–2 at the end of Chapter 1. Make a list of the aspects of your teaching you would most like to change.
2. Using the list you developed above, read through the following chapter descriptions and decide which chapter would be the most useful starting place for you.
   Chapter 3: Basing assessment at the institutional, academic program, and/or course level on sound assessment principles.

Chapter 4: Developing intended learning outcomes for your courses, academic program, or institution.

Chapter 5: Identifying techniques for actively involving students in your courses and for gathering their feedback about how to improve the learning environment; learning how to receive and interpret feedback so that faculty and students can be partners in learning.

Chapter 6: Identifying and communicating the characteristics of excellent work to help students shape and evaluate their work and to help faculty provide useful feedback for improvement; learning how to give useful feedback to students to improve their learning.

Chapter 7: Developing assessments that evaluate students' abilities to think critically, solve enduring and emerging problems in their discipline, communicate effectively, work in teams, and so forth.

Chapter 8: Using portfolios in assessment so that faculty and students together can assess what students know and how they know it; helping students to become more sophisticated learners and shift to a learner-centered paradigm.

Chapter 9: Examining the organizational and individual implications of making a paradigm shift. Participating in a faculty development program that provides support and guidance for becoming learner-centered.

## REFERENCES

Aguayo, R. (1990). *Dr. Deming: The man who taught the Japanese about quality.* Secaucus, NJ: Carol Publishing Group.

Angelo, T. A. (1994). Classroom assessment: Involving faculty and students where it matters most. *Assessment Update, 6* (4), 1–10.

Angelo, T. A., & Cross, K. P. (1993). *Classroom assessment techniques* (2nd ed.). San Francisco: Jossey-Bass.

Barr, R. B., & Tagg, J. (1995, November/December). From teaching to learning: A new paradigm for undergraduate education. *Change,* 13–25.

Baxter Magolda, M. B. (1992). Students' epistemologies and academic experiences: Implications for pedagogy. *The Review of Higher Education, 15* (3), 265–287.

Baxter Magolda, M. B. (1995). The integration of relational and impersonal knowing in young adults' epistemological development. *Journal of College Student Development, 36* (3), 205–216.

Baxter Magolda, M. B. (1996). Epistemological development in graduate and professional education. *The Review of Higher Education, 19* (3), 283–304.

Bonstingl, J. J. (1996). *Schools of quality.* Alexandria, VA: Association for Supervision and Curriculum Development.

Bransford, J. D., Brown, A. L., & Cocking, R. R. (Eds.). (1999). *How people learn: Brain, mind, experience, and school.* Washington, DC: National Academy Press.

Bransford, J. D., & Vye, N. J. (1989). A perspective on cognitive research and its implications for instruction. In L. B. Resnick & L. E. Klopfer (Eds.), *Toward the thinking curriculum: Current cognitive research, 1989 ASCD Yearbook* (pp. 173–205). Alexandria, VA: Association for Supervision and Curriculum Development.

Brookfield, S. (1995). *Becoming a critically reflective teacher.* San Francisco: Jossey-Bass.

Brooks, J. G., & Brooks, M. G. (1993). *In search of understanding: The case for constructivist classrooms.* Alexandria, VA: Association for Supervision and Curriculum Development.

Chickering, A. W., & Gamson, Z. F. (1987, March). Seven principles for good practice. *AAHE Bulletin, 39*, 3–7.

Copple, C., Sigel, I. E., & Saunders, R. (1984). *Educating the young thinker: Classroom strategies for cognitive growth.* Hillsdale, NJ: Lawrence Erlbaum Associates.

Cornesky, R., & Lazarus, W. (1995). *Continuous quality improvement in the classroom: A collaborative approach.* Port Orange, FL: Cornesky & Associates.

Cross, K. P. (1996, March-April). New lenses on learning. *About Campus,* 4–9.

Deming, W. E. (1986). *Out of the crisis.* Cambridge, MA: Massachusetts Institute of Technology Center for Advanced Engineering Study.

Department of Forestry Faculty. (1998). Unpublished program and course materials. Ames, IA: Iowa State University.

Department of Statistics. (1996). *Annual student outcomes assessment report.* Unpublished document. Ames, IA: Iowa State University.

Duffy, T. M., & Cunningham, D. J. (1996). Constructivism: Implications for the design and delivery of instruction. In D. H. Jonassen (Ed.), *Handbook of research on educational communications and technology* (pp. 170–198). London: MacMillan.

Fosnot, C. T. (Ed.) (1996). *Constructivism: Theory, perspective, and practice.* New York: Teachers College Press.

Freed, J. E., & Klugman, M. R. (1997). *Quality principles and practices in higher education: Different questions for different times.* Phoenix, AZ: American Council on Education and The Oryx Press.

Gardner, H. (1991). *The unschooled mind: How children think and how schools should teach.* New York: Basic Books.

Greenwood, M. S., & Gaunt, H. J. (1994). *Total quality management for schools.* London: Cassell.

Griffith, J., McLure, J., & Weitzel, J. (1995). Total quality management, assessment, and large class size. *Assessment Update, 7* (3), 1–7.

Jahren, C. T., & Kipp, R. (1999). A mock bid-letting for learning assessment. *Journal of Professional Issues in Engineering Education and Practice, American Society of Civil Engineers, 125* (3), 103–107.

Joint Task Force on Student Learning. (1998a). *Learning principles and collaborative action.* Washington, DC: American Association for Higher Education.

Joint Task Force on Student Learning. (1998b). *Powerful partnerships: A shared responsibility for learning.* Washington, DC: American College Personnel Association. http://www.aahe.org, http://www.acpa.nche.edu, or http://www.naspa.org

Keane, B. (1997, July 8). The Family Circus, *The Des Moines Register,* p. 5T.

Keane, B. (1998, May 19). The Family Circus, *The Des Moines Register,* p. 5T.

Keller, B. A., Russell, C. A., & Thompson, H. A. (1999). Effects of student-centered teaching on student evaluations in calculus. *Educational Research Quarterly, 23* (1), 59–73.

Ketcham. (1997a, July 5). Dennis the Menace, *The Des Moines Register,* p. 5T.

Ketcham. (1997b, July 14). Dennis the Menace, *The Des Moines Register,* p. 5T.

King, P. M., & Kitchener, K. S. (1994). *Developing reflective judgment: Understanding and promoting intellectual growth and critical thinking in adolescents and adults.* San Francisco: Jossey-Bass.

Kuh, G. (1997). Working together to enhance student learning inside and outside the classroom. In *Assessing Impact: Evidence and Action* (pp. 67–78). Washington, DC: American Association of Higher Education.

Kurfiss, J. G. (1988). *Critical thinking: Theory, research, practice, and possibilities.* (ASHE-ERIC Higher Education Report No. 2). College Station, TX: Association for the Study of Higher Education.

Loacker, G., Cromwell, L., & O'Brien, K. (1986). Assessment in higher education: To serve the learner. In C. Adelman (Ed.), *Assessment in American higher education* (pp. 47–62). Washington, DC: U.S. Department of Education. Office of Educational Research and Improvement.

Marchese, T. J. (1997). The new conversation about learning. In *Assessing Impact: Evidence and Action* (pp. 79–95). Washington, DC: American Association for Higher Education.

Martinez, M. E. (1998). What is problem solving? *Phi Delta Kappan, 79,* 605–609.

Milton, O., Pollio, H. R., & Eison, J. A. (1986). *Making sense of college grades: Why the grading system does not work and what can be done about it.* San Francisco: Jossey-Bass.

Okere, M. (1997). Unpublished course materials. Ames, IA: Iowa State University, Department of Sociology.

Resnick, L. B., & Klopfer, L. E. (1989). Toward the thinking curriculum: An overview. In L. B. Resnick & L. E. Klopfer (Eds.), *Toward the thinking curriculum: Current cognitive research, 1989 ASCD Yearbook* (pp. 1–18). Alexandria, VA: Association for Supervision and Curriculum Development.

Resnick, L., & Resnick, D. (1992). Assessing the thinking curriculum: New tools for educational reform. In B. R. Gifford & M. C. O'Connor (Eds.), *Changing assessments: Alternative views of aptitude, achievement and instruction* (pp. 37–75). Boston: Kluwer Academic Publishers.

Seymour, D., & Chaffee, E. E. (1992). TQM for student outcomes assessment. *AGB Reports, 34* (1), 26–30.

Tribus, M. (1994, June). *When quality goes to school, what do leaders do to put it to work?* Paper presented at the Annual AAHE Conference on Assessment and Quality, Washington, DC.

Ulrichson, D. (1998). Unpublished materials from Chemical Engineering 430. Ames, IA: Iowa State University, Department of Chemical Engineering.

Wandersee, J. H., Mintzes, J. L., & Novak, J. D. (1994). Research on alternative conceptions in science. In D. L. Gabel (Ed.), *Handbook of research on science teaching and learning* (pp. 177–210). New York: MacMillan.

Warren, R. G. (1997, March-April). Engaging students in active learning. *About Campus,* 16–20.

Whitehead, A. N. (1929). *The aims of education.* New York: MacMillan.

Wiggins, G. (1993). *Assessing student performance: Exploring the limits and purpose of testing.* San Francisco: Jossey-Bass.

Wiggins, G. (1997). Feedback: How learning occurs. In *Assessing Impact: Evidence and Action* (pp. 31–39). Washington, DC: American Association of Higher Education.

Wiggins, G., & McTighe, J. (1998). *Understanding by design.* Alexandria, VA: Association for Supervision and Curriculum Development.

# CHAPTER 5

# BASIC COURSE COMPONENTS

With the first four chapters of *New Strategies in College Teaching*, we have sought to lay a philosophical foundation that integrates the accountability and student-focused perspectives driving today's higher education environment. The remaining chapters seek to foster the development of more specific skills that dovetail with this new paradigm, as well as provide a richer professional experience to those employing them.

In the following chapter, David Royse focuses our attention on the basic course-planning issues elevated to increased importance in today's environment such as the strategy and specific contents of our syllabus, the development of more effective and rewarding course assignments, grading strategies, and others. His insights are certain to trigger self-assessing questions capable of leading to improvements in our classroom-management tactics that we may not have considered for quite some time. The checklists and bulleted lists included significantly influence the usability of this well developed chapter.

# BASIC COURSE COMPONENTS

Chapter 2 from *Teaching Tips for College and University Instructors*
David Royse
Allyn & Bacon, © 2001

*Overview: This chapter focuses on three of the four main essentials needed in a course of educational instruction (the syllabus, a text or body of readings, and assignments). Although it is not uncommon for instructors to go hunting for texts before drafting a syllabus, the entire course should not be centered on one book. Texts are resources, aids in accomplishing the educational objectives—not the prime reason a course exists. Developing a syllabus should, ideally, precede textbook selection. Writing a syllabus for the first time, even revising an old one, is a complex project—more difficult than simply allocating readings over an academic term and deciding on assignments.*

*The first portion of this chapter identifies the components that go into a well-constructed syllabus, and this is followed by a segment that discusses textbook selection. The next segment examines the purpose of assignments and their use as instructional devices. This is followed by several topics that relate to issues that arise whenever instructors require assignments and presentations.*

## CONSTRUCTING THE SYLLABUS

The compass that guides and keeps students and faculty on the right educational path in a particular course of instruction is the syllabus. The syllabus should clearly communicate course objectives, assignments, required readings, and grading policies. Every student should receive his or her own copy of the syllabus on the first meeting of the class—certainly no later than the second meeting.

Fewer misunderstandings and problems will occur if you take the time to be as specific as possible in writing the syllabus, exactly defining your expectations. Think of the syllabus as a stand-alone document. Those students who miss the first or second meeting of class should be able to learn most of what they need to know about the requirements of the course from reading the syllabus.

Start with collecting syllabi from colleagues who have recently taught the course you will be teaching. Particularly your first year, you may want to make only minor changes to the way the course has been taught over the past several years—unless you've been asked to make a major overhaul. Look for the common threads and themes if you gather syllabi from several instructors.

Creating a syllabus for a course you've never taught before is not the easiest of tasks. It forces you to plan three or four months ahead of time and to anticipate how the class will progress. You'll need to guess how much time will be spent on each topic, on in-class group projects, and on student debates. What topics will you treat superficially, which ones in-depth? The syllabus will reflect your philosophy of teaching and the pertinent educational objectives (e.g., knowledge, comprehension, application, analysis, synthesis, and evaluation; see the discussion on Bloom's Taxonomy later in this chapter) you hope to accomplish. Many curriculum specialists urge teachers to include a statement of intended learning outcomes. This makes perfect sense, both from the standpoint that students have the right to know what they are expected to learn and from the perspective that stating learning outcomes helps keep instructors from drifting too far afield. As much as possible, your objectives should indicate what students will be able to do once they have completed the course.

If your course is one in a series (e.g., the second calculus course), you will also need to consider what students should have mastered prior to the proposed course and how much they ought to accomplish to be fully prepared for the next one. If the course is being taught in the evening, or by Internet or television, or off campus, there may be special considerations in terms of the facilities or supporting resources available to students. In short, many "pieces" go into the construction of a syllabus.

## THE BASICS: WHAT NEEDS TO BE IN A SYLLABUS

These are the essential components of a well-designed syllabus:

TOP OF SYLLABUS
1. Course title and university course identifier (e.g., PSY 100: Introduction to Psychology)
2. Location of classroom as well as days and hours the class meets
3. Your name, office location, office hours, phone number, and e-mail address (Some faculty list their home phone numbers; however, there is no compelling reason for you to do this. If you choose to, you might want to include "No phone calls after 11 P.M.")
4. Course description (Usually this comes directly from the college bulletin; any prerequisites should be identified. You may want to identify

how this course fits into the student's program of instruction—for example, the third of four required calculus courses.)

5. Course objectives or statement of intended learning outcomes (These are usually common to all sections of the class being taught within the department.)

**MIDDLE OF SYLLABUS**

6. Schedule of topics to be discussed (Check the school calendar and plan for holidays, spring break, etc. Identify any field trips or required activities outside of the class.)

7. Texts and/or equipment needed (Note required and supplementary titles, authors, publishers, and editions of any books the students are expected to read; full citations are necessary for any journal articles in a required reading list. If materials are placed on reserve, indicate where.)

8. Explanation of assignments and dates when they are due (Do not have "floating dates." Be specific, even if you have to make some adjustments later.)

**LAST THIRD OF SYLLABUS**

9. Scheduled tests (and locations if different from the regular classroom)

10. Policy on attendance, tardiness, and participation in class

11. Policy on work that is submitted late

12. Explanation of how overall grade will be computed (Provide students with specific information about the weighting of attendance, homework, major assignments, examinations, etc.)

13. Grading scale (e.g., 100 to 92 = A)

14. Miscellaneous information (This section may contain statements about plagiarism, the University's Honor Code, your policy on missed tests, class rules regarding such matters as talking or eating in class, computer and e-mail skills required, availability of instructional support services, course drop dates, etc.)

Do you need to put *everything* in writing? Probably not. In the first class, you might discuss, say, your philosophy of teaching and you shouldn't feel guilty about that material not being in the syllabus. Ideally, the syllabus should cover the basics about the course in 3 or 4 pages. Not too many students will read a 15 single-spaced course outline. Handouts of such things as lab safety procedures can be distributed separately from the syllabus.

Once you have composed a draft of your syllabus containing all of the essential items you want to convey, take a little more time to look at it from a student's perspective. If, for instance, you placed in heavy bold type that your office hours are available *only by appointment*, does this send the message that you don't want to be disturbed? On the other hand, if you orally mention your willingness to meet with students before or after class, or whenever they don't understand the material, then you have identified yourself as a student-friendly, concerned educator. Similarly, providing students with options regarding their assignments will set you apart from other educators who do not allow students to personalize their courses. Even the amount of time you choose to spend on the various points to be covered makes a statement about what you emphasize and value.

Often, syllabi are so concerned with stating requirements, policies, and penalties that little effort is made to stimulate student interest in the course. One way to create involvement is by posing a few challenging questions that the course will attempt to answer. Why should students be interested in your class? Whet their appetites by posing some questions that will be examined during the term.

No matter the length of your syllabus, be sure to use lots of headings to divide the various sections. Consider using a table of contents if the syllabus is extremely lengthy. Finally, keep a copy of the syllabus to make ongoing notes to yourself about needed revisions. These might be reminders to insert more detailed instruction on a particular assignment, that supplementary readings are outdated or have gone out of print, and so forth.

**EXAMPLE OF A SYLLABUS**

SW 650 RESEARCH METHODS IN THE SOCIAL SCIENCES (3 CREDIT HOURS)

| | |
|---|---|
| Fall, 2000 | George Gipper, Ph.D. |
| MWF 3:00–4:15 | 555-293-6645 or (gipper.@blt.edu) |
| 17 Belding Classroom Building | 641 Patterson Tower |
| | Office Hours M,W, F noon to 4:00 |
| | (Other times by appointment) |

### I. Course Description

Introduction to systematic approaches to scientific thinking necessary for building basic knowledge as applied to problems in society. Issues addressed include conceptualization of research, measurement, ethical use of scientific inquiry, and appropriate analytical procedures. (The first of three required research courses.)

### II. Course Objectives

A. To introduce the process of research as a sequence of rationally and systematically organized events. (What are the steps needed to conduct research in the social sciences?)

B. To acquaint students with the basic concepts necessary to understand written reports of research. (What terms, expressions, and statistics do I need to know in order to fully comprehend journal articles and reports?)

C. To teach students how to design research projects capable of making scientific contributions. (How do I craft a research design capable of providing objective, scientific information?)

| III.  Class Outline | Assignment for Class |
| --- | --- |
| 9/2: Introduction to course and each other | None |
| 9/9: The research process & operationalizing variables | Read Chapters 1 and 2 |
| | Write a hypothesis or research question that interests you, one that could be completed within one semester; (2) operationalize your dependent variable; (3) list three independent variables you will need. |
| 9/16: Continuing discussion of Chapter 2 | Find five references related to your topic from a computerized database. Write at least one page describing (1) the amount of material you found on your topic and (2) your experience in locating relevant material. |
| 9/23: Single subject design | Read Chapter 3. |
| | Develop a single system design for some realistic problem that a client might have. Graph fictitious data for baseline and intervention. Write at least a paragraph describing (1) the client's presenting problem and (2) the intervention. |
| 9/30: Group research designs | Read Chapter 4. |
| | Write a research design for an experiment. State (1) your hypothesis, (2) your operationalized dependent variable, (3) the intervention, (4) the type of design, and (5) how you will procure your research subjects. (1 to 2 pages, typewritten) |
| 10/7: Measurement issues | Read Chapter 5. |
| | Find a scale or instrument that you could use in some research project. Address its reliability, validity, and how you might use it. Attach a copy of the scale to your paper. |
| 10/14: Survey research | Read Chapter 6. |
| | Find an article in a professional journal that employed a survey, then, in 2–3 paragraphs, discuss (1) the confidence you have in it because of the sampling design, sample size, |

etc., and (2) Would you generalize from the finding? If so, how far? Alternatively, find a survey in an issue of the *Gallup Poll Monthly* or the *Harris Poll* and explore the same issues. Attach the article to your paper.

10/21: Questionnaire design & review for exam

Prepare 5 items suitable for measuring self-esteem; bring questions for the review.

10/28: Midterm exam

11/4: Qualitative research

Read Chapter 11.

Propose a qualitative study that you would be interested in implementing (1.5 pages, typewritten).

11/11: Secondary data analysis & content analysis

Read Chapter 8.

Propose a realistic study that would draw on secondary data or rely on content analysis. State your hypothesis, your methodology (including how you operationalized your dependent variable), and the limitations of your research.

11/18: Program evaluation

Read Chapter 10.

Choose from 1, 2, 3, or 4: (1) find a journal article reporting a program evaluation and critique it in 250 words or so; (2) locate a program evaluation from a local agency and critique it; (3) propose a program evaluation that could or should be done; or (4) critique "Evaluation of a Residential Center for Emotionally Disturbed Teens."

11/25: Data analysis

Read Chapter 9.

11/27: THANKSGIVING!!!

12/2: Data analysis (cont.), application of research

Design a table showing fictitious data. Make at least one comparison that is statistically significant and indicate the appropriate statistical procedure.

12/9: Ethical issues & review

Read Chapter 12, skim Chapter 13; bring questions for the review.

12/16: Final exam

## IV. Required Text

Gipper, G. (1997). *Research Methods for Knowledge Building* (2nd ed.). Chicago: Hall & Taylor.

## V. Expectations and Student Evaluation

Students are expected to keep current with their reading of the text. If the instructor detects that the class as a whole is not reading the material, he reserves the right to conduct unannounced quizzes which will count as in-class assignments. Students are further expected to contribute to class discussions and to raise questions. All assignments are due at the *beginning* of class and unexcused *late* assignments will be penalized.

A. Exams: There will be a midterm exam plus a final exam which will be averaged together for **60%** of final grade. Missed exams will not be made up unless there is a valid excuse *and* the instructor is notified beforehand.

B. Assignments: **30%** of final grade

C. Attendance & Participation: These are required and will constitute **10%** of final grade. Participation in class discussion is highly desired. Class will start as scheduled. Please be present on time.

## VI. Grading Scale

100 to 92 = A    82 to 74 = C

91 to 83 = B    73 to 65 = D

## VII. Additional Scholarly Resources

Tabbie, E., and Talley, F. (1994). *Adventures in Social Research.* New York: Guru Publications.

Canebridge, E. S. (1989). *Survey Research: A Computer-Assisted Approach.* Wildflower, CA: Smart Books, Inc.

Loom, M., Wischer, J., and Arme, J. G. (1995). *Evaluating Your Practice: An Introduction.* Boston: Hamilton Books.

Korcoran, K., and Lister, J. (1994). *Measures for Social Research* (2nd ed.). New York: Knotty Books, Inc.

Judson, W. W., and Natters, P. S. (1994). *Controversial Issues in Research Methods.* Boston: Get-Reading Book Co.

Windle, Q. S., and Judson, W. W. (1993). *Research Methods in Human Services.* Pacific Grove, CA: Surfside Books.

---

## DEPARTING FROM THE SYLLABUS

The syllabus is a contract between you as the university's representative and the student. For this reason, it should be thoughtfully prepared and not changed for capricious reasons during the course of the academic term. It is almost always a bad idea to add additional requirements or to change the syllabus substantially once it has been distributed to students. With four weeks to go in the semester, don't surprise your students with an announce-ment that you've decided to make the 4-page minor assignment due next Monday an 18-page major term paper because the class did so poorly on the last quiz. That kind of thing will always generate a rash of complaints. Simi-larly, if you failed to state any expectations about attendance, don't announce half-way through the semester that because of your concern about high ab-senteeism, you are going to start grading students on their attendance. Learn from your mistakes and craft a better syllabus next time.

As a general rule, don't ask students to do *more* than the syllabus states; however, you probably won't have any trouble if you ask students to do a little less. For instance, suppose you underestimated the amount of work re-quired for students to complete their assignments. Even though the syllabus stated that they had to turn in 12 of these, you might decide to require only 10. If you are going to cancel some assignments, make this decision early enough that students won't have already invested time working on the one you are thinking about canceling.

Even though you should think of the syllabus as a contract, there's no reason to be paranoid about it. Sometimes adjustments are necessary. If a blizzard blows in and no one can get to class on the date of a scheduled exam or when a major paper was due, accommodations must be made.

Note, too, that in preparing the syllabus you may discover a desire to establish certain "rules" to keep order and ensure that students perform to expectation, but at the same time you might experience a conflict because of the knowledge that too many rules smother creativity and interfere with learning. Finding one's place on the no rules/rules continuum is not always easy and is very much a personal decision. Experience suggests that unnec-essary rules can be relaxed if they are not needed. And while, in theory, new rules can be promulgated at any time during the academic term, once a class has met together for several weeks, each class develops its own customs and traditions and the imposition of new standards is not always tolerated with-out much complaining and protest.

## SELECTING A TEXT

There are more options available to instructors today than in years past. First of all, you might opt not to require a textbook but to scan your lecture notes and other relevant materials into an Internet site that students can read on their computers. On campuses where most of the students have their own computers and easy access to the World Wide Web, this is becoming an in-creasingly popular way of providing instructional material. Note that it is necessary to secure copyright permission when electronically reproducing chapters from books, articles from journals, or graphs, charts, or illustrations appearing in commercially prepared publications.

Another possibility is to assemble a collection of readings that you like and to have them reproduced at your local photocopy center. These can be compiled in a number of different forms, from loose-leaf, three-hole punched for notebooks, to plastic spiral binding, to being bound like paperback books. This option allows you to finely tune the material your students will learn and to overcome the shortcomings of some texts. You get to choose the very best journal articles and to arrange the readings in a way that makes the most sense according to the way you teach the content.

The third choice, of course, is to adopt a text from one of many already on the market. There's a lot to be said for staying with a commercially produced text. For one thing, it provides continuity and, over time, standardizes content. Knowing what material students learned when they are transferring from or to another school is made a lot easier when a well-known text is used. Furthermore, texts often have features such as review questions and potential assignments or projects that will be lacking in collections of journal articles, unless you take the time to create them.

Choosing the right text to use with your class is an important decision—not only for you but for your students, too. After all, they will spend hundreds of dollars on these purchases each academic term. The textbook extends your instruction outside of the classroom; it is your representative outside of class. The text needs to be informative, current, and written on a level accessible to students. Students prefer that their books be inexpensive to purchase, not too densely packed with verbiage, and generously endowed with illustrations and graphics for visual interest.

Students are savvy consumers. About a third of the students in your classroom may not purchase their own copy of the text or texts you assign. Bookstores, of course, know this and often order substantially fewer books than there are students enrolled in courses. Students on tight budgets might borrow the assigned text from the library or from a friend, make their own photocopy of it, or go in with a classmate and jointly purchase the text. The bookstore managers also know that first-year students tend to buy proportionately more of their books than students in their third or fourth year. The student's decision to buy a text may hinge on what you say about it.

If, for instance, you suggest the book is only a supplement to the *required* text, or that the class will read portions of it—not the whole book—fewer students will make the purchase than if you clearly state that there will be weekly reading assignments from the book or that students should bring it to class with them at each meeting. All other factors being equal, students are more likely to buy books that are (1) not terribly expensive, (2) appear interesting and relevant, and (3) perceived as necessary in order to get a good grade.

As a new instructor, you may be faced with the decision of whether to adopt a new text or to stay with the one that has been popular with the other instructors in your department. If you stay with the current text, students will often be happier, because of the availability of used books—some students will have already purchased the old one from friends or roommates just completing the course. However, sometimes the very features of a book that were responsible for it being adopted change or get dropped in new editions and there is less reason to stick with it. Students will have to buy new books anyway when revised editions come out, so if you want to change texts, that might not be a bad time. Conversely, another time to go on the market for a new text is when the current one hasn't been revised for many years.

When you wish to consider a new text, what should you look for? Start with the preface. What does the author tell you about the book? Is it written for undergraduate or graduate students? Is it best suited for an introductory-level or an intermediate-level course? Next, browse the table of contents. Does the organization of the material make sense? Does there seem to be sufficient coverage of important topics and issues? Is it proportioned in a way that fits your teaching emphasis or academic term?

Read several chapters. Does the author have a writing style that is appropriate for your students? Is the content up to date? Is it presented in an interesting way? Would it stimulate thinking and class discussion? Is the content relevant? Are the ideas expressed clearly? Is the level of abstraction appropriate? Does the author make frequent use of headings and subheadings? When new terms are introduced, does the author highlight these? Is the index detailed?

There are also book features that especially benefit students—for instance, review questions or problems (with answers) at the end of each chapter. Recommendations of supplemental readings can also be helpful—particularly if they are current. In some disciplines, it might be important to have glossaries in the back of texts. You may also want to adopt a text that has an accompanying instructor's manual or test bank.

Although we know better than to "judge a book by its cover," we probably all do fall into that trap, at least occasionally. In fact, a colleague told me that he once chose one book over another because it looked more substantial. He chose a text of almost 800 pages over one about half that size. Although he usually was unable to get through the whole book, he thought that the smaller book suggested there wasn't as much for students to learn as there really was. Obviously, a smaller book that students are inclined to read and able to understand will do more to further their education than large, obtuse texts that they don't read.

Choosing texts always involves trade-offs. The book you choose may not be organized the way you like and it might be necessary to assign chapters out of order, or to assign additional readings for particularly weak chapters. However, students prefer to read chapters straight through rather than skip around. The best advice is: Choose the book with the most features you deem essential and the one with the fewest disadvantages.

If you make a mistake and choose a text that you later discover to be less than satisfactory, don't bemoan this all through the academic term. Students will wonder why you didn't give the decision more thought and may be troubled by the fact that your announcement of plans to change texts next term means they won't be able to sell their used copies back to the bookstore. Even a text with certain flaws will seldom cause students irreparable harm. The only problem will be that you will probably have to work a little harder to bring in material to cover its deficiencies. Doubtlessly, you will not choose any texts where there are factual errors or where the author's biases show too clearly.

---

**QUICK CHECKLIST FOR EVALUATING TEXTS**

_____    1. Is the material pertinent to course objectives?
_____    2. Is the content up to date?
_____    3. Is the book organized and logical?
_____    4. Is it clearly written?
_____    5. Will students find the book interesting and accessible?
_____    6. Does it conform to general departmental or professional standards?
_____    7. Will students find its cost reasonable?
_____    8. Is this book well suited for the way I teach?
_____    9. Is this book/edition available in time for the start of class?
_____   10. Is there a test bank or instructor's manual available?

---

While you are reviewing texts, it is a good idea to keep on hand one or two that you like although you may not adopt. These will allow you to draw lecture material, examples, and so forth from texts other than the one you have chosen for the class. This is one way to provide variety to students and to keep them from knowing that you are "only one chapter ahead of them" (Sawyer, Prichard, & Hostetler, 1992, p. 188).

## PROBLEMS TO AVOID

Although there are many ways in which instructors may communicate less directly or clearly than they intend, one mistake commonly made by educators teaching a course for the first time is that they may have rich and intricate visions of how they want students to demonstrate comprehension and synthesis of the material, but they somehow fail to convey this information to those enrolled. Before you send the final version of your syllabus off to be duplicated, check to make sure your expectations have been fully articulated. Be very specific. Avoid vaguely worded instructions, as in the following instructions in the left-hand column:

**EXAMPLES**

| _Instruction_ | _Students May Interpret As:_ |
|---|---|
| "Write a short paper." | Write a paragraph. |
| | Write a half a page. |
| | Type a two- to three-page paper. |

| | |
|---|---|
| "Keep a log of your experiences." | Make daily entries. Make weekly entries. |
| | Make an entry whenever the spirit moves me. At the end of the term, record what I recall. Record what interesting things I learned from the material, how I might be able to use it, questions that arose, how I reacted to the material on an emotional level. |
| "Obtain an article from a periodical in the library." | Any magazine article. An article from a professional journal. A *recent* journal article. A column from a newsletter. A journal article written in 1896. A journal article under three pages in length. |

Is it important that all the papers be typed? If you leave the instructions open, some students will type and others will write in longhand. With no required word count (e.g., at least 500 words), one or two students will set their margins on 2 inches on all sides to make their skimpy papers seem longer. Others will handwrite in large, loopy letters to use as much space as possible. Similarly, if you expect that students should employ five references in their papers, then you need to include that in the instructions. And you might want to define what "counts" as a reference: Their textbook? Something they find on the Internet? Must it be from a professional journal?

With undergraduates, it is often useful to specify in the syllabus that assignments are due at the *beginning* of each class. Otherwise, there will always be a few students who forgot and who then proceed to do their homework while you are lecturing or attempting to involve the class in a discussion or group activity. Although it is possible to go overboard and to be *too detailed* in your instructions (I once heard of a 50-page syllabus), it is generally better to produce more guidelines than too few.

## WEIGHTING TESTS, ASSIGNMENTS, AND PARTICIPATION/ATTENDANCE

Some otherwise intelligent students perform very badly on in-class tests. Other students with underdeveloped written communication skills do poorly on assignments that require composition and logical argument, but obtain the highest scores on multiple-choice tests. Putting too much weight on a single term paper without other controls can almost guarantee that students will get help (to say it nicely) or have someone else author their papers. And what professor hasn't experienced students who can't or won't attend class? Few individuals do all things well. So, how does one decide the best balance for assessing students?

The most fair way is to use a mixture of assessment approaches. Over the years, I've learned that I'm a soft-touch for students when it comes to grading their papers and assignments. Usually if they don't do well, I blame inadequate instructions and resolve to revise the syllabus. I tend to find some kernel of merit even in the vaguest of responses. Knowing this about myself, I almost always construct my syllabi so that the most weight comes from at least two objective (multiple-choice type) tests. With undergraduates, I frequently assess their performance with three objective tests. I prefer that 60 to 75 percent of a student's grade is based on such examinations. The weight given to everything else centers on that decision. However, in courses where there is less emphasis on content and more on creativity and original thinking, objective tests are not going to be the best method for assessment. These may need to be replaced with in-class writing assignments or projects that allow students to showcase their talents.

Assignments can also be structured so that subjectivity is minimized. However, homework where students are all working on the same problems makes it difficult for the instructor to know to what extent students shared information or helped each other. Of course, sometimes instructors want students to interact and collaborate on assignments. (See Chapter 4 for more discussion on the use of groups.) When collaboration is not wanted, one approach is to create assignments that produce individualized responses. These tend to be more enjoyable to read but require more time to grade. I tend to favor giving multiple (7 to 10) brief one- to two-page assignments that can be graded quickly. Even if a student doesn't do well on several of these, there are many other occasions when he or she should perform more successfully. These assignments can create opportunities for students to reflect on what they are learning and inform me whether the material is being understood. Short, 10-question quizzes could accomplish the second objective, but not the first.

Building in an expectation of attendance (e.g., 10 percent of their grade) conveys the message that it is important to attend class. This can also be communicated by including questions on every test that come from the lecture or class discussion and that would not be found in the text. Requiring attendance, however, is not a point of strong consensus among all faculty. Some adopt the position that if students learn (whether from the notes of comrades, reading independently, or even audiotaping)—that is the key issue, not whether students actually sit in a classroom during a given hour. Other faculty insist on attendance because they use Socratic dialogue or small group techniques or simply don't like lecturing to a bunch of tape recorders in a mostly empty room (a problem, I learned recently, that faculty in a medical school were experiencing).

Because I want to minimize subjectivity in grading, I usually do not distinguish between attendance and participation. If the two concepts are separated, the issue that arises involves judging the *quality* of a student's contributions versus their *quantity*. For instance, should participation be counted if a student regularly asks if the class can take its break? Is one astute question that generates stimulating class discussion better than three "staged" questions where the answers are obvious and possibly already known to the questioner?

However, over the years there have been times when I wished I had stated in the syllabus that attendance *and* participation were going to be evaluated separately. One semester I taught a class by interactive television (ITV) and the students were so hesitant to raise questions that the quality of the course was affected. I learned my lesson and vowed that if I taught that same class by ITV again, students *would be graded* on their participation.

Objective assessment may not be possible in every course. Creative writing is one example that comes to mind where objectivity in grading is not possible to the same extent as in the math or physics department. Great variation will also be found in how instructors develop their weights. The only caution is that basing too much of the final grade on attendance or a combination of attendance and participation can inflate a student's final grade. The following illustration shows how weighting can affect a mediocre student's grade:

**HEAVY WEIGHTING OF ATTENDANCE/PARTICIPATION**

|  | Average | Weight |
|---|---|---|
| Objective test scores | 75 | (40%) |
| Minor assignments | 85 | (30%) |
| *Attendance and participation* | 95 | (30%) |
| Final Grade | **84** | |

**HEAVY WEIGHTING OF OBJECTIVE TESTS**

|  | Average | Weight |
|---|---|---|
| *Objective test scores* | 75 | (70%) |
| Minor assignments | 85 | (20%) |
| Attendance and participation | 95 | (10%) |
| Final Grade | **79** | |

All things being equal, giving more weight to attendance and participation can help weaker students earn higher grades than they might expect otherwise. Also, try to match the weighting of assignments and tests as much as possible to the course objectives. An assignment that covers two or three course objectives should be worth more than one peripherally related to a single or minor objective. Similarly, a comprehensive exam should count more than a test for a single unit.

## ASSIGNMENTS AS PEDAGOGICAL TOOLS

Most of us can recall, either from high school or our own college experiences, courses where the assignments could best be characterized as simply dreary, mind-numbing busywork. Instructors in high school who favored this legalized form of torture seemed to do so as a means of crowd control—students stayed occupied and quieter than they ordinarily would be. College instructors who engage in this behavior are just poor teachers.

In the best of all possible worlds, every assignment should be instructive—helping students make new discoveries while encouraging them to think independently and creatively. Now it's true, any one assignment that you think is strategic and essential might be viewed by students as a waste of time. If students complain more than you think they should, several factors may be at work: You may not have explained the importance of the assignment sufficiently, they may have already completed similar assignments recently for another instructor, or perhaps you are asking too much. What is it you want to accomplish with your assignments? Each one should have an objective and lend itself in some way to the overall plan of what students should be learning, but too much repetition kills interest.

Benjamin Bloom (1956) published a widely heralded set of educational objectives that may provide you with a useful starting place to begin thinking about the assignments you require.

### BLOOM'S COGNITIVE TAXONOMY

(Arranged from concrete to abstract and simple to complex levels)

**Knowledge:**     (Remembering factual materials)

Students must remember, memorize, recognize, describe, and recall.

Sample verbs that would be used: *define, describe, list, name, cite, recall, state, identify*

**Comprehension:**     (Grasping the meaning of materials)

Students must interpret, describe, and explain knowledge.

Sample verbs that would be used: *discuss, explain, interpret, extrapolate, arrange, sort, classify*

**Application:**     (Problem solving)

Students must apply facts, rules, and principles to produce some result.

**Analysis:**                Sample verbs that would be used: apply,
                             illustrate, sketch, solve, demonstrate, use
                             (An understanding of the structure and
                             components of knowledge)
                             Students must be able to break down knowledge
                             and show relationships among the parts.
                             Sample verbs that would be used: *analyze,*
                             *appraise, categorize, contrast, criticize, distinguish,*
                             *examine, differentiate, compare*

**Synthesis:**               (Creating a unique, original product; combining
                             ideas to form a new whole)
                             Students must bring together parts and
                             components of knowledge to form a whole and
                             build relationships for new situations.
                             Sample verbs that would be used: *compose, create,*
                             *construct, formulate, propose, plan, design, organize,*
                             *prescribe*

**Evaluation:**              (Making value decisions about issues; resolving
                             controversies)
                             Students must make judgments about the value
                             of material for given purposes.
                             Sample verbs that would be used: *appraise, argue,*
                             *assess, attack, compare, evaluate, predict, support,*
                             *defend, recommend*

In the lower-division courses, it is natural to expect students to commit new terms and vocabularies to memory, but few educators would be happy if that is all that students learned. Besides providing us with a structure to help us think about the assignments we create, Bloom's taxonomy is also useful for evaluating the types of questions we might employ when developing examinations.

Another consideration is the timing of the assignments. One or two opportunities to assess what students are learning before a major exam or project can be beneficial to all parties. Similarly, scheduling minor projects or quizzes through the academic term will encourage students to stay current and is preferable to a single, heavily weighted project or exam in the final week of the academic term. Many students will procrastinate and delay working until they absolutely have to, and the quality of classroom discussions will suffer when they are not reading and preparing for class.

*Mastery learning* is a concept proposing that students could, for example, be allowed to redo an assignment on multiple occasions—until they get it right. Many students like this idea because those who are willing to work hard and to put in the hours feel that they will eventually get a desirable grade. Pedagogically, the concept is sound. Students who receive feedback and revise and then get additional advice and revise have several (many?) opportunities to learn from their mistakes. Although only the most motivated of students will pursue this option, instructors who are considering adopting this teaching technique should realize that it also requires more of their own time for grading. Another point for consideration is whether students revising their assignments should get the same grade as students who got it correct on the first attempt. McKeachie (1999) recommended discounting the rewritten papers somewhat so that they are not counted as equivalent to those that have not been rewritten.

## CRITICAL THINKING

As we struggle to keep up with the latest developments in our field, most educators are well aware of how fast knowledge is multiplying. And, it is not just the amount of information that must be processed, but new ideas and research attack cherished theories and assumptions. What we learned only a handful of years ago may tomorrow become as outmoded as the manual typewriter. As a result, almost all college and university educators accept that the teaching of critical thinking should be a fundamental goal of education (Keeley et al., 1995). Unlike teaching in simpler eras, teaching in 2002 and beyond cannot consist solely of a one-way transfer of knowledge from the instructor to his or her students. Our pupils, the future leaders of this country and the world, must be taught how to find creative solutions to problems in an environment where the major feature is a constant barrage of new information. We cannot simply ladle out facts, theorems, or formulae and return to our offices. We must teach students how to think.

What is critical thinking? It is teaching students to analyze data and solve problems—to think—by examining, evaluating, and challenging the assumptions, premises, interpretations, and evidence that others have taken for granted. It is thinking "outside of the box." Critical thinking is sometimes known as developing *higher-order thinking* and is exemplified in the last three categories in Bloom's taxonomy (analysis, synthesis, and evaluation).

The Socratic method of teaching using probing questions instead of lectures is commonly cited as a model for helping students develop their reasoning skills. In this approach, the questions that are asked are not designed to test for acquisition of knowledge where there is a single correct answer, but to help the student examine alternative ways of viewing a problem and discover general principles or solutions. Critical thinking centers on the questions—lively, interesting, "deep" questions that stimulate self-reflection and debate within the class. Educators using this approach can ask questions regarding:[1]

- Interpretation (What underlying meanings or values are inherent?)
- Point of view (What other perspectives are possible?)
- Assumptions (What is being taken for granted?)
- Implications (What is the logical conclusion?)
- Relevance (Does the statement directly relate to the issue?)
- Accuracy (Is it true?)
- Logic (Do the parts fit together?)
- Evidence (Are the data reasonable?)

Teaching in this manner requires much skill in keeping the discussion focused. Each student's response must be carefully considered as implications and logical extensions are traced out. Students are not always comfortable with a Socratic style because they fear that they will give an "incorrect" answer and look stupid. Overholser (1997) recommended that if a student responds by stating, "I don't know," the instructor ought to rephrase the question or provide an example. "Simply repeating the question or dropping it entirely does nothing to facilitate the learning process. Inducing students to persist and attack the problem from several different vantage points can help them answer the question and can give them an important coping skill" (p. 15).

Instructors must model openness and integrity and be willing to explain their thinking—indeed, to expose it to public debate (Brookfield, 1987). You must create a climate in the classroom where most everyone feels comfortable to speculate and exchange ideas, where members can disagree with each other without feeling insulted or belittled. Brookfield has noted:

> There is no point in...asking critically insightful questions and practicing a devastating critique of generally accepted assumptions, if people are insulted or intimidated in the process. The worst thing...is to suggest, by a verbal response or some kind of body language (smirk, sigh, quizzically raised eyebrow) that someone's comment, writing, or other form of contribution falls pitifully short of some desired critical standard. (p. 72)

Students who volunteer information in the Socratic classroom very likely feel that they are taking huge risks. They are volunteering personal material, in some instances, that they may have never spoken aloud. Their thoughts may not be expressed eloquently; they may speak hesitantly with many false starts and stops. Because as instructors we have the decided advantage in having planned the questions ahead of time, reflected on them, and perhaps devoted considerable time to preparing with reading and discussion with colleagues, we must not intellectually bully our students. Once again, to quote Brookfield, "Humility is essential to teachers, lest they slip into the all-too-seductive (but appallingly arrogant) role of omniscient guru of critical thinking" (p. 81).

## TECHNIQUES FOR DEVELOPING CRITICAL THINKING

Here are a few ideas that you might be able to use in the classroom to help students develop higher-order thinking skills:[2]

- Have students develop flowcharts, models, concept maps, or decision trees.
- Schedule mock trials or debates.
- After a presentation or reading, have students write a critique, rebuttal, or rejoinder.
- Implement minute papers, reflection logs, student learning journals, or learning portfolios. Be creative: Ask for a 100-word analysis of the last class.
- Ask students to prepare abstracts of articles, reviews of books, or outlines with commentary of presentations.
- When there is a great deal of supplemental reading, request that students develop a taxonomy or categorization of the articles. Ask that they conceptualize three different ways the articles could be categorized.
- Practice brainstorming on some problem or issue.
- Involve the class in a nominal group decision-making process.
- Present a case that demonstrates a particular point. Ask students to analyze the case for factual errors, erroneous assumptions, or interpretations. Alternatively, ask them to write another case with the same basic information but to change it so that a different solution can be found.
- Around one central point, have students identify two different analogies to support the example and then two that contradict it. (Collaborative learning techniques are further discussed in Chapter 4.)

## ASSIGNMENTS: HOW MUCH IS TOO MUCH, TOO LITTLE?

In one class I heard about, the instructor assigned hundreds of pages of reading every week as well as a short reaction paper. The students complained vigorously but the instructor did little to reduce their workload. As the end of the semester approached, the students staged a mutiny and refused to do any additional reading because so much was expected of them that they hadn't been able to work on their end-of-the-term paper. When students en masse express their unhappiness about the amount of work required or the quantity of assignments, you need to listen. They often have talked with other students who have had the same course with different teachers and have a good sense of the amount of work being required by your colleagues. Sometimes we *do* get carried away. If you are hearing a lot of complaining, then talk with a more senior colleague about what you are having the students do. A different perspective is often helpful. It is also quite possible that other instructors are not demanding enough of their students and that the right thing to do is to expect your pupils to do more.

Pedagogically, there seems to be real value in requesting that students turn in some of their own handiwork at least once a week. These don't have to be long, complicated assignments requiring a great deal of research. Weekly assignments or quizzes communicate that you take the business of teaching seriously, that your course is the real McCoy, that students may not succeed if they don't give it a good effort. Weekly assignments provide a structure that many students need to keep them from procrastinating themselves into a deep hole at the end of the semester.

Many students will be delighted if their only assignment is a single paper due at the end of the term. Even though you know that in order to get a grade of A, they will need to be working on the paper each week, you shouldn't be surprised to find that some of your students will wait until the last minute before doing any work at all. If you don't require attendance (or if you do but you don't build in tests or assignments to be completed on a periodic basis), you may find that fewer students will attend and participate in class than if you expect more from them. Although a single end-of-the-term paper can require as much or more work than a series of weekly assignments, students who procrastinate until the last minute won't be as involved in the class and will contribute less to discussions.

In terms of the number of hours that students can be expected to work outside of class on their assignments, there are few hard and fast rules. However, there is some evidence that many instructors in the United States expect about two hours of involvement per week per credit hour; however, students *on average* actually spend less than one hour per week per credit hour (cited in McKeachie, 1999). Planning for students to spend *at least* three hours each week out of class in reading, studying, and involved with assignments for every three-hour course doesn't seem at all unreasonable—to the contrary, it may strike some instructors as much too little. Instructors concerned about the amount of time to require of students outside of class might want to estimate how much time is needed for their reading, library work, and so on, and then to approximate the amount of time required for the planned assignments. These estimates could then be checked with a more experienced colleague for reasonableness.

Another idea for arriving at the amount of time students spend out of class on course-related work would be to offer, at the beginning of the term, extra credit points to any students who keep *detailed* logs of the amount of time that they spend on the course outside of class. Alternatively, this could be a course requirement (an assignment). The instructor could then collect these logs periodically and adjust or fine-tune the amount of work levied on the students. A benefit of these logs could be that they might be diagnostically useful when students are not doing well in your class.


## DO I HAVE TO READ EVERY SENTENCE?

If you are requiring a lot (e.g., daily) of assignments from students and are hard-pressed to get them all graded, one option is to collect the papers and then pair each student with another for peer evaluation. Criteria can be prepared ahead of time to guide students in their grading. Sometimes the questions that emerge when students are asked to grade peers' papers serve as a review of points that may not have been well understood by the class.

Another option is to grade simply for completion of the assignment— students might get a check mark or a zero or four out of five possible points. There's also no reason why you can't take up homework on a more or less random basis. Grade the first four assignments but then don't take up the fifth assignment, grade the sixth assignment, skip the next one. As long as you don't make the announcement ahead of time, most students will do the assignments because you'll keep them guessing as to whether you'll be collecting the homework or not. But if students have invested a lot of time on an assignment, they will be miffed if you don't take up their work and give them the good grades they think they have earned.

When you are able to determine that the majority of students seem to have a good understanding of the material (e.g., by randomly calling on several students) one other option is to announce that you won't be grading that day's or that set of assignments, but that you will give feedback to any student who is concerned that he or she might not have done the assignment correctly. As a general rule, if you plan to *not* grade every daily or weekly assignment, tell the students this at the beginning of the academic term.


## SHOULD SPELLING AND GRAMMATICAL ERRORS BE OVERLOOKED?

It can be very difficult to focus on the content of a student's paper and to give it any credibility if every other word is misspelled. Similarly, students who don't know when to capitalize or insert commas can distract and frustrate even the most tolerant of readers. Should instructors overlook grammatical and spelling errors? Not if your goal is to educate students. Oftentimes it is possible for student to go pretty far in college without knowing basics that should have been learned earlier. When you find yourself covering a student's paper with red correction marks on more than one occasion, this suggests that the student could benefit from a referral to a writing center.

Unless you are in the English department, students will probably think it unfair of you to grade down their papers because of spelling or grammatical errors. That doesn't mean you shouldn't maintain high standards. If you are a stickler for well-written papers, alert your students to this. Share with them the criteria you will use to grade their work. Encourage them to do more than one draft and to have someone else proof their rough drafts. Be specific. If you recommend in your syllabus that students spell-check all of their papers before turning them in, you will get a better-quality paper than if you don't emphasize the importance of good writing.

How much should you "punish" a student who has horrible written communication skills? This is a judgment call. Students seem comfortable with no more than 5 or 10 percent of their grades on assignments being affected by their own poor grammar or spelling. However, you could defend dropping the grade on a particular paper by a whole letter if you have stated the grading criteria in the syllabus. Suppose you are inclined to fail the student altogether just because of poor communication skills. Is that fair? Maybe, if you are in the English department, but it probably isn't if your discipline is geology. A wiser course of action might be to offer the student the chance to revise and resubmit the paper. This is one of those areas where you would be well advised to consult with your departmental colleagues first. What would they do in such a case? As a new instructor, you may not want to generate too many student complaints your first year.

## WHAT STUDENT PRESENTATIONS COULD AND SHOULD ACCOMPLISH

Like a steady diet of chips and cookies, too much lecturing, even if you think of yourself as a skilled communicator, might not be as educationally "healthy" for students as allowing them to participate more actively. Variety is good. Using a mixture of approaches to convey material that students need to learn helps keep them interested and involved. One way to get out of the rut of lecturing every class meeting is to structure time for student presentations.

Educators usually incorporate student presentations for all of the following reasons:

- Presentations provide students with the opportunity to be creative and to demonstrate, often in an innovative way, what they have learned.
- Presentations help students learn organizational skills.
- Presentations provide students with the opportunity to hone their public speaking skills.

- Presentations (especially those coupled with discussion of the topic afterwards) encourage intellectual exchange and help students gain different perspectives and interpretations.
- Presentations give students a different motivation for learning class material and involve them actively in learning.
- Presentations reduce the amount of time or material that the instructor has to prepare.

This last reason is a terrible rationale for building in student presentations into the syllabus. However, realistically, many new faculty do rely on students to help shoulder some of the responsibility for their courses—for instance, the instructor might be scheduled to present a major paper at a conference in November and knows that he or she won't have the time to prepare a lecture in the week afterward. Also, many courses lend themselves to a format where students would naturally be expected to summarize and share with classmates their research projects at the end of the academic term.

When you decide to include student presentations in your course, be advised of the following problems you may encounter:

| PROBLEM | SOLUTION |
| --- | --- |
| 1. Many students will read their presentations word for word and make even the most attentive class slumberous. | Instruct students not to read, but to *tell* in their own words; encourage them to use transparencies or note cards. |
| 2. Students may take too much time. | Explain how this might be a problem and you will therefore need to interrupt if they run over their allotment; bring a stopwatch or a kitchen timer to class; appoint a student to be the time-keeper. |
| 3. Students (particularly group presentations) run well short of the time (i.e., a whole class period) allotted. | Clearly instruct the students to practice their group presentations—to hold "dress rehearsals" and to time themselves. Inform them that they will lose points if their presentation is too short. |
| 4. Students who are not presenting don't pay enough attention or may not come to class. | Announce ahead of time that you will draw several test questions from the presentations; don't allow students or groups to show lengthy videos that may have been widely seen. Require and take attendance. |

Above all else, student presentations should provide your class with another opportunity to learn. This means that students must wrestle with their material—integrating and organizing it differently than they would if just cramming for a test. When you hold the expectation that students will learn from these projects, they will be much more serious than when they suspect you don't value their presentations. If you create the right climate, students may relish the role of being educators, too. In order to make a good showing, they may put far more hours into preparation or into library research than they would if they weren't expected to make a presentation. However, you should be prepared to meet with students outside of class to give them ideas and resources, and, if necessary, to approve their plans.

## REFERENCES AND RESOURCES

Bloom, B. (1956). *Taxonomy of educational objectives. Vol 1: Cognitive domain.* New York: McKay.

Brookfield, S. D. (1987). Effective strategies for facilitating critical thinking. *Developing critical thinkers: Challenging adults to explore alternative ways of thinking and acting.* San Francisco: Jossey-Bass.

Diamond, R. M. (1989). *Designing and improving courses and curricula in higher education: A systematic approach.* San Francisco: Jossey-Bass.

Keeley, S. M., Shemberg, K. M., Cowell, B. S., & Zinnbauer, B. J. (1995). Coping with student resistance to critical thinking: What the psychotherapy literature can tell us. *College Teaching, 43,* 140–145.

McKeachie, W. J. (1999). *McKeachie's teaching tips: Strategies, research, and theory for college and university teachers.* Boston: Houghton Mifflin.

Overholser, J. C. (1997). Socrates in the classroom. *College Teaching, 40,* 14–19.

Sawyer, R. M., Prichard, K. W., & Hostetler, K. D. (1992). *The art and politics of college teaching.* New York: Peter Lang.

## ENDNOTES

1. Many of these questions were drawn from the following website on "The Role of Questions in Thinking, Teaching, and Learning" at <www.sonoma.edu/cthink/>.

2. Most of these ideas were derived from a chapter entitled "Learner-Centered Web Instruction for Higher-Order Thinking, Teamwork, and Apprenticeship" by C. J. Bonk and T. H. Reynolds (1997) in Badrul Khan (Ed.), *Web-based instruction.* Englewood Cliffs, NJ: Educational Technology Publications, pp. 167–178.

# CHAPTER 6

# DEVELOPING, ADMINISTERING, AND ANALYZING EXAMS

The seasoned, insightful professor has learned that there are two key mileposts in a course that account for the overwhelming majority of student dropouts—the first meeting of the class and the first examination. *The Adjunct Professor's Guide to Success* devotes a chapter to the former, as well as the chapter included here that addresses the full range of issues impacting successful exams.

This chapter emphasizes the need to employ exam formats and questions that dovetail with the level within Bloom's Taxonomy at which instruction is delivered. Well-developed, professionally administered, and effectively evaluated exams markedly impact the value students perceive from their courses, as well as their motivation to complete the course and their degree program. The chapter's closing feature, *Through the Adjuncts' Eyes*, which presents diverse, contemporary scenarios of today's higher education environments, has been acclaimed as especially valuable for most professors, regardless of status.

# DEVELOPING, ADMINISTERING, AND ANALYZING EXAMS

Chapter 10 from *Adjunct Professor's Guide to Success*
Richard E. Lyons, Marcella L. Kysilka, & George E. Pawlas
Allyn & Bacon, © 1999

## FOCUS QUESTIONS

- What are the characteristics of an effective college-level course examination?
- How should the professor approach constructing the examination?
- What special precautions should be taken when administering a test?
- What are the critical follow-up activities to an examination?

Few activities of teaching cause the new professor as much concern as developing examinations that accurately evaluate students' learning. Although examinations serve to provide data upon which the professor formulates course grades, they play significant additional roles for both the instructor and students. Effective exams provide feedback for both students and professors to build assessments of their success, and for some students to make decisions that influence their continuation in the course and, perhaps, the discipline. Examination results can build students' self-confidence or inhibit its development. In discussions with their support network of peers and family members, students often reveal that test results can be either a great source of pride or of severe disappointment and embarrassment. Far more than many instructors seem to realize, the results of exams dramatically affect the morale of both students and teachers and contribute to the quality of the learning environment within the classroom.

## EXAMINATION DEVELOPMENT STRATEGY

Most of us can probably cite horror stories from our own lives about a test-taking experience. One of the authors of this book recalls being asked on the final examination of a particular course to identify the author of the course textbook. Its author was not a person cited during the course or otherwise known to have made a significant contribution to the discipline. Few students studied that bit of trivia and consequently missed a question whose only purpose seemed to be to round out the total number of questions required to make the exam scores simpler to calculate. Clearly, the professor developing the exam should have invested a few more minutes in the development of his test, so that the final perception of his teaching was far more positive. As in this case, much of students' perception about the effectiveness of an instructor flows from how tests were managed. Probably the most common negative student perception is that the test was punitive in its approach, relying on tricky or trivial questions. As you begin formulating a strategy of test development, be especially mindful that tests:

- Are necessary for instructors to determine if students are learning
- Must be well-designed if they are to be effective
- Are only *estimates* of what students have learned
- Can be abused, even by well-intentioned instructors

Therefore, your approach to testing must incorporate several perspectives—the student's, your instructional leader's, perhaps the textbook author's, and your own. Students grow best when they receive appropriate, timely, specific, and positive feedback. Students suffer when tests are punitive, vague, disconnected to the material, or capricious.

Though we typically associate one overriding type of instructor decision with examinations—grade determination—there are others which are at least, if not more, important. Tests should accurately assess how well students are progressing toward the achievement of their overall educational goals. Exams should also contribute to making better instructional decisions, such as how much class time should be dedicated to concepts that students did not sufficiently understand. Finally, well-designed exams should contribute to diagnostic decisions related to directing students to resources that might contribute to their success. With so much riding on the results, the examination must be developed based on sound principles and a sensitive, constructive approach focused on long-term learning goals.

Often, the novice professor waits to "cover the material" to be included on a particular examination before beginning its development. Out of an effort to either save time or to ensure that all test items were covered, this practice typically leads to less-than-ideal results. Given the many demands on their time, adjunct professors are seldom able to construct effective test items, word process, and print the examination in the timeframe between finishing the coverage of the material and the actual administration of the examination. Waiting so late to develop the exam also provides insufficient time to de-bug questions and proofread the final draft, raising the possibility that errors will affect the results of the test, create problems for students, and embarrass the professor.

By developing the examination prior to covering its contents in class, the professor will be more likely to emphasize the most critical points at the appropriate time. In its most extreme form, this practice is referred to as "teaching to the test." Though it is often criticized by traditionalists, this practice might be understood best when positioned at the end of a continuum whose opposite end is "not giving students a clue to the content of a test." Based on your own values and the ability, motivation, and time availability of students, together with common practices of the department you must decide where to be on that continuum. Since the ramifications of test results are so great, you are encouraged to discuss this issue thoroughly with your discipline leader or mentor prior to developing your first examination.

## QUALITIES OF AN EFFECTIVE EXAMINATION

Traditionally, experts in educational testing have emphasized the importance of three qualities of an effective examination.

- *Content validity* refers to a test's ability to effectively evaluate what it is supposed to measure. More specifically, did the test items, i.e., questions, elicit responses that demonstrated student mastery of a particular concept? A "comprehensive" final exam that derived 50% of its questions from a single chapter in a textbook that was covered in its entirety would lack content validity.
- *Reliability* refers to the dependability or consistency of students' scores. Stated another way, if the test were repeated, would the scores remain essentially the same? A test with questions that engender a great deal of guessing by most students would lack reliability, because results in a similarly prepared group of students would probably vary greatly.
- *Objectivity* refers to a test's score flowing primarily from the student performance being measured, rather than the idiosyncrasies of the instructor constructing the exam. Tests with many questions worded as if they were "fact," when they are actually the opinion of the test developer, lack objectivity.

These three general test properties should undergird your test development strategy. Also, in order to create fair and effective examinations, you should consider the following principles:

- An effective examination should be a learning, as well as an evaluative, experience. It should serve as a thorough review of the content addressed, enabling students to deepen their mastery of the concepts included.
- Each examination should be a win–win situation for students and the professor, rather than the battle of wits that has so often been the case.

If many students regularly must re-read test questions several times to clarify what the wording of the questions seeks to elicit, students are losing.

- An effective examination should evaluate the most critical concepts and not blatantly trivial information.
- An effective examination consistently differentiates levels of students mastery by including a mix of basic, intermediate, and difficult questions. Your examinations should contribute to your teaching strategy of building *meaningful* rather than *surface* knowledge by including an appropriate ratio of higher-level questions.
- An effective examination has no significant surprises for the well-prepared student.
- A well-developed examination will reflect the time spent on the concept in class or otherwise emphasized by the instructor. As students, we all hated it when questions not covered at all in class appeared on the examination. Nearly as much, we felt cheated when an activity requiring a large chunk of class time was not included among the questions, and we probably paid less attention the next time such an activity was conducted.

Although the task of incorporating so many properties might seem a little overwhelming, you will be rewarded richly when you experience the results of your first well-designed exam. While students are known to commonly experience "test anxiety," it also is common for instructors to become anxious over the administration of an exam. Invest the extra time to develop a valid, reliable, and objective first exam so that after the test you experience the type of "rush" that successful students feel.

## DEVELOPING OBJECTIVE TEST ITEMS

Novice teachers often wonder about the best format for their tests. As is often the case in teaching, there is no single "best" answer—it depends on the nature of the learning, the level of the students' knowledge and experience, and other factors. In selecting the appropriate format for your tests, first ask "Where does my course fall in the sequence of the curriculum?" Introductory courses especially often employ *forced choice* test items, e.g., true–false, multiple choice, matching, and so on. The term *objective* test, defined somewhat differently in another context earlier in this chapter, is often used synonymously with forced choice. Perhaps the single most important thing to remember is to **test at the level you have taught.** Among students' greatest test frustrations is to be taught at Bloom's knowledge and application levels only, then to be tested at the application and synthesis levels. That is not only unfair to students but is inherently ineffective in the teaching and learning process.

On the surface, true–false items are easy for the instructor to develop and use in a test. However, to make a true–false question the least bit challenging, the instructor must employ tactics which are often regarded as tricky by students. This leads to heated discussions when scored exams are being reviewed in class, and reinforces the adversarial relationship we should be trying to avoid. Regardless of how well, or how poorly, written, true–false test items provide students with a 50% chance of success—even without reading the question! On balance, true–false questions are not as effective in most college course environments as other types of test items.

Well-written "matching-item questions can be very effective for evaluating students' mastery of vocabulary words or for linking knowledge items to one another. Typically they are not appropriate for more sophisticated levels of learning. The exercise found in Appendix 10.1 will enable you to refine your skills in developing matching-item sets for examinations.

"Multiple-choice" items are no doubt the favorite testing method for most instructors of undergraduate classes. When properly worded, multiple-choice items can be valid, reliable and objective in situations calling for knowledge, comprehension, application and even limited analysis learning situations. Therefore, it clearly would be in most instructors' best interest to develop their skills in creating effective multiple-choice test items. Some tips for creating effective multiple-choice items follow.

- Tailor (or adapt, if you are beginning with test bank questions) the difficulty level of the test item to the reading comprehension level of your students.
- Ensure that correct answers are objective, rather than opinions, unless you clearly indicate what famous person or recognized body held the opinion.
- To reduce guessing, offer 4 to 6 response options to each question, ensuring that the wrong choices ("distractors") are plausible responses rather than "throw-aways."
- Arrange the question so that the opening statement ("stem") includes all necessary qualifications needed for answer selection, creating response options that are relatively short.
- Ensure that both the correct response and distractors are approximately the same length, with similar amounts of detail and levels of complexity.
- Ensure that none of the wrong choices could be considered correct by someone truly knowledgeable in the field.
- Avoid "clangers," such as having the subject–verb agreement correct for only one option, or the last word of the stem being "an" when the correct response begins with a vowel.
- Omit nonfunctional words and trivial facts.
- Avoid negative constructions. For example, rather than "Which of the following is *not*...," use "All of the following are true, *except*."

- Although limited use of phrases such as "Both A and B are correct," "None of the above," or "All of the above" might contribute to the effectiveness of a test, be careful that such items are not disproportionately the correct response. Too often in many tests, "All of the above" is the correct answer.
- Avoid response options that overlap or include each other. For example, "Less than 25%" overlaps with the choice "Less than 50%."
- Whenever possible, for *application* and *analysis* questions use situations to which students can easily relate, thus encouraging longer-term retention.

Since instructors are often anxious about developing effective exams, many rely on test banks provided by the publishers of their textbooks to generate questions for their exams. There seems to be an inherent confidence that questions included in test banks have been validated through extensive classroom use. While many test banks are valuable resources for effective questions as well as great time-savers, be aware that some have poor questions that have not been validated at all. Some test bank questions are totally unusable, while others require editing before they can be used effectively. Your students deserve a valid, reliable exam and have the right to expect you to provide it. Poor questions, whether from test banks, or any other source, are inexcusable. The exercise in Appendix 10.2 will equip you to develop more effective multiple-choice test items.

## EFFECTIVE ESSAY TEST ITEMS

Although objective tests clearly are convenient to score, many observers attribute an overdependence on their use as a contributing factor to a marked decline in the writing and critical thinking abilities of students. In contrast, essay questions are relatively easy for the instructor to write and they eliminate student guessing and emphasize the sophisticated communications skills that society and the marketplace increasingly demand. When managed properly, essay writing is widely accepted as contributing to the development of higher level thinking, encompassing Bloom's application, analysis, synthesis and evaluation levels. More specifically, essay questions help students achieve the following learning outcomes:

- Establish meaningful connections between theoretical principles and practical situations
- Compare and/or contrast two or more approaches to an issue
- Explain the range of factors which contribute to a particular situation
- Integrate information from several sources to explain a particular situation
- Propose and defend a grounded solution to a problem
- Evaluate the quality or appropriateness of a product, process or action

In addition to the time required, scoring essay questions presents other challenges. Students often have been conditioned to equate "quantity of words" to "quality of response" in an essay—a perception that unfortunately has been reinforced in some classrooms. That paradigm of wordiness sometimes invades the minds of instructors who score longer essay responses higher even when they contain extraneous or "bluff" material. Scored essay question responses may also contribute to uncomfortable interchanges with disagreeable students. Let us offer some suggestions for minimizing these occurrences.

Before the exam, instructors employing essay test questions might invest some class time in teaching students to write an effective essay response. One effective way likely to be well received by students is to provide the class with an essay question that could plausibly appear on the first exam. On the chalkboard or overhead, succinctly write and explain the content and writing standards you will employ in scoring responses. Solicit feedback before moving on to ensure that your point was understood. Then, emphasize that each response will be scored beginning with "0" and that points will be awarded for positive achievement, rather than starting with "10" (or whatever the possible score is) and taking points off for making incorrect statements or writing improperly. Provide all the students written copies of your criteria to guide their preparation for the exam.

Then, divide the class into groups of two or three students, and provide them, one at a time, three written responses to the question. Based on the scoring standards you presented (leave the overhead or chalkboard display in place), they are to score each response. You probably would want to give them a clearly poor response, an average one, and an outstanding response—in that order. Following their analysis, discuss the experience and provide your score for each of the three. For the outstanding response, emphasize the key correct components and points awarded for each. Students are thus equipped to begin their preparation with a clear understanding of your expectations.

Your time in scoring essay responses will be made more efficient if you carefully plan your questions. First, compose essay items with clear parameters within their wording so students will not be tempted to write unnecessarily long responses. After writing your initial essay questions, you might want to have your mentor or other veteran instructor review them with this focus, as well as difficulty level, in mind. Next, based on the criteria provided to students, outline the specific content, organization, and process you expect to be included in each effective response and assign objective point values for their attainment. Be prepared to share this rubric with the class when you return their scored exams. To ensure your objectivity when scoring essay items, conceal the student's identity by covering the name or having them use the last four numbers of their Social Security number on the response pages. If you assign more than one essay on the same test, score all of the responses to the same question at the same time, before proceeding to score any of the responses to subsequent essay items. Minimize delays between scoring sessions to maximize your continuity of thought and minimize the impact of your mood.

Once your exam is fully developed, with its probable combination of objective and essay items, enlist the help of your mentor or other veteran instructor to give it a final review prior to printing. Develop your scoring key and use it to guide your exam review. Besides the correct answers, your key should include margin notes of why particular choices are correct or incorrect and the source of the question, e.g., page number in the textbook.

## FACILITATING STUDENT SUCCESS

All instructors want students to accept full responsibility for their performance on tests, but enlightened professors realize they themselves have a stake, and therefore a role to play, in facilitating success. Several tactics are possible; as the instructor, you must weigh the costs and benefits of each tactic to arrive at a position that fits your values, the experience level of students in the course, and departmental and institutional standards. You might want to consider the following information as you formulate a position on this issue, especially as it relates to the first test in a course when students are often grappling to overcome anxieties.

Most instructors would agree that students have a right to enter each exam with a clear and accurate expectation of test content and format. At a minimum, the professor should clarify that expectation through a detailed review conducted the class meeting prior to the exam. An effective review can utilize varied formats, depending on the maturity level of students, the format of test items, the complexity of the material, and other factors. For example, if the exam is largely "objective," the instructor might take a sample of questions from the exam, reword them slightly, and provide a handout. Students can then be assigned to groups of no more than three (they should not form their own groups, which are likely to be comprised of individuals too similar to each other) and provided a single copy of the handout. Allow perhaps ten minutes for students to formulate responses to explain to the rest of the class. The professor can then debrief the collective responses, focusing on the concepts that give students the most difficulty. The handout can then either be collected, or each student given a copy from which to study.

For classes with especially anxious students, a week or so before the first exam you might provide a study guide with a simple listing of the concepts that will be included on the exam. In addition, you might want to divide the class into small groups during the last 20 to 30 minutes of class and encourage them to discuss possible responses while you circulate throughout the classroom. Since students have become acquainted somewhat with each other largely through your earlier icebreaker activity, you should once again encourage them to form study groups outside of class to prepare for the exam.

Before releasing students from the class meeting prior to the exam, describe for students your procedures for administering the exam, including:

- Supplies (for example, Scantron answer sheets or blue books) they will need for the exam
- Special seating arrangements or other procedures you plan to employ to ensure that a secure and quiet environment is created
- The schedule you will follow in administering the exam, including time parameters you will employ. If your class periods are long, plan to give the exam at the beginning of the period, rather than cover additional material. Also explain the activities that will follow the test administration, and any other critical information
- A restatement of penalties for not taking the exam (which should also be in your syllabus)

Reviewing these details in advance will contribute to a positive perception by students and increase their sense of confidence as they embark on the exam.

## ADMINISTERING THE EXAMINATION

Arrive especially early for the class period during which an exam is to be administered, allowing yourself time to adjust the temperature and other factors, as well as meet students who might have arrived early with questions about the exam. Designate a seating area near the door for any students who arrive late to minimize disruption to students who will be engaged in the test. If you have not already done so, proofread the final copy of the exam carefully, marking any typos or factual errors that might have withstood earlier scrutiny.

When students begin arriving, it is critical to create an atmosphere of positive expectancy and trust. Greet students as they enter and ask each an open-ended question about their readiness, such as "How are you feeling about this?" and in other ways proactively deflate their anxieties. Avoid jokes or remarks that might be perceived as flippant, since these can contribute to an adversarial dynamic within anxious students.

When the scheduled time for beginning class arrives, ask the class as a whole if there are any final questions you need to clarify prior to starting the exam. If there are, answer them in a constructive manner, avoiding lengthy, highly detailed responses. Be patient and reassuring. Ask students to have only the materials required to take the exam on their desk and place everything else on the floor (or in some other specific out-of-the-way area). Direct them where to bring their exams and answer sheets when completed and remind them of time parameters and your procedures for scoring and returning the exams. If you found any typos or other mistakes on the exam, direct students to delay beginning the exam until all are distributed, then review the corrections that should be made on the test. Remind them once again of the time parameters of the test. Wish them good luck.

# DEALING PROACTIVELY WITH STUDENT CHEATING

Perhaps the single most unpleasant aspect of teaching is dealing with cheating. We inherently feel we were fair in developing the exam and resist believing *our* students feel the pressure to make grades that fuels dishonorable behavior. When we allow ourselves to feel that way, we sometimes fail to take the proactive measures necessary to create the classroom security and clear positive expectations that can minimize, though not eliminate, the pressure to cheat. Students who perceive that their peers are cheating and that the instructor does nothing to prevent it often lack the self-discipline to resist cheating themselves at the next opportunity.

Peeking at other students' papers and using crib sheets continue to be widely employed as test-cheating methods. However, technology, larger classes, the use of machine-graded answer sheets, and the risk-taking mindset so common among students today have evoked more brazen methods, some of the which are described next.

- Students use calculators, micro-cassette recorders, and other electronic devices to store potential answers.
- Students well prepared for the exam write responses on a second Scantron answer sheet which they surreptitiously give to a friend as they leave the classroom.
- Students adhere potential answers to body areas that instructors cannot readily see and therefore are less likely to investigate.
- Students have someone else take an exam for them.
- Students accuse the instructor of losing an exam that was not submitted.

Clearly, prevention is the most effective strategy to minimize cheating. (Therefore, avoid having someone else proctor your exam because it increases the incidence of cheating.) It is critical to create a trusting classroom atmosphere where students know that you want them to perform well. Asking students in a positive tone and monitoring their placing of books and notes in secure places prior to distributing the exam will help. Having students disburse themselves throughout the entire classroom, rather than clustering in the same area, will also send the message that you care about ensuring the chances of success for the better-prepared students. For classes with large numbers of students, it takes little additional work for you to develop a second version of the exam that scrambles the order of questions.

Another preventive technique is to develop exams that are perceived as fair and secure by students. Often, the accusation by students that certain questions were tricky is valid, as it relates to ambiguous language and trivial material. Ask your mentor or other experienced instructor to closely review the final draft of your first few exams for these factors.

## SCORING OBJECTIVE EXAMINATIONS

Since multiple choice and matching questions require a single letter answer, they are inherently easy to score. Traditionally, scoring of such items was facilitated through use of an answer sheet and a corresponding key that could be positioned next to it. In recent years, this process has been made even easier through the use of scoring machines and especially designed answer sheets. The most common of such systems have been developed by the Scantron Company. The machine first reads an answer sheet marked as a key, then scores each student answer sheet, marks incorrect answers (advanced models even print the correct answer) and prints the total number of correct responses. Obviously, this can be a great time-saver, especially when there are many students in the class. However, Scantron machines provide an even greater advantage by providing analytical information for the instructor.

Scantron systems enable the instructor to insert an item-analysis form into the machine following the scoring of all student answer sheets, providing a count of the number of times each question is answered incorrectly. Thus, the instructor can easily focus on questions missed most frequently, evaluate their clarity and accuracy, and contemplate corrective actions that might be taken.

The logical next step in analyzing the test results is to list the scores, from highest to lowest, and calculate the average score. Since the results on the first exam are so critical for both you and the students, you might want to meet with your mentor or other veteran teacher—ideally familiar with this particular course—to review the exam results. Resist the temptation to curve the test by adding a certain number of points to all scores. Curving grades discounts students' success on exams and places responsibility on the instructor. It also raises the expectation that future exams will be curved. Should you decide that one or more questions were poor, think about eliminating the question(s) and re-calculating the scores. While it might take a few additional minutes, this corrective action reinforces to students that they are being held responsible for their own success.

## REVIEWING RESULTS OF EXAMS WITH STUDENTS

Since immediate feedback enhances effective learning, always review the results of exams no later than the period immediately following its administration. Do not allow a student who has missed the exam and not taken a makeup delay the critical review process. Instead, make arrangements for such students to take an alternative version of the test prior to rejoining the class. (To minimize possible negative reactions to this procedure, you would be wise to explain it during the pre-exam review.)

If answer sheets were used in administering the exam, initially return only the exams themselves and review each question thoroughly. Students therefore will more likely focus on their understanding of each question rather than which they answered incorrectly. Be prepared, from the Scantron or other form of test-item analysis, to identify how many times each question was missed. Thoroughly double-check the questions missed most often and dedicate extra time during the review to ensure that students leave with a clear understanding of the correct answers. Be prepared to deal constructively with argumentative or otherwise emotional students by building "common ground." If appropriate, be willing to lead them through the process of logically determining the correct answer. Compliment their effort and provide reassurance.

Before distributing the corrected answer sheets, write the scores in a ranked list on the board (without students' names), together with the class average, so students can clearly see where they stand within the group. Return scored answer sheets in random fashion, rather than from highest to lowest scores. Make eye contact with each student and make a quiet, constructive comment.

Realize anew that exam results are interpreted by each student through a very personalized lens. Affected by the expectations of employers (whose degree of tuition reimbursement may depend on the final course grade) and expectations of family members (who might prefer mom or dad not to be giving up limited time to attend school), students often put a great deal of pressure on themselves to perform. Schedule a break immediately following the review of exam results and offer to meet individually with students. In addition, extend an invitation for them to meet with you at the end of the class meeting to discuss their concerns. Employ the transactional analysis skills you learned earlier in the book to ensure that students leave the class meeting with as constructive a view of the test results as possible. Each of us retains for a long time the memories of those who influenced us during the periods of our lives when situations were most challenging. Students are very much that way with exams!

## THROUGH THE ADJUNCTS' EYES

JUAN:

In administering my first exam, I was struck again by the dichotomy between community college and university undergraduate students. The range of the exam scores was 42 to 98, and the average score was 74. The distribution of scores was nothing like the bell-shaped curve I had expected! There were more A's than B's or C's, no D's, and more F's than C's. I was flabbergasted! Upon reflection, I realize that university students largely study in groups—in the dormitories or, in a few cases, in fraternity and sorority houses. Community college students, who work and commute to campus, usually study alone. The overachievers do well, because they are motivated to improve themselves at work or prove something to their children, their spouses, or themselves. Those who get behind usually have no one at home who has gone to college capable of helping, and often find it hard time-wise to access the help that is available in tutoring labs.

The class period following the exam, when I returned and reviewed their papers, was more difficult than I expected. Several students were primed as soon as I walked in the room. Although they maintained their composure, I could see frustration built up in their eyes. As we reviewed the exam, some common complaints emerged. The first was that the test included a lot of material that wasn't sufficiently covered in class. When I responded that it was in their reading assignment, one student asked why she needed to come to class if the exam was going to be taken totally from the textbook. Several students then said that some of the things we spent a lot of time on in class were not included on the exam. While university students would probably not have verbalized any complaint, the community college students were vehement. Although their complaints were stinging, I listened closely, and upon reflection, have to admit there was a lot of truth in their complaints. I think the fact that I showed concern and listened carefully was a positive. I told them I would re-think the results of the test and develop some sort of remedy. They seemed to accept that—reluctantly.

**KAREN:**

I gave my first exam last night—a mid-term. Mr. Jackson planned only two exams for the course, both of which I will be using. Each has 100 multiple choice questions and covers 8 to 10 chapters from the textbook. As students were taking the exam, I reviewed it closely for the first time. There were 6 or 8 questions that were challenging to me! A good number of the questions required an evaluation of actions taken by the courts—not a level at which I had delivered the material. Several questions had a convoluted format that tested the students' test-taking ability more than it did their knowledge of the material.

I dedicated the entire class meeting to the exam. When students left, several looked like they had seen a ghost. I left the classroom feeling like I had really let the students down. Having the exam cover so much material and waiting so late in the term to give the first exam were big mistakes. My not reviewing the exam earlier in the term, simplifying some of the questions, and making sure I addressed the material in my lectures were even bigger mistakes!

MARGARET:

Two weeks before giving my first exam, I had the students work in small groups to provide input into its development. While a few made suggestions that were overly elementary, most of their ideas on what should be included were practical and appropriate. Since we had good results working in small groups to solve case problems, I included on the exam several case problems similar to the previous situations. In class the week before, I reviewed extensively for the exam, gave them a study guide that included the concepts I expected them to have mastered, and told them the number and format of questions. To me, the process should work just like it does at work, where you give employees a job description and performance appraisal form, show them what to do, then give them feedback on how well they are doing. I also encouraged students to study together outside of class.

When they came to take the exam, most students looked confident and relaxed. Overall, the results were outstanding, although a few students lack sufficient writing skills for this level. As we reviewed the scored exam, there were no complaints, even though three students got failing scores. Two of those saw me at the end of class and apologized for not having dedicated more time to preparing for the exam.

## TIPS FOR THRIVING

As stated earlier, feedback on results is the most effective of motivating factors. Anxious students are especially hungry for positive feedback. You can quickly and easily provide it by simply writing "Great job!" or "Terrific" on the answer sheets or tests of students who did especially well. For students who performed less than ideally, a brief note such as "I'd love to talk with you at the end of class" can be especially reassuring. Again, the key is to be proactive and maintain high standards, while requiring students to retain ownership of their own success in the course.

Since your major goal is empowering students to achieve their own success and the first exam in a course is typically the major departure point for students dropping out of a course, you might want to develop a contingency plan to deal with disappointing scores. One which works quite well, while maintaining student responsibility for success, is "Plan B." On your syllabus, you outlined your grading procedure for the course ("Plan A"), similar to that in the model syllabus in Appendix 4.1. If you used a simple scheme, where each component was weighted at 20% of the final course grade, you can easily offer students not scoring up to their expectations a win–win alternative. If they choose, they may drop the score on the first exam only (*not* the lowest score of all their exams) by recalculating the weights on the remaining components to 25% each. Since there are many understandable reasons why students might get off to a slow start in a class (for example, added the course after the term began, were unable to purchase the expensive textbook in a timely fashion, and so on), "Plan B" is very defendable from the professor's position and protects the students' self-efficacy. In addition, this plan requires the student to intensify his or her commitment for the remainder of the course.

This chapter contains many tips for effectively developing, administering, and following up examinations. The common thread is that testing can and should be a rewarding experience for both students and you. With that idea solidly in mind, you can very effectively overcome for yourself, and help students overcome for themselves, the anxiety that accompanies testing.

---

**REVIEW OF KEY POINTS**

- Examinations contribute significantly to the overall perception students develop of an instructor.
- Develop a draft of your exam early to ensure that material on it is properly addressed in class.
- Ensure that your exams are valid, reliable, and objective.
- The test item format selected should dovetail with the learning domain and level within Bloom's Taxonomy.
- Well-written test items employ easily understood criteria.
- Essay test items encourage effective writing and critical thinking skill development.
- Proactively manage student success on exams by clarifying mutual expectations and holding a thorough, interactive review of material it will include.
- Meticulously organize every detail of administering the exam.
- Avoid having someone else proctor an exam for you.
- Thoroughly analyze overall exam results before returning them to students.
- Return scored exams no later than the next regularly scheduled class meeting.
- Demonstrate sensitivity to the anxiety that many students feel before, during, and after taking exams.

## SUGGESTED READINGS

Jacobs, L., & Chase, C. (1992). *Developing and using tests effectively*. San Francisco: Jossey-Bass.
Kubisyn, T., & Borich, G. (1996). *Educational testing and measurement: Classroom application and practice* (5th ed.). New York: HarperCollins.

## APPENDIX 10.1   MATCHING-ITEM EXERCISE

This exercise is designed to increase your sensitivity to the ineffective dynamics of many matching exercises. As you respond to questions, note any characteristics of the exercise that might create unfair disadvantages or advantages for students.

*Directions:* Match the name from the left column to the achievement in the right column. Enter its letter in the appropriate space. Each correct answer is worth 10 points.

|  |  |  |  |
|---|---|---|---|
| ____ | 1. Madame Curie | a. | Father of psychoanalysis |
| ____ | 2. Adolph Hitler | b. | *Fuhrer* of the Third Reich |
| ____ | 3. Charles DeGaulle | c. | Wrote *The Communist Manifesto* |
| ____ | 4. Peter Tchaikovsky | d. | French inventor |
| ____ | 5. Karl Marx | e. | Leader of France during World War II |
| ____ | 6. Sigmund Freud | f. | Wrote *The 1812 Overture* |
| ____ | 7. Louis Pasteur | g. | Developed process for purifying milk |
| ____ | 8. Nicholas II | h. | His assassination led to start of World War I |
| ____ | 9. Georgi Zhukov | i. | Last czar of Russia |
| ____ | 10. Archduke Ferdinand | j. | Russian general, led WW II assault on Berlin |

What situations did you find which might be problems for students taking the test, or the instructor who will base grades on its results? Check your findings against some of the faults listed below.

*Incomplete Directions.*   There are *two* "French inventors" in the list. Does the student put both correct answers down, or through process of elimination determine that since "g" goes with "7", then "d" must go with "1"?

*Easy Guessing.*   Two of the questions—2 and 7—were on the same line with their correct answers—"b" and "g" respectively. There are ten total items and equal numbers in both lists, making the overall "process of elimination" especially easy. If there were two or three extra achievements listed, the chances of guessing correctly would be markedly reduced.

*Position of Lists.* The material would be more logical and less time-consuming for the student to process if the achievements, i.e. long phrases, were in the left column and the names, i.e. shorter phrases, in the right column.

*Lack of Commonality in Lists.* The list includes politicians, royalty, writers, inventors, a physician, and a composer. The exercise would be much more effective if all were of very similar roles and if the historical period were more limited.

*Order of Names.* While not a major problem in a list of ten names, the fact that names are not given in alphabetical order could make a longer exercise much more time-consuming and confusing for students to complete.

*Clangers.* The use of certain terms contributes to a mental "clanging" clue for students, providing an extra, inappropriate tip to the correct answer. "Pasteur" and "milk," "DeGaulle" and "France," and "Hitler" and "fuhrer" produce such a clanging sound. "His" rules out Madame Curie as a possible choice.

---

**APPENDIX 10.2   MULTIPLE-CHOICE ITEM EXERCISE**

As you review each of the following questions, determine any obstacle it might create for students completing the exercise. For ease of focus, the content of each question is derived from material in this book.

*Directions:* Select the **best** answer to each of the following and enter its letter on the answer sheet. Each correct answer is worth X points.

1.  Which of the following would a department chairperson and dean expect of you during your teaching of a semester-long course?
    A. Telling lots of "war stories" and actively promoting your full-time career
    B. Arriving a few minutes before to the scheduled starting time of each class meeting and staying a few minutes afterward
    C. Canceling a class whenever you had a business, medical, or personal reason
    D. Speaking up vehemently for the "one best way" on all issues within the course

E. Assigning at least 20% of students a "D" or "F" as a final course grade

2. Which of the following is not true of an effective course syllabus?
   A. It serves as a contract between the instructor and the student.
   B. It includes a "tentative schedule" that the instructor should expect to modify.
   C. It provides answers to most reasonable questions students would have.
   D. It is especially clear on the issues of grading and attendance/participation.
   E. None of the above.

3. During the first meeting of your class,
   A. distribute your syllabus, but don't review it until the second meeting.
   B. the classroom and your handout materials should create a positive first impression.
   C. wait for 10 minutes before starting to allow all students time to arrive.
   D. take about 15 minutes to review your professional and personal background.
   E. be sure to tell students if the class was assigned to you on short notice.

4. During the first class meeting, avoid
   A. "heavy stuff," like reviewing the goals and limitations of the course.
   B. learning students' names, because if they drop the course you have wasted time.
   C. going into great depth with the material of the course.
   D. introducing yourself to individual students.
   E. gathering any detailed information about students.

5. Which of the following is the most important reason for conducting "icebreakers"?
   A. Break down barriers between students who are likely to be passive
   B. Give students a chance to have some fun as a balance against the "heavy stuff"
   C. Provide students a chance to satisfy their need to "fit in"
   D. Create a positive learning atmosphere
   E. Encourage students to begin relationships that might lead to forming study groups

6. Which of the following is true of "learning domains"?
   A. The psychomotor domain refers to the thought processes.
   B. The effective domain refers to attitudes, character issues, and appreciation of beauty.
   C. The cognitive domain refers to physical skills and dexterity.
   D. All of the above are true.
   E. None of the above are true.

7. Which of the following lists the correct sequence of "Bloom's Taxonomy"?
   A. Application, analysis, knowledge, comprehension, evaluation, synthesis
   B. Knowledge, comprehension, analysis, application, synthesis, evaluation
   C. Analysis, knowledge, comprehension, application, evaluation, synthesis
   D. Knowledge, comprehension, application, analysis, synthesis, evaluation
   E. Comprehension, knowledge, analysis, application, evaluation, synthesis

8. Which of the following are true of the effective use of "cooperative learning"?
   A. Students work in small groups to process information or solve problems
   B. Groups work best when members are alike in age, gender, etc.
   C. Students should work with the same group of students throughout the term
   D. Groups should include no more than 4 students so everyone is encouraged to contribute
   E. Both A and D are true.

---

## DISCUSSION

These questions may well seem very much like some you have taken as a student, but let's analyze each more closely.

The correct answer to 1 is clearly B. That answer was easy to determine because "distractor" (choice) A (and perhaps others) was a "throwaway." Although many instructors believe the first question on any exam should be relatively easy, in order to relieve student anxiety and build confidence, this question is probably too easy for our intended audience, i.e., the readers of this book.

Questions 2 is messy. First, many test-takers would have difficulty focusing on the key issue in question, largely because of the negative nature of its stem. Rewording the stem to read, "All of the following are true of an effective course syllabus, *except:*" would prompt the attention of the student more effectively. In addition, given the stated choices, the "correct" answer is E, i.e., "none of the above." However, the pattern of the original question— "Which is...not" is "none..." is confusing to anybody, but especially to anxious students. Many bright students who otherwise knew the correct answer would probably not select E as the correct answer because of the flawed phrasing.

Question 3 looks pretty good doesn't it? The choices required you to process and analyze appropriate concepts for your level of teaching experience. Did you select the "correct" answer, B? Although you probably didn't need it, there was a clue. Notice all of choices except B began with a verb, which probably created a subliminal "clanging" in your mind. The question would be more valid if choice B were reworded to also begin with a verb.

Question 4 also requires an appropriate degree of analysis. But, it would confuse some students because the trigger word in the stem, "avoid," is negative. The human mind has a challenging time focusing on a negative, and thus the question has an uneasy feeling about it. "All of the following are appropriate activities of the first class meeting, *except:*" is a more effectively worded stem.

The purpose of question 5—encouraging recall of valid reasons for conducting an "icebreaker"—is appropriate in a quiz for a reader of this book. But the way the test item is written, the "correct" choice is largely the opinion of the writer of the question. Again, the question could be rewritten with an "all of the following, *except:*" stem. Or, the existing stem could be used if four of the choices were reworded to make them objectively incorrect.

To many people, question 6 has a "giveaway" answer. A and C are clearly wrong, so D is also wrong. While B seems like the correct answer, "affective" is the actual term for the described domain. Unless correct spelling of terms is critical in your course, students should not be evaluated with such relatively trivial choices. Such questions are perceived as mean-spirited by students, and they serve to stifle their motivation and increase their test-anxiety for the remainder of the course.

Were you tempted to look back to Chapter 5 before answering 7? The correct answer is D. While this question might be appropriate for a student majoring in education, it requires an inappropriate level of exactness for a reader of this book. It is very easy to make a similar mistake in exams you develop for your students. Such questions serve to encourage students to memorize facts that are forgotten soon after the exam, rather than develop an appreciation for the overall concept.

Like Question 3, the final test item also has a hidden clue. The plural verb "are" in the stem serves as a "clanger" for choice E. A number of students who did not fully understand the material would probably get this answer correct. In the process, the overall value of the exam is discounted.

Finally, did you notice the pattern of the responses? Three of the eight questions (not counting the "opinion" Question 5), or 38%, were correctly answered B. Since each question had 5 choices, B should be the correct answer on only about 20% of the questions in this multiple-choice exercise. Many teachers unknowingly fall into patterns in which they disproportionately use a particular letter as the "correct" response. Such patterns are discerned by some students, often those who were not necessarily the best prepared for the exam.

---

**APPENDIX 10.3    MODEL STUDY GUIDE**

**Principles of Management**
**Exam No. 2, Study Guide**

**Chapter 5**
1. Explain Gantt charts, uses
2. Explain PERT diagrams, uses
3. Calculate "break-even point"
4. Common ways of determining how much inventory to hold in stock
5. Explain "just in time" inventory system, when used

**Chapter 6**
1. Explain measurable characteristics of jobs that improve employee motivation
2. Challenges facing the job designer
3. Explain "self directed work teams"
4. Advantages/disadvantages of job specialization
5. Characteristics of enriched jobs
6. Compare/contrast methods of nontraditional job scheduling
7. Advantages/disadvantages of telecommuting

**Chapter 7**
1. Advantages/disadvantages of a bureaucracy
2. Compare/contrast types of authority
3. Explain function, applications of organizational chart
4. Methods of departmentalization
5. Advantages/disadvantages of flat organizations over tall ones
6. Explain components of delegation
7. Factors affecting size of span of control
8. Explain foundation, development of organizational culture

**Chapter 8**
1. Contrast "personnel management" with "human resource management"
2. Identify key shifts in workforce
3. Components of staffing function
4. Compare/contrast job analysis, job specifications, job description
5. Explain, cite cases of "reverse discrimination"
6. Explain the Americans with Disabilities Act
7. Compare/contrast types and examples of sexual harassment

# CHAPTER 7

# EXPERIENCING A PARADIGM SHIFT THROUGH ASSESSMENT

This second of three chapters included from Mary Huba's and Jann Freed's *Learner-Centered Assessment on College Campuses* effectively presents the key elements of ongoing learner assessment practices. It emphasizes the importance of implementing a systems approach, in which clearly delineated learning outcome objectives are assessed as an integrated activity of the learning process rather than the disjointed activity it often is in an instructor-centered environment.

An especially valuable feature of this book is the "making connections" dialogue boxes that serve as an advance organizer for each chapter, and the "self reflection" exercises provided following each concept. Each exercise poses questions that trigger analysis of the reader's current teaching practices and foster contemplation of approaches likely to improve learners' success. Such insights are critical to the orchestration of a true learner-center paradigm.

# EXPERIENCING A PARADIGM SHIFT THROUGH ASSESSMENT

Chapter 1 from *Learner-Centered Assessment on College Campuses*
Mary E. Huba & Jann E. Freed
Allyn & Bacon, © 2000

---

Definition of insanity: Doing the same thing, the same way, all the time—but expecting different results (Anonymous).

It is tradition. It was a part of my training, and seems like what I should be doing. I feel somehow guilty when I am not lecturing (Creed, 1986, p. 25).

Suddenly I *saw* things differently, and because I *saw* differently, I *thought* differently, I *felt* differently, and I *behaved* differently (Covey, 1989, p. 31).

---

## MAKING CONNECTIONS

*As you begin to read the chapter, think about ideas and experiences you've already had that are related to experiencing a paradigm shift...*

- What are your assumptions about how learners learn?
- What are your assumptions about the best way to teach?
- How do you know if your teaching has been successful?
- How have your ideas about teaching and learning changed over the years?
- How can you help your students improve what they learn and how they learn?
- What are your students learning that will help them be successful in the information age?

- In your role as a teacher, what is your relationship to the rest of your institution?
- What do you know about the assessment movement in higher education?
- How do assessment results help you understand what your students know and don't know, what they can do and can't do?

*What else do you know about experiencing a paradigm shift?*

*What questions do you have about experiencing a paradigm shift?*

Tomorrow's citizens, tomorrow's leaders, tomorrow's experts are sitting in today's college classrooms. Are they learning what they need to know? Are faculty using teaching methods that prepare them for future roles?

Struggling to answer these questions, those of us who teach in higher education are looking at how we teach and trying to evaluate what we do. This is not an easy task. The many years we spent as students shaped our notions of what teaching is all about. These notions may be so deeply embedded in our world views that they are virtually invisible to us, eluding objective examination. On top of that, many of us have spent additional years teaching as we were taught—practicing the "old ways." Few of us have had opportunities to study teaching the way we study topics in our own disciplines. It is difficult to step back, analyze current approaches critically, make revisions, and move ahead, confident that the new direction is the right one.

## TEACHER-CENTERED AND LEARNER-CENTERED PARADIGMS OF INSTRUCTION

Most of us learned to teach using the lecture method, and research has shown that traditional, teacher-centered methods are "not *in*effective...but the evidence is equally clear that these conventional methods are *not* as effective as some other, far less frequently used methods" (Terenzini & Pascarella, 1994, p. 29). In fact, the lecture method is clearly *less effective* than other methods in changing thoughts and attitudes (Bligh, 1972; Eison & Bonwell, 1988). These findings suggest that a change in the traditional method of college teaching is needed in order to enhance student learning (Kellogg Commission on the Future of State and Land-Grant Universities, 1997, 1999).

> The primary learning environment for undergraduate students, the fairly passive lecture–discussion format where faculty talk and most students listen, is contrary to almost every principle of an optimal student learning setting ...Intimate faculty-student contact that encourages feedback, that motivates students, that allows students to perform is the exception and not the norm (Guskin, 1997, pp. 6–7).

The current view in higher education is that we should focus on student learning rather than teaching in order to improve students' college experiences (e.g., Cross, 1998). The reason is not so much that our current approach is "broken" and in need of "fixing," but rather that we are underperforming (Engelkemeyer & Brown, 1998). We are failing to use existing knowledge about learning and our own institutional resources to produce graduates who leave the institution ready to succeed in the information age.

"We have failed to realize the synergistic effect of designing, developing, and delivering curricula, programs, and services that collaboratively and collectively deepen, enhance, and enable higher levels of learning" (p. 10).

As shown in Figure 1.1, the shift from teaching to learning has been endorsed by many prominent leaders and theorists in higher education since the mid-1980s. In addition, in 1998, the Joint Task Force on Student Learning

**FIGURE 1.1    Importance of Learner-Centered Teaching from the Viewpoint of Prominent Leaders in Higher Education**

- Students learn by becoming involved...Student involvement refers to the amount of physical and psychological energy that the student devotes to the academic experience (Astin, 1985, pp. 133–134).

- The routine is always the same: Begin the unit, teach the unit, give the students a test, correct the test, return the test, review the "right" answers with the class, collect the test, and record the grades. Then move on to the next unit. If we continue this practice, how will students learn to use experiences from past units to improve the work they do on future units? (Bonstingl, 1996, p. 30)

- Learning is not a spectator sport. Students do not learn much just by sitting in class listening to teachers, memorizing prepackaged assignments, and spitting out answers. They must talk about what they are learning, write about it, relate it to past experiences, apply it to their daily lives. They must make what they learn part of themselves (Chickering & Gamson, 1987, p. 3).

- The ultimate criterion of good teaching is effective learning (Cross, 1993, p. 20).

- We also know, from research on cognition, that students who reflect on their learning are better learners than those who do not (Cross, 1996, p. 6).

- Learning is, after all, the goal of *all* education, and it is through a lens that focuses on learning that we must ultimately examine and judge our effectiveness as educators (Cross, 1996, p. 9).

- Students learn what they care about and remember what they understand (Erickson, 1984, p. 51).

- Our entire educational system is designed to teach people to do things the one right way as defined by the authority figure. We are taught to recite what we hear or read without critically interacting with the information as it moves in and out of short-term memory. In this exchange, the information leaves no tracks, and independent thinking skills are not developed (Lynch, 1991, p. 64).

- Classes in which students are expected to receive information passively rather than to participate actively will probably not be effective in encouraging students to think reflectively. Similarly, tests and assignments that emphasize only others' definitions of the issues or others' conclusions will not help students learn to define and conclude for themselves (King & Kitchener, 1994, p. 239).

appointed by the American Association for Higher Education (AAHE), the American College Personnel Association (ACPA), and the National Association of Student Personnel Administrators (Joint Task Force, 1998a, 1998b) alerted us to the need for all segments of a college campus to work together to enhance and deepen student learning. The Task Force developed a set of propositions about learning that can be used by both faculty and student affairs professionals to guide future practice. These propositions are presented in Chapter 2.

The idea of focusing on learning rather than teaching requires that we rethink our role and the role of students in the learning process. To focus on learning rather than teaching, we must challenge our basic assumptions about how people learn and what the roles of a teacher should be. We must unlearn previously acquired teaching habits. We must grapple with fundamental questions about the roles of assessment and feedback in learning. We must change the culture we create in the courses we teach. In other words, we must experience a paradigm shift.

What is a paradigm? Paradigm means model, pattern, or example. A paradigm establishes rules, defines boundaries, and describes how things behave within those boundaries (Barker, 1992). A paradigm is like the rules of a game that define the playing field and the domain of possibilities on that field. A new paradigm changes the playing field by making it larger or smaller, or even moving it somewhere else, which in turn affects the domain of possibilities. Those of us who shift our paradigm regarding teaching and learning have new rules, new boundaries, and new ways of behaving.

To develop new conceptualizations, we must analyze our old ways of thinking and make continuous changes. If our ways of thinking are not analyzed, they remain unchanged, existing patterns continue, and "structures of which we are unaware hold us prisoner" (Senge, 1990, p. 60). When people challenge present paradigms, paradigm structures loosen their hold and individuals begin to alter their behaviors to improve processes and systems. As expressed by Covey (1989) in the quote at the beginning of this chapter, to shift the paradigm, we must experience a personal change. To focus on student learning, we must shift from a traditional teaching paradigm to a learner-centered paradigm.

> Changing the question from *How will I teach this?* to *How will students learn this?* lays bare tacit assumptions about what should be learned and how it should be taught. Specifying what "this" is turns out to be a difficult problem. All too often what is learned turns out not to be what was intended, which often is different also from what was actually taught (Hakel, 1997, p. 19).

Figure 1.2 is a comparison of the traditional teaching paradigm and the emerging learner-centered paradigm. Similar comparisons can be found in Barr and Tagg (1995); Bonstingl (1992); Boyatzis, Cowen, Kolb and Associates

**FIGURE 1.2    Comparison of Teacher-Centered and Learner-Centered Paradigms**

| TEACHER-CENTERED PARADIGM | LEARNER-CENTERED PARADIGM |
|---|---|
| Knowledge is transmitted from professor to students. | Students construct knowledge through gathering and synthesizing information and integrating it with the general skills of inquiry, communication, critical thinking, problem solving, and so on. |
| Students passively receive information. | Students are actively involved. |
| Emphasis is on acquisition of knowledge outside the context in which it will be used. | Emphasis is on using and communicating knowledge effectively to address enduring and emerging issues and problems in real-life contexts. |
| Professor's role is to be primary information giver and primary evaluator. | Professor's role is to coach and facilitate.    Professor and students evaluate learning together. |
| Teaching and assessing are separate. | Teaching and assessing are intertwined. |
| Assessment is used to monitor learning. | Assessment is used to promote and diagnose learning. |
| Emphasis is on right answers. | Emphasis is on generating better questions and learning from errors. |
| Desired learning is assessed indirectly through the use of objectively scored tests. | Desired learning is assessed directly through papers, projects, performances, portfolios, and the like. |
| Focus is on a single discipline. | Approach is compatible with interdisciplinary investigation. |
| Culture is competitive and individualistic. | Culture is cooperative, collaborative, and supportive. |
| Only students are viewed as learners. | Professor and students learn together. |

See also Barr and Tagg (1995); Bonstingl (1992); Boyatzis, Cowen, Kolb and Associates (1995); Duffy and Jones (1995); and Kleinsasser (1995).

(1995); and Duffy and Jones (1995). When we examine this figure, we see that our thinking about teaching is based on assumptions about the role of students in learning, about our roles as teachers, and about the role of assessment. Our paradigm also includes assumptions about how people learn and about the type of environment or culture that supports learning. A thorough discussion of the differences between traditional and learner-centered paradigms is presented in Chapter 2, along with an opportunity to examine our own teaching practices and the assumptions that support them.

---

**REFLECTIONS**

*As you create your own meaning from the ideas in this section, begin to think about…*

- Which characteristics in Figure 1.2 best describe my beliefs and practice as a teacher?

- In what ways does my practice seem to fall within the traditional paradigm?
- In what ways does my practice seem to fall within the learner-centered paradigm?

---

## A SYSTEMS PERSPECTIVE ON LEARNER- CENTERED TEACHING

In addition to examining our own teaching practices as we shift to a learner-centered approach, we must also consider our relationship to the institution in which we teach. This is because we and our students are part of an entire educational system that has developed at our institution from its teaching mission. In a system, each part affects the behaviors and properties of the whole system (Ackoff, 1995). Whenever there is a need for improvement, efforts should be targeted at the system as a whole as well as at the parts individually.

Thus, efforts to promote student-centered teaching and assessing should be made at the academic program and institutional levels, as well as at the level of the individual professor or course. According to Senge (1990), systems thinking is a conceptual "framework for seeing interrelationships rather than things, for seeing patterns of change rather than static snapshots" (p. 68). The outcome of a system is based on how each part is interacting with the rest of the parts, not on how each part is doing (Kofman & Senge, 1993).

Conceptualizing higher education as a system may make more sense to students than it does to professors. As professors, we tend to focus on preparing and delivering our own courses, whereas students enroll in and experience a program as a whole. Chapter 2 emphasizes that students are driven to make sense of their experiences and to actively construct their knowledge by integrating new information with current understanding. This means that, throughout their academic programs, students are developing their general skills and disciplinary expertise by making sense of the curriculum as they experience it. The knowledge, skills, and abilities that students achieve at the end of their programs are affected by how well courses and other experiences in the curriculum fit together and build on each other throughout the undergraduate years.

In this systems view of the curriculum, we must examine how the system fosters student learning. When and where are skills and content knowledge introduced? In which courses are they developed and reinforced? Is there unnecessary duplication of emphasis for some topics, but incomplete coverage for others? Are courses designed to be taken in an order that supports learning? Are the teaching styles and approaches of the faculty who deliver the curriculum compatible with each other and with the principles of student-centered learning? Are they effective?

When we begin to view our programs as systems, we think about our own courses differently. For example, we become aware that prerequisite courses are important inputs into our own courses and that our courses are the inputs for subsequent courses that students will take. The following story illustrates one professor's understanding that students' efforts to make sense of new information will be more effective when courses in a curriculum build on one another.

> I taught the first-level theory course and I was asked to teach the second level. Since I did not know what the third level required, I enrolled in the third level course so that I would know how to teach the second level (Freed & Klugman, 1997, p. 35).

In a systems framework, we work together to design and deliver a curriculum that is coherent to students rather than work separately to design individual courses that we find personally satisfying. We also seek partners in other academic departments, student affairs, the library, the computer center, and other segments of the institution that provide services to enhance learning. Systems thinking continually reminds us that our courses are components of an entire system to support learning.

This type of systems thinking has been encouraged by the assessment movement in higher education. Assessment is a learner-centered movement which encourages us to focus on the student learning component of our teaching as it takes place within the entire system of our institution and within the smaller systems of our academic programs and courses.

---

**REFLECTIONS**

*As you create your own meaning from the ideas in this section, begin to think about...*

- What kind of "system" am I a part of? How do my courses fit into the curriculum of my academic program?

- How can my faculty colleagues and I dialogue about the interrelationship of courses and experiences in our program?

- How can we involve appropriate colleagues from other parts of the institution?

## DEFINITION OF ASSESSMENT

Learning is the focus and ultimate goal of the learner-centered paradigm. Because of this, assessment plays a key role in shifting to a learner-centered approach. When we assess our students' learning, we force the questions, "What have our students learned and how well have they learned it?" "How successful have we been at what we are trying to accomplish?" Because of this focus on learning, assessment in higher education is sometimes referred to as outcomes assessment or student outcomes assessment.

As shown in Figure 1.2, assessment in a learner-centered paradigm is also an integral part of teaching. In other words, through assessment, we not only monitor learning, but we also promote learning. As will be explained throughout this book, we can both encourage and shape the type of learning we desire through the types of assessment we use.

We define assessment as follows:

Assessment is the process of gathering and discussing information from multiple and diverse sources in order to develop a deep understanding of what students know, understand, and can do with their knowledge as a result of their educational experiences; the process culminates when assessment results are used to improve subsequent learning.

In a college or university at which the faculty take a learner-centered approach, the assessment process takes place at all levels—institutional, program, and course. The process is fundamentally the same at all levels, although the focus, methods, and interested parties may change somewhat from level to level.

Furthermore, the process at one level is related to the process at another. For example, the quality of student learning at the end of a program—the focus of program or institutional assessment—depends in part on how and how well we are assessing student learning in our courses. As individuals, are we focusing on developing the knowledge, skills, and abilities that the faculty as a whole have agreed are important? Are we using appropriate teaching and assessing strategies?

In turn, the quality of student learning in courses depends in part on the type of information yielded by program assessment data. Do the programmatic data reveal that we should focus more on student writing? Do they indicate that a particular concept is poorly understood by graduates and needs greater coverage? Do students report that some courses seem outdated or that a prerequisite is misplaced? Program assessment and classroom assessment interact to provide data to enhance student learning.

A practical sense of the many ways in which faculty have approached assessment at their institutions can be found in the 82 case examples provided by Banta, Lund, Black, and Oblander (1996). Illustrations of assessment in general education and various major disciplines are provided from a number of different institutions.

---

**REFLECTIONS**

*As you create your own meaning from the ideas in this section, begin to think about...*

- How is the definition of assessment presented in this section similar to my own view of assessment?
- How is it different?
- What do I know about assessment at my institution?

- What do I know about assessment in my academic program?
- How do I assess student learning in my courses?
- How does my approach to assessment support learning in my academic program?
- What changes have I made in my courses based on assessment results gathered in my academic program?

---

## ELEMENTS OF THE ASSESSMENT PROCESS

There are four fundamental elements of learner-centered assessment. These are shown in Figure 1.3.

### Formulating Statements of Intended Learning Outcomes

The first element of the assessment process is that, as faculty, we develop a set of intended learning outcomes, statements describing our intentions about what students should know, understand, and be able to do with their knowledge when they graduate. Faculty at many institutions have formulated common learning outcomes for all students at the institution. Intended learning outcomes reflecting the discipline should also be developed for each academic program and for each course in the program.

Discussed at length in Chapter 4, these statements typically begin with the phrase, "Students will be able to..." The statements are obviously learner-centered, and developing them reflects a systems approach to teaching in the program. When we collectively decide what graduates of an institution or program should know, understand, and be able to do, we are working as a team, rather than as individuals. We are collectively confronting perhaps the most fundamental question in higher education, "What does the degree or certificate that we award mean and how can we prove it?" (Plater, 1998, p. 12)

When assessment takes place at the institutional or academic program level rather than the course level, only the most important goals of the insti-

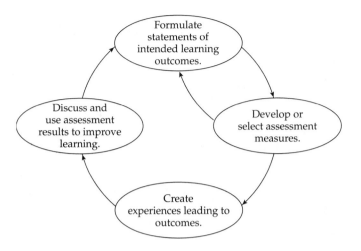

**FIGURE 1.3    The Assessment Process**

tution or program are addressed in assessment. As will be discussed in Chapter 4, learning goals at the institutional level are likely to be more broadly stated than those at the program level, and those at the program level are likely to be more broadly stated than those at the course level. However, achieving the more specific learning goals that we develop for a course or even for a specific class period should help students make progress toward achieving program and/or institutional goals.

---

**REFLECTIONS**

*As you create your own meaning from the ideas in this section, begin to think about…*

- How successfully have faculty in my program worked together to formulate intended learning outcomes for our program?

- How could we work together to do this?
- What intended outcomes would I develop for my courses that would support program/institutional outcomes?

---

## Developing or Selecting Assessment Measures

The second element of the assessment process is designing or selecting data gathering measures to assess whether or not our intended learning outcomes have been achieved. This element not only provides the foundation for data gathering, but it also brings to a culmination the previous step of determining learning outcomes. This is because the process of designing assessment measures forces us to come to a thorough understanding of what we really mean by our intended learning outcomes (Wiggins & McTighe, 1998). As we develop our assessment measures, we may find ourselves fine-tuning our learning outcomes.

Our assessment measures should include both direct and indirect assessments of student learning (Palomba & Banta, 1999). Direct assessments may take a variety of forms—projects, products, papers/theses, exhibitions, performances, case studies, clinical evaluations, portfolios, interviews, and oral exams (see Chapters 6, 7, and 8). In all of these assessments, we ask students to demonstrate what they know or can do with their knowledge. Most, if not all, of these forms of assessment can be incorporated into typical college courses, although a few (e.g., clinical evaluations) are likely to be used more in some disciplines than in others. At the program level, we can gather assessment data from assessments embedded in courses or design additional assessments that we administer outside of courses.

Indirect assessments of learning include self-report measures such as surveys distributed to students which can be used both in courses and at the program and institutional levels. (Designing measures for gathering feedback from students in courses is discussed in Chapter 5 of this book.) Other indirect measures used in program or institutional assessment, although not a focus of this book, include surveys of graduates or employers in which respondents share their perceptions about what graduates know or can do with their knowledge.

Both direct and indirect assessment measures should be chosen to provide accurate and useful information for making decisions about learning. In order to do so, they must evaluate the type of learning we desire in our students. For this reason, in this book there will be little discussion of tests comprised of objectively scored paper and pencil test items like multiple-choice and true–false. Many of us use these types of items heavily because they can be easily scored—even by machine—and we rely on the scores that result as the primary contributors to students' final grades. This type of evaluation is appealing because we can collect information efficiently and the results seem easy to interpret.

However, these items typically test only factual knowledge. It is possible to write multiple-choice and true–false items that go beyond checking recall of facts to measure higher-order thinking, and items that do so appear on standardized tests prepared by professional test developers at companies like the Educational Testing Service. However, when objectively scored items are written by individuals without professional training in test development, they tend to focus on factual knowledge.

Another criticism of objectively scored test items is that they assess knowledge bit by bit, item by item, typically with no reference to any eventual real-world application (Resnick & Resnick, 1992). They are only *indirect* indicators of more complex abilities such as reasoning about cutting-edge issues or using information to solve important problems in a particular field. Furthermore, objectively scored tests always have a right answer. For these reasons, when we use them, we send students the message that it is important to master isolated facts and skills and to always know the right answers.

However, the challenges faced by adults in general and by professionals in particular fields tend to be those that require the simultaneous coordination and integration of many aspects of knowledge and skill in situations with few right answers. As Howard Gardner (1991) points out, the ability to take objectively scored tests successfully is a useless skill as soon as one graduates from college. The rest of one's life, he says, is a series of projects.

The perspective of this book is that, in learner-centered teaching, we should design "assessments" to evaluate students' ability to think critically and use their knowledge to address enduring and emerging issues and problems in their disciplines. We define an assessment in the following way:

> An assessment is an activity, assigned by the professor, that yields comprehensive information for analyzing, discussing, and judging a learner's performance of valued abilities and skills.

This book discusses the development and use of assessments like projects, papers, performances, portfolios, or exhibitions that evaluate higher-order thinking and require students to *directly* reveal the very abilities that professors desire. Sometimes these are referred to as authentic assessments because of their intrinsic value (Wiggins, 1989); at other times, they are referred to as performance assessments because they require students to demonstrate their learning. At still other times, they are termed qualitative assessments because they allow us to evaluate the nature and quality of students' work. Further, our scoring is based on subjective judgment using criteria we develop, rather than on an answer key that permits us to objectively sum correct answers. Whatever they are called, these assessments are effective tools for assessing mastery of factual knowledge, but more importantly, for finding out if students can *use* their knowledge effectively to reason and solve problems.

For those of us who would like to continue using objectively scored tests, several excellent resources are available (e.g., Airasian, 1994; Brookhart, 1999; Gronlund & Linn, 1990; Payne, 1997; Stiggins, 1994; Thorndike, Cunningham, Thorndike, & Hagen, 1991). These books include guidelines for writing effective test items, and they give examples of items that measure more than recall of facts.

## Creating Experiences Leading to Outcomes

The third element in the assessment process is ensuring that students have experiences both in and outside their courses that help them achieve the intended learning outcomes. If we expect students to achieve our intended outcomes, we must provide them with opportunities to learn what they need to learn. We should design the curriculum as a set of interrelated courses and experiences that will help students achieve the intended learning outcomes.

Students' learning will be affected by the way courses and other required experiences like independent studies, practica, and internships are organized in the curriculum and the order in which they are taken. The appropriateness of the prerequisite courses we designate will also influence how well students learn. Designing the curriculum by working backward from learning outcomes helps make the curriculum a coherent "story of learning" (Plater, 1998, p. 11).

Orchestrating stages in the skill development of students is also part of curriculum development. Where in the curriculum will students learn and practice skills like writing, speaking, teamwork, and problem solving? What teaching strategies will faculty use to help students develop these skills, and how will professors give feedback to students on their progress? Will all professors be responsible for these skills? Will the skills be addressed only in the general education component of the curriculum? Will some courses throughout the course of study be targeted as "intensives" (e.g., writing intensive, problem solving intensive, etc.)? All of these questions are curriculum questions that are central to an assessment program.

As we develop or revise the curriculum, we should include activities and experiences that will help students acquire the knowledge, skills, and understanding that *each* of our learning outcomes requires. Conversely, we should scrutinize each of the activities and experiences that we create in our courses and programs and ask ourselves, "How will this help students achieve the intended learning outcomes of the institution, program, or course?"

---

**REFLECTIONS**

*As you create your own meaning from the ideas in this section, begin to think about...*

- To what extent do my faculty colleagues and I design and revise curriculum with learning outcomes in mind?

- How could we change our approach to curricular design and revision so that we focus more on helping students achieve intended learning outcomes?
- How could we help students develop more effective skills

---

## Discussing and Using Assessment Results to Improve Learning

The fourth element is a process for discussing and using the assessment results to improve learning. Within courses, these discussions take place between us and our students, and the focus is on using the results to improve individual student performance. At the program or institutional level, discussions take place among the faculty as a whole.

Through our discussions of assessment results, we gain insights into the type of learning occurring in the program, and we are better able to make informed decisions about needed program changes. We understand what students can do well and in what areas they have not succeeded. We raise questions about the design of the curriculum or about the teaching strategies we use (Walvoord, Bardes, & Denton, 1998). We also develop a better understanding of how to assess learning in a useful manner.

In order to seek additional perspectives, we should share summaries of the process with key stakeholder groups (e.g., students, alumni, advisory groups) who may also provide insights about whether changes are needed in the program's intended learning outcomes, in the curriculum, in teaching strategies used by faculty, or in assessment techniques used. In this stage of the process, we reveal the nature and process of a college education to a broad audience, and we help build trust for institutions of higher education.

With information from the assessment itself as well as the perspectives of students, alumni, advisory groups and others, we can proceed to recommend and implement changes that will improve both the curriculum and the teaching taking place in the program. As discussed in Chapter 3, assessment data should also be used to inform processes like planning and resource allocation, catalog revision, and program review.

---

**REFLECTIONS**

*As you create your own meaning from the ideas in this section, begin to think about...*

- When and with whom have I discussed assessment findings

- and their implications for learning?
- What stakeholder groups would be interested in knowing about learning in my courses and program?

---

## A BRIEF HISTORY OF THE ASSESSMENT MOVEMENT IN HIGHER EDUCATION

Our role as faculty in assuming primary ownership for assessing academic programs is critical. We are responsible for developing the intended learning outcomes of our academic programs, for developing the curricula on which the programs are based, and for delivering the curricula through our teaching. It naturally follows that we should be responsible for building quality into the programs through evaluating the learning that takes place within them.

Assuming the responsibility for assessment provides us with several opportunities. One is the opportunity to ask important questions about the value and effectiveness of our instructional programs. Another is the opportunity to engage in conversations about student learning with each other. The final opportunity is to use data about student learning to strengthen the way decisions are made, leading to improvement in the curriculum and in instruction.

However, many faculty have been reluctant to engage in assessment because, in some states or regions of the country, assessment has been introduced as a requirement by external agencies such as legislatures or regional or specialized accreditation associations. The reasons for this can be traced historically.

### Changing Resources and the Seeds of Reform

The post-war period of the 1950s and 1960s was a time of expansion in higher education (Brubacher & Rudy, 1976). "The enrollment [sic] of World War II veterans created the most rapid growth of colleges and universities in the history of higher education" (Henry, 1975, p. 55). Between 1955 and 1970, the number of students pursuing academic degrees tripled (Henry, 1975,

p. 101). Generous support from federal and state governments helped institutions keep pace, culminating in the Johnson years, "golden ones for all of education and not the least for higher education" (Pusey, 1978, p. 109). During this time, the value of a college education was assumed, and universities functioned in a relatively autonomous fashion. There was little need to reveal to external audiences what was happening in college classrooms.

However, by the 1970s, higher education was in a grave financial crisis. Resources available to higher education could not keep pace with rising costs and inflation. Large private donations to institutions, common in the first half of the century, had declined sharply; inflation had reduced institutional income, and it had become increasingly difficult to raise tuition to offset costs and still maintain access to a college education (Brubacher & Rudy, 1976). Politicians were faced with the increasing need to fund welfare, hospitals, prisons (Erwin, 1991), schools, highways, and public utilities (Henry, 1975).

In addition, by the 1970s, the population of students attending college had become more diverse. As the goal of a college education for all became more widespread, college faculties were faced with challenges they had never experienced before. Concerns that college graduates did not have the skills and abilities needed in the workplace surfaced. The public and the politicians who represented them began to question the value of higher education. A movement to bring about reform in higher education—and education at all levels—began (Ewell, 1991).

As a result, in 1984 and 1985 alone, four reports were issued addressing the need for reform on the college campus (Ewell, 1991): *Access to Quality Undergraduate Education* (Southern Regional Education Board, 1985), *Integrity in the College Curriculum* (Association of American Colleges, 1985), *Involvement in Learning* (National Institute of Education, 1984), and *To Reclaim a Legacy* (Bennett, 1984). These reports received less attention than *A Nation at Risk*, the report that triggered the reform movement in elementary and secondary schools. However, according to Ewell, their messages were clear and strong: instruction in higher education must become learner-centered, and learners, faculty, and institutions all need feedback in order to improve.

## Calls for Accountability

In some states, politicians assumed the responsibility for initiating reform. A number of legislatures (e.g., Arkansas, Colorado, Florida, Kentucky, Missouri, Ohio, Tennessee) have implemented performance funding programs, and although many such programs have floundered, additional states continue to consider this approach (Ewell, 1998; Serban, 1998). In performance funding, some portion of the public monies earmarked for higher education are allocated to institutions based on institutional ability to meet performance targets like retention rates, graduation rates, or demonstrations of student learning.

For example, the Tennessee legislature mandated that institutions pre- and post-test students, with incentive funding following, based on improvements (Astin, 1993). Florida instituted a "rising junior" test at its public institutions in order to ensure that students were prepared to enter the upper division or receive an associate in arts degree. However, the test was not sensitive to institutional differences and needs, but rather was a common instrument for use at all state-funded institutions and was developed by faculty members from across the state (Astin, 1993; McCabe, 1988).

In part to curtail the direct involvement of state legislatures in higher education, regional accreditation agencies—organizations comprised of institutions of higher education themselves—became involved. Accreditation agencies declared that they would require member institutions to conduct outcomes assessment in order to maintain their status as accredited institutions.

For example, in 1989, the Commission on Institutions of Higher Education of the North Central Association of Colleges and Schools introduced the requirement that every affiliated institution conduct outcomes assessment (Commission on Institutions of Higher Education, 1996). This was one of the few times in its 100-year history that the organization established a program and required every affiliated institution to give evidence within a limited period of time of making a good faith effort to implement it (S. Crow, personal communication, October 29, 1998). As time passed, specialized accrediting bodies—those that accredit professional programs rather than institutions (e.g., business, veterinary medicine, engineering, counseling, architecture)—also began to adopt an outcomes approach to program evaluation.

## The Continuous Improvement Movement

Another factor influencing the assessment movement was the continuous improvement movement. Just as higher education was influenced by the business processes of long-range planning in the late 1970s and strategic planning in the mid-1980s, it was influenced in the late 1980s by the use of quality principles and practices. American businesses become involved in quality improvement because of the intense competition resulting from the introduction of better products from foreign countries. Likewise, colleges and universities pursued continuous improvement because of competition for students, the need to reduce costs and improve quality of services, and the desire to enhance learning. The introduction of quality improvement in higher education paralleled the development of the assessment movement, and the two initiatives have much in common.

W. E. Deming is recognized as one of the founders of the quality improvement movement. He believed that continuous improvement is the path to improved quality, greater productivity (less rework and more efficiency), and reduced cost (Deming, 1986). Deming's Fourteen Points (1986), the most cited set of principles for continuous improvement, have been reframed for other settings, one of which is education (Cornesky, 1993, 1994; Greenwood & Gaunt, 1994). Figure 1.4 outlines the original Fourteen Points according to Deming. Figure 1.5 presents one example of how Deming's interpretation of quality improvement has been adapted for education.

Gathering data for informed decision making is at the heart of Deming's philosophy of improvement. Deming advocated cross-functional teamwork and partnerships by stressing that barriers must be removed so that people can work together effectively and creatively. Deming believed that people need to have pride in what they do. Therefore, he encouraged education, professional development, and personal self-improvement for everyone (Deming, 1986).

At the end of the 1980s and the beginning of the 1990s, the quality movement in higher education was relatively new and existed only on the fringes of campus concerns. Research reveals that even though continuous improvement started and has made more progress on the administrative side of most institutions, its principles are becoming increasingly used on the academic side to improve learning and teaching (Freed & Klugman, 1997; Schnell, 1996).

**FIGURE 1.4  Abbreviated Statement of W. Edwards Deming's Fourteen Points for Continuous Improvement**

1. Create constancy of purpose toward improvement of product and service.
2. Adopt the new philosophy and take on leadership for change.
3. Cease dependence on inspection to achieve quality by building quality into the product in the first place.
4. Develop long-term relationships of loyalty and trust with suppliers.
5. Constantly improve systems and processes.
6. Institute training on the job.
7. Institute leadership—the aim of supervision should be to help people do a better job.
8. Drive out fear so that everyone may work effectively.
9. Break down barriers between departments—people must work as a team.
10. Eliminate zero-defect work targets and slogans. Recognize that the causes of low quality and productivity belong to the system, thus lying beyond the power of the workforce.
11. Eliminate numerical quotas and management by objective, substituting leadership instead.
12. Remove barriers to pride of workmanship.
13. Promote education and self-improvement.
14. Involve everyone in accomplishing the transformation.

**FIGURE 1.5   Deming's Fourteen Points Adapted for Education**

1. Pursue continuous improvement of curriculum and learning diligently and constantly.
2. Adopt the system of profound knowledge in your classroom and [institution] as the prime management tool.
3. Build quality into teaching and learning and reduce the inspection of quality into work after the event.
4. Build a partnership relationship with colleagues, students, and...employers.
5. Constantly improve the system within which teaching/learning takes place.
6. Take every opportunity to train in new skills and to learn from your pupils.
7. Lead—do not drive or manipulate.
8. Drive out fear of punishment—create joy in learning.
9. Collaborate with colleagues from other departments and functions.
10. Communicate honestly, not through jargon and slogans.
11. So far as possible create a world without grades and rank order.
12. Encourage and celebrate to develop your students' pride in work.
13. Promote the development of the whole person in students and colleagues.
14. Wed your students to learning by the negotiation with them of a quality experience.

[From Greenwood & Gaunt, *Total Quality Management for Schools* (London: Cassell plc). Source: W. E. Deming, 'Out of Crisis,' 1982 (adapted to school rather than manufacturing context by L. Richelou and M. S. Greenwood).]

## Improvement as Accountability

The preceding discussion illustrates the fact that assessment is a movement that began outside the academy in order to make institutions more accountable to external constituencies. However, it is becoming increasingly clear that the best way for institutions to be accountable to any audience is to incorporate the evaluation of student learning into the way they operate on a regular basis. When faculty collectively take charge of their educational programs, making visible their purpose and intent, and putting in place a data-based system of evaluation that focuses on improving student learning, the institution itself is the primary beneficiary while external audiences are satisfied as well.

---

**REFLECTIONS**

*As you create your own meaning from the ideas in this section, begin to think about...*

- How have the historical factors leading to the assessment movement influenced my environment?

- How have these factors affected faculty *knowledge* about assessment?
- How have these factors affected faculty *attitude* toward assessment?

## ASSESSMENT AND THE IMPROVEMENT
## OF UNDERGRADUATE EDUCATION

In its report, *Making Quality Count in Undergraduate Education,* the Education Commission of the States proposed twelve quality attributes of good practice in delivering an undergraduate education (1995). "Extensive research on American college students reveals...that when colleges and universities systematically engage in these good practices, student performance and satisfaction will improve" (Education Commission of the States, 1996, p. 5). Shown in Figure 1.6, these attributes address aspects of an institution's organizational culture and values, its curriculum, and the type of instruction that takes place within it (Education Commission of the States, 1996).

One of the attributes is "assessment and prompt feedback," and it is included in the list as an intrinsic element of quality instruction. However, we believe that learner-centered assessment, as discussed in this book, promotes or enhances all the attributes of quality that are listed in Figure 1.6. Assessment can thus be a powerful tool for improving—even transforming—undergraduate education (Angelo, 1999).

In the following sections, we briefly point out ways in which learner-centered assessment supports the attributes of a quality undergraduate education. Chapter 2 provides a more extended discussion in its review of the hallmarks of learner-centered teaching and assessment.

**FIGURE 1.6  Attributes of Quality Undergraduate Education: What the Research Says**

QUALITY BEGINS WITH AN ORGANIZATIONAL CULTURE THAT VALUES:
1. High expectations
2. Respect for diverse talents and learning styles
3. Emphasis on the early years of study

A QUALITY CURRICULUM REQUIRES:
4. Coherence in learning
5. Synthesizing experiences
6. Ongoing practice of learned skills
7. Integrating education and experience

QUALITY INSTRUCTION BUILDS IN:
8. Active learning
9. Assessment and prompt feedback
10. Collaboration
11. Adequate time on task
12. Out-of-class contact with faculty

(Education Commission of the States, 1995, 1996)

## Learner-Centered Assessment Promotes High Expectations

"Students learn more effectively when expectations for learning are placed at high but attainable levels, and when these expectations are communicated clearly from the onset" (Education Commission of the States, 1996, p. 5). Learner-centered assessment clearly supports the principle of high expectations. In a learner-centered assessment environment, students are aware of the faculty's intended learning outcomes before instruction begins. They thus know what we expect them to know, understand, and be able to do with their knowledge. We give them challenging assessment tasks to evaluate their achievement, and using scoring rubrics, we describe for them the characteristics that are present in excellent work. These characteristics derive from the standards to which we hold educated people and practicing professionals in their disciplines.

## Learner-Centered Assessment Respects Diverse Talents and Learning Styles

In learner-centered assessment, assessment tasks are designed so that students can complete them effectively in many different ways. There is not just one right answer, but rather students have the opportunity to do excellent work that reflects their own unique way of implementing their abilities and skills.

## Learner-Centered Assessment Enhances the Early Years of Study

"A consensus is emerging that the first years of undergraduate study—particularly the freshman year—are critical to student success" (Education Commission of the States, 1996, p. 6). Learner-centered assessment enhances the first year of study by engaging students in meaningful intellectual work and helping them discover connections between what they learn in college and the ways in which they will use their knowledge in society or the professions after graduation. This is accomplished by designing assessment tasks that derive from challenging real-world problems and call upon students to use and extend their skills in critical thinking and problem solving.

## Learner-Centered Assessment Promotes Coherence in Learning

> Students should be presented with a set of learning experiences that consist of more than merely a required number of courses or credit hours. Instead, the curriculum should be structured in a way that sequences individual courses to reinforce specific outcomes and consciously directs instruction toward meeting those ends (Education Commission of the States, 1996, pp. 6–7).

Learner-centered assessment promotes a coherent curriculum by providing data to guide the curriculum development and revision process. If we want to know whether thve curriculum as a whole or the experiences in individual courses are coherent to students, we can ask for their opinions directly. In learner-centered assessment, students give us feedback on their learning in a continual fashion, suggesting ways in which instruction and the curriculum can be improved to help achieve our intended learning outcomes. In addition, through assessment that takes place at the program level, as well as in courses, we can find out what students have learned well and in what areas they need to improve. The resulting information provides direction for curricular improvement.

## Learner-Centered Assessment Synthesizes Experiences, Fosters Ongoing Practice of Learned Skills, and Integrates Education and Experience

Learner-centered assessment tasks frequently take the form of projects, papers, exhibitions, and so forth, in which students synthesize the knowledge, abilities, and skills they have learned in the general education curriculum, in their major field, and in their course experiences. These assessments also focus on *using* knowledge to address issues and problems that are important in students' chosen disciplines. Critical thinking, problem solving, and written and oral communication are the vehicles through which students employ their knowledge in the pursuit of important goals in the assessment tasks we give them.

## Learner-Centered Assessment Actively Involves Students in Learning and Promotes Adequate Time on Task

All of the forms of learner-centered assessment we have discussed require active learning. Assessment tasks like projects, papers, and so on cannot be completed in a 50-minute time period. They actively involve students in learning over a period of several days or weeks. During this time, we can structure in-class activities to help students acquire the knowledge and skills they need to complete the assessment task. In this way, students are continually focused on achieving the intended learning outcomes of the course and program.

## Learner-Centered Assessment Provides Prompt Feedback

When students are completing the assessments we have discussed in this chapter, we can assess their learning as it takes place and provide revelant feedback to guide the process. A major theme of this book is that learners cannot learn anything without feedback. Feedback is part and parcel of learner-centered assessment, whether students are giving feedback to us or we are giving feedback to them. Both types of feedback improve student learning, and this book emphasizes strategies to make feedback both timely and useful.

## Learner-Centered Assessment Fosters Collaboration

"Students learn better when engaged in a team effort rather than working on their own...it is the way the world outside the academy works" (Education Commission of the States, 1996, p. 8). Unlike conventional tests which students complete silently and alone—and which are often graded on a competitive basis—learner-centered assessments provide opportunities for students to work together and develop their skills in teamwork and cooperation. As students talk about what they know and what they are learning, their knowledge and understanding deepen.

## Learner-Centered Assessment Depends on Increased Student-Faculty Contact

In learner-centered assessment, we guide and coach students as they learn to do important things worth doing. We give students feedback on their learning, and we seek feedback from students about how to improve the learning environment. Through the use of portfolios and other self-evaluation activities, we and our students confer together about students' progress toward the intended learning outcomes of the program. This increases contact between us and our students both in and outside the classroom.

---

**REFLECTIONS**

*As you create your own meaning from the ideas in this section, begin to think about...*

- Which attributes of a quality undergraduate education are present in my courses and my program?

- Which attributes would I most like to enhance?

---

## LEARNER-CENTERED ASSESSMENT AND TIME

Using learner-centered assessment may be more time consuming than previous approaches, particularly in the beginning. We will need to take time to confer with our colleagues about fundamental issues like learning outcomes and the coherence of the curriculum. Initially, this will require an extra investment of time and energy as we attempt "to transcend the privacy of our own courses, syllabi, or student programs, let alone our departments, divisions, or schools" (Plater, 1998, p. 13). In our courses, when we try new techniques, we will undoubtedly spend more time analyzing and questioning our past approach to pedagogy and evaluating the new techniques we employ.

We will also discover that our institutions are structured to accommodate the traditional paradigm (Barr, 1998). It takes time and effort to implement a new approach when factors like schedules, room arrangements, reward systems—even the structures of our buildings—have been designed to make the traditional paradigm work efficiently.

Helping students change paradigms will take time as well (Warren, 1997). As we create new learning environments and use new teaching strategies, we will have to guide students to understand new ways of learning.

However, as we, our colleagues, and our students become more familiar and comfortable with learner-centered strategies, the overall time spent on teaching will probably decrease to former levels. We may have to learn to use time more efficiently and effectively at faculty meetings so that we can find the time we need to confer about issues related to learning and assessment on a continuing basis.

In our courses, as Figure 1.7 shows, we will learn to spend time *differently* than we have in the past. When we prepare to teach, we will continue to keep up-to-date in our disciplines. However, we will spend more time developing materials to facilitate learning and less time organizing presentations of information or constructing objectively scored tests.

Preparing to facilitate learning rather than lecture about what we know involves designing an approach to teaching that allows students to create their own understanding of the material. We will need to find time to develop materials like statements of intended learning outcomes, questions to guide student discussion of assigned readings, activities that involve students actively in their learning, criteria describing the characteristics of excellent work to use in grading, and assessments that promote enhanced learning.

Facilitating learning rather than imparting information may require the development of new teaching techniques as well. We may have to learn to ask questions that guide student thinking, to facilitate student discussion in ways that lead to increased understanding, to coach students as they work in pairs or groups, and to coordinate in-class student activities. We will have to learn to share our learning outcomes with students and to devote time to periodic discussions of the progress students are making in achieving them. We should seek student input as we develop grading criteria, eliciting students' ideas about the characteristics of excellent work and sharing our ideas as well.

In a learner-centered environment, we will spend more time using these public criteria to discuss students' work with them and evaluate it at various stages of development. The need to monitor how well our students are doing by studying grade distributions will be replaced by more direct involvement in helping students improve their work.

**FIGURE 1.7    Allocation of Professor's Time/Effort/Emphasis in Teacher-Centered and Learner-Centered Paradigms**

|  | TEACHER-CENTERED PARADIGM | LEARNER-CENTERED PARADIGM |
| --- | :---: | :---: |
| *Preparing to teach* | | |
| Keeping up-to-date | +++ | +++ |
| Developing materials to facilitate learning | — | +++ |
| Preparing a presentation of information | ++++ | + |
| Developing objectively scored tests to monitor learning efficiently | +++ | — |
| *Teaching* | | |
| Facilitating learning | — | +++ |
| Imparting information | ++++ | + |
| Giving feedback to improve learning | — | +++ |
| *Following up* | | |
| Examining grade distributions to monitor learning | +++ | — |
| Using student input to improve the course | —— | +++ |

Finally, in each course, we will need to seek and review student feedback about how well the course is helping students to learn and then spend the time to make adjustments that will enhance the learning environment. The payoff of better prepared students justifies the time it takes to make the transformation from teacher-centered to learner-centered practices.

---

**REFLECTIONS**

*As you create your own meaning from the ideas in this section, begin to think about...*

- On which of the practices in Figure 1.7 do I spend the most time?
- On which practices would I spend more time if I became more learner-centered?

- On which practices would I spend less time if I became more learner-centered?
- What characteristics of my institution would interfere with a learner-centered approach?

## LOOKING AHEAD

In Chapter 2, we will discuss several hallmarks of learner-centered teaching and assessment. We will provide examples, as well as an opportunity to examine our own teaching practices in terms of the traditional vs. learner-centered paradigms. Chapter 3 examines several guidelines and practices that will foster the development of strong assessment programs on college campuses, thereby providing a foundation for refocusing the campus culture on learning rather than teaching.

Chapters 4 through 8 address several specific techniques for assessing student learning in a learner-centered environment: formulating intended learning outcomes (Chapter 4), gathering feedback from students to continually guide improvement in courses (Chapter 5), developing criteria for shaping and judging student work in the form of scoring rubrics (Chapter 6), designing assessments that promote and evaluate students' ability to think critically, solve problems, and use their discipline related knowledge (Chapter 7), and using portfolios to understand what and how students learn (Chapter 8). In Chapter 9, we discuss the implications for both us and our institutions of making the shift to a learner-centered paradigm.

## TRY SOMETHING NEW

As authors, we have tried to design this book using current principles of learning. One of these principles is that individuals learn best when they have opportunities to examine what they already know about a topic before they encounter new information. This fosters deep learning by helping learners prepare to make connections between current and new knowledge. For this reason, we begin each chapter of this book with a series of questions entitled Making Connections.

We have also referred to the fact that adults learn best when they have opportunities to reflect upon their current knowledge and practice in the light of new information. Throughout this chapter, as well as the others in this book, we have provided opportunities for reflection in the several series of questions entitled Reflections.

A final aspect of the book is the opportunity at the end of each chapter to Try Something New. We suggest that you review your answers to the questions in the Making Connections and Reflections sections in this chapter. Then pursue one or more of the suggested activities below to begin shifting from teaching to learning.

1. Read an article from this chapter and identify three points that have implications for your teaching.

2. Invite a colleague to lunch and bring along a copy of Figure 1.2. Discuss together those features of your teaching that could be considered elements of the traditional paradigm and those that could be considered learner-centered.

3. Make a list of all the ways that you assess learning in your courses. Discuss your assessment approach with a colleague and seek his/her reactions.

4. Find out what your institution is doing to support the shift from teaching to learning, as well as to establish an assessment culture on campus.

## REFERENCES

Ackoff, R. L. (1995, June). *The challenges of change and the need for systems thinking.* Paper presented at the AAHE Conference on Assessment and Quality, Boston, Massachusetts.

Airasian, P. W. (1994). *Classroom assessment* (2nd ed.). New York: McGraw-Hill, Inc.

Angelo, T. A. (1999, May). Doing assessment as if learning matters most. *AAHE Bulletin,* 3–6.

Association of American Colleges. (1985). *Integrity in the college curriculum: A report to the academic community.* Washington, DC: Association of American Colleges.

Astin, A. W. (1985). *Achieving educational excellence.* San Francisco: Jossey-Bass.

Astin, A. W. (1993). *Assessment for excellence.* Phoenix, AZ: Oryx Press.

Banta, T. W., Lund, J. P., Black, K. E., & Oblander, F. W. (1996). *Assessment in practice: Putting principles to work on college campuses.* San Francisco: Jossey-Bass.

Barker, J. A. (1992). *Paradigms: The business of discovering the future.* New York: Harper Business.

Barr, R. B. (1998, September-October). Obstacles to implementing the learning paradigm— What it takes to overcome them. *About Campus,* 18–25.

Barr, R. B., & Tagg, J. (1995, November/December). From teaching to learning: A new paradigm for undergraduate education. *Change,* 13–25.

Bennett, W. J. (1984). *To reclaim a legacy: A report on the humanities in higher education.* Washington, DC: National Endowment for the Humanities.

Bligh, D. A. (1972). *What's the use of lectures?* Baltimore: Penguin Books.

Bonstingl, J. J. (1992). The total quality classroom. *Educational Leadership, 49* (6), 66–70.

Bonstingl, J. J. (1996). *Schools of quality.* Alexandria, VA: Association for Supervision and Curriculum Development.

Boyatzis, Cowen, Kolb, & Associates. (1995). *Innovation in professional education.* San Francisco: Jossey-Bass.

Brookhart, S. M. (1999). *The art and science of classroom assessment: The missing part of pedagogy.* (ASHE-ERIC Higher Education Report: Vol. 27, No 1). Washington, DC: The George Washington University, Graduate School of Education and Human Development.

Brubacher, J. S., & Rudy, W. (1976). *Higher education in transition (3rd ed.).* New York: Harper and Row.

Chickering, A. W., & Gamson, Z. F. (1987, March). Seven principles for good practice. *AAHE Bulletin,* 3–7.

Commission on Institutions of Higher Education of the North Central Association. (1996, February 22). *Commission statement on assessment of student academic achievement.* Chicago: North Central Association.

Cornesky, R. (1993). *The quality professor: Implementing TQM in the classroom.* Madison, WI: Magna Publications.

Cornesky, R. (1994). *Quality classroom practices for professors.* Port Orange, FL: Cornesky & Associates.

Covey, S. R. (1989). *The 7 habits of highly effective people.* New York: Simon & Schuster.

Creed, T. (Winter 1986). Why we lecture. *Symposium: A Saint John's Faculty Journal, 5,* 17–32.

Cross, K. P. (1993, February-March). Involving faculty in TQM. *AACC Journal,* 15–20.

Cross, K. P. (1996, March-April). New lenses on learning. *About Campus,* 4–9.

Cross, K. P. (1998, July-August). *Why* learning communities? *Why now? About Campus,* 4–11.

Deming, W. E. (1986). *Out of the crisis.* Cambridge, MA: Massachusetts Institute of Technology Center for Advanced Engineering Study.

Duffy, D. K., & Jones, J. W. (1995). *Teaching within the rhythms of the semester.* San Francisco: Jossey-Bass.

Education Commission of the States. (1995). *Making quality count in undergraduate education.* Denver, CO: Education Commission of the States.

Education Commission of the States. (1996, April). What research says about improving undergraduate education. *AAHE Bulletin,* 5–8.

Eison, J., & Bonwell, C. (1988, March). *Making real the promise of active learning.* Paper presented at the meeting of the American Association for Higher Education, Washington, DC.

Engelkemeyer, S. W., & Brown, S. C. (1998, October). Powerful partnerships: A shared responsibility for learning. *AAHE Bulletin,* 10–12.

Erickson, S. C. (1984). *The essence of good teaching.* San Francisco: Jossey-Bass.

Erwin, T. D. (1991). *Assessing student learning and development.* San Francisco: Jossey-Bass.

Ewell, P. T. (1991). To capture the ineffable: New forms of assessment in higher education. In G. Grant, (Ed.). *Review of Research in Education, 17,* 75–125. Washington, DC: American Educational Research Association.

Ewell, P. T. (1998, May-June). From the states—implementing performance funding in Washington state: Some new takes on an old problem. *Assessment Update, 10* (3), 7–8, 13.

Freed, J. E., & Klugman, M. R. (1997). *Quality principles and practices in higher education: Different questions for different times.* Phoenix, AZ: American Council on Education and The Oryx Press.

Gardner, H. (1991). *The unschooled mind: How children think and how schools should teach.* New York: Basic Books.

Greenwood, M. S., & Gaunt, H. J. (1994). *Total quality management for schools.* London: Cassell.

Gronlund, N. E., & Linn, R. L. (1990). *Measurement and evaluation in teaching* (6th ed.). New York: MacMillan Publishing Company.

Guskin, A. (1997, July-August). Learning more, spending less. *About Campus,* 4–9.

Hakel, M. D. (1997, July-August). What we must learn from Alverno. *About Campus,* 16–21.

Henry, D. D. (1975). *Challenges past, challenges present: An analysis of American higher education since 1930.* San Francisco: Jossey-Bass.

Joint Task Force on Student Learning. (1998a). *Learning principles and collaborative action.* Washington, DC: American Association for Higher Education.

Joint Task Force on Student Learning. (1998b). *Powerful partnerships: A shared responsibility for learning.* Washington, DC: American College Personnel Association. http://www.aahe.org, http://www.acpa.nche.edu, or http://www.naspa.org

Kellogg Commission on the Future of State and Land-Grant Universities. (1997). *Returning to our roots: The student experience.* Washington, DC: National Association of State Universities and Land-Grant Colleges. http://www.nasulgc.org

Kellogg Commission on the Future of State and Land-Grant Universities. (1999). *Returning to our roots: The engaged institution.* Washington, DC: National Association of State Universities and Land-Grant Colleges. http://www.nasulgc.org

King, P. M., & Kitchener, K. S. (1994). *Developing reflective judgment: Understanding and promoting intellectual growth and critical thinking in adolescents and adults.* San Francisco: Jossey-Bass.

Kleinsasser, A. M. (1995, March/April). Assessment culture and national testing. *The Clearing House,* 205–210.

Kofman, F., & Senge, P. M. (1993). Communities of commitment: The heart of learning organizations. *American Management Association*, 5–23.

Lynch, R. F. (1991, April). Shedding the shackles of George Patton, Henry Ford, and first-grade teachers. *Quality Progress*, 64.

McCabe, R. H. (1988). The assessment movement: What next? Who cares? In J. S. Stark & A. Thomas, (Eds.), *Assessment and program evaluation* (pp. 199–203). ASHE Reader Series. Needham Heights, MA: Simon & Schuster Custom Publishing.

National Institute of Education, Study Group on the Conditions of Excellence in American Higher Education. (1984). *Involvement in learning: Realizing the potential of American higher education.* Washington, DC: U. S. Government Printing Office.

Palomba, C. A., & Banta, T. W. (1999). *Assessment essentials.* San Francisco: Jossey-Bass.

Payne, D. A. (1997). *Applied educational assessment.* Belmont, CA: Wadsworth.

Plater, W. M. (1998, November-December). So…Why *aren't* we taking learning seriously? *About Campus*, 9–14.

Pusey, N. M. (1978). *American higher education: 1945–1970.* Cambridge, MA: Harvard University Press.

Resnick, L., & Resnick, D. (1992). Assessing the thinking curriculum: New tools for educational reform. In B. R. Gifford & M. C. O'Connor (Eds.), *Changing assessments: Alternative views of aptitude, achievement and instruction* (pp. 37–75). Boston: Kluwer Academic Publishers.

Schnell, M. S. (1996, April). Could collaboration be on the horizon? *AAHE Bulletin*, 15–17.

Senge, P. M. (1990). *The fifth discipline: The art and practice of the learning organization.* New York: Doubleday/Currency.

Serban, A. (1998, March-April). The performance funding wave: Views of state policymakers and campus leaders. *Assessment Update, 10* (2), 1–2, 10–11.

Southern Regional Education Board. (1985). *Access to quality undergraduate education: A report to the Southern Regional Education Board by its Commission for Educational Quality.* Atlanta: Southern Regional Education Board.

Stiggins, R. J. (1994). *Student-centered classroom assessment.* New York: Merrill.

Terenzini, P. T., & Pascarella, E. T. (1994, January/February). Living with myths: Undergraduate education in America. *Change*, 28–30.

Thorndike, R. M., Cunningham, G. K., Thorndike, R. L., & Hagen, E. P. (1991). *Measurement and evaluation in psychology and education* (5th ed.). New York: MacMillan.

Walvoord, B. E., Bardes, B., & Denton, J. (1998, September-October). Closing the feedback loop in classroom-based assessment. *Assessment Update, 10* (5), 1–2, 10–11.

Warren, R. G. (1997, March-April). Engaging students in active learning. *About Campus*, 16–20.

Wiggins, G. (1989, May). A true test: Toward more authentic and equitable assessment. *Phi Delta Kappan*, 703–713.

Wiggins, G., & McTighe, J. (1998). *Understanding by design.* Alexandria, VA: Association for Supervision and Curriculum Development.

# CHAPTER 8

# USING FEEDBACK FROM STUDENTS TO IMPROVE LEARNING

Countless studies have confirmed the positive impact of feedback on individual motivation. But in today's fast-paced environment, we sometimes seem to have lost sight of its power and the enhanced quality it can engender. In the final inclusion from their book, Mary Huba and Jann Freed provide a summary of literature on Classroom Assessment Techniques then effectively explain specific tools for gathering student feedback. They proceed to detail measures the professor can take to create a complete feedback loop, fostering the type of Continuous Quality Improvement cycle that has enabled leading-edge business organizations to foster huge leaps in their productivity.

This chapter includes a fast feedback questionnaire and model course evaluation instrument suitable for implementation in an array of instructional environments. In addition, the bulleted lists of key points, and the "making connections" and "self reflection" dialogue boxes foster a more grounded understanding of the concepts discussed.

# USING FEEDBACK FROM STUDENTS TO IMPROVE LEARNING

Chapter 5 from *Learner-Centered Assessment on College Campuses*
**Mary E. Huba & Jann E. Freed**
**Allyn & Bacon, © 2000**

If you are serious about quality, everybody has to know how they're doing (Marchese, 1991, p. 5).

You don't get good at anything without feedback—not feedback in the sense that an expert translates things for you, but feedback in the sense of watching the ball, where it goes and where it doesn't go, and realizing what the result means for your next actions (Wiggins, 1997, pp. 31–32).

Feedback is not praise or blame. It's what you did and did not do, whether you realized it or intended it. Assessment should make its chief business the confronting of performers with the effect of their work, including performers called teachers. And then performers must do something about the effect, either to explain it, to justify it, or correct it (Wiggins, 1997, p. 39).

**MAKING CONNECTIONS**

*As you begin to read the chapter, think about the ideas and experiences you've already had that are related to gathering feedback from students to improve learning...*

- How do you collect feedback from your students to help you improve your teaching and their learning?

- What tools and techniques are you aware of to help you collect feedback from students?
- How would your students react if you asked them for feedback?
- When and how do you reflect on your teaching?

*What else do you know about using assessment information to improve learning?*

*What questions do you have about using assessment information to improve learning?*

Continuous improvement in education means constantly looking for new learning systems and processes. As we shift from a teacher-centered paradigm to a learner-centered paradigm, we must make fundamental changes in the way we teach. We also need to gather information about the effectiveness of the changes we make. Christensen (1991) claims that people "live life forward but understand it backward" (p. 99). Gathering feedback from others and spending time reflecting on our teaching are critical in helping us understand our practice as teachers.

To illustrate, think about your most recent learning experience. Was it learning how to write a grant proposal, swing a golf club, invest your money wisely, or something else? In all cases, you undoubtedly received feedback on your performance.

If you wrote a grant proposal, what did you learn when your grant proposal did or did not get funded? What did you learn from reviewers' comments? If you were seeking expertise on the golf course, what did you learn from the feelings you experienced when you either missed the ball completely or when you made a clean connection with it? How did your instructor's comments affect you? Finally, what factors have affected your investment strategies? Market fluctuations and their consequences? Feelings resulting from violating your level of risk tolerance?

Most importantly, in each case, what did you do because of the internal and external feedback you received? Did you decide to tailor your grant proposal more closely to RFP guidelines? Did you practice keeping your head down while swinging? Have you decided that the time is right to pursue growth as an investment goal? Useful feedback lets you know not only how you are doing, but what you should do next to improve.

Just as we all need feedback to help us understand how well we are learning to write proposals, play golf, or invest our money, we also need feedback to help us improve our teaching so that students in our courses will learn more effectively. Students can play an important role in providing the kind of feedback we need. According to Chaffee (1997),

> Compared with other kinds of enterprise, universities and colleges are systematically deprived of input from the people we serve.... An enterprise that cared

deeply about the people it serves would mount an extensive system to gather feedback.... Instead, we typically have a weak system, with end-of-term surveys, if that—too late to improve a course while the student is still enrolled in it (p. 46).

Brookfield (1995) calls gathering information about the effects of our teaching on students "seeing ourselves through our students' eyes" (p. 92) and believes that this is one of the trickiest, yet most crucial, tasks for teachers.

## TECHNIQUES FOR COLLECTING FEEDBACK FROM STUDENTS

This chapter discusses several techniques we can use to involve and engage our students in providing data that can help us improve teaching and learning. These approaches are in harmony with two key elements of quality improvement, sometimes known as total quality management (TQM) or continuous quality improvement (CQI): involving and engaging participants and making decisions based on data (Chaffee, 1997; Cross, 1993; Freed & Klugman 1997). They allow us to gather assessment information from our students as a group *during* a course—formative assessment. This approach is quick and efficient, and most importantly, it helps us make immediate changes to our courses to improve student learning. Waiting until the end of the course to distribute course evaluation forms—summative assessment— is just too late to get feedback in a continuously improving culture.

It could be said that the techniques discussed in this chapter provide us with "fast feedback." *Fast feedback* is a term derived from management practice, but it can be applied to education as well. Faculty who use the activities described in this chapter report learning more ways to improve their courses than they ever learned from end-of-course student evaluation forms (Bateman & Roberts, 1992). The techniques described require a small amount of effort, are easy to practice, are flexible, and use little class time. Feedback is a critical component if we are to learn how to become more effective teachers.

Using the techniques of this chapter benefits students directly as well. As discussed in Chapters 1 and 2, active involvement in learning promotes excellence in undergraduate education (Cross & Steadman, 1996; Study Group on the Conditions of Excellence in American Higher Education, 1984). Research suggests that "the more time and effort students invest in the learning process and the more intensely they engage in their own education, the greater will be their growth and achievement, their satisfaction with their educational experiences, and their persistence in college, and the more likely they are to continue their learning" (Study Group on the Conditions of Excellence in American Higher Education, 1984, p. 17). Assessment techniques like the ones discussed in this chapter help students learn to become more effective learners.

In a learner-centered environment, "teaching and learning are inseparable parts of a single continuum—more Mobius strip than circle—of reciprocal giving and receiving.... All teach, and all learn" (Christensen, 1991, p. 99). Feedback and assessment are used to help both students and teachers continuously improve.

---

**REFLECTIONS**

As you create your own meaning from the ideas in these sections, begin to think about...

- What do I look like "through students' eyes"? How do I know?

Do I need better sources of information?

- Would I benefit by reflecting more frequently on my teaching?

---

## Classroom Assessment Techniques (CATs)

Angelo and Cross (1993) have developed a number of classroom assessment techniques (CATs) to help faculty become better able to understand and promote learning, and they have described ways in which they can be used in a variety of disciplines. These techniques increase our ability to help students become more effective, self-assessing, self-directed learners.

Classroom assessment is based on the assumption that the best way to improve learning is to improve teaching. The question that drives classroom assessment is: What are students learning? "The purpose of Classroom Assessment is to make both teachers and students more aware of the learning that is taking place—or perhaps not taking place—in the classroom; it is an assessment of learning in process, during the semester, in a given classroom" (Cross & Steadman, 1996, p. xvii). When we observe students while they are learning and collect frequent feedback from them, we can learn much about how they learn and, more specifically, about how they respond to particular teaching practices (Angelo & Cross, 1993).

Cross and Steadman (1996) define classroom assessment as "small-scale assessments conducted continually in college classrooms by discipline-based teachers to determine what students are learning in that class" (p. 8). Data are collected with the understanding that results are shared with students. By using classroom assessment, both professors and students continually use information to improve their performance.

Characteristics of classroom assessment conform to principles of good practice for continuously improving student learning. According to Angelo and Cross (1993), classroom assessment is learner-centered, teacher-directed, mutually beneficial, formative, context-specific, ongoing, and rooted in good teaching practice. The model of classroom assessment is based on seven assumptions.

1. The quality of student learning is directly, although not exclusively, related to the quality of teaching. Therefore, one of the most promising ways to improve learning is to improve teaching (p. 7).
2. To improve their effectiveness, teachers need first to make their goals and objectives explicit and then to get specific, comprehensible feedback on the extent to which they are achieving those goals and objectives (p. 8).
3. To improve their learning, students need to receive appropriate and focused feedback early and often; they also need to learn how to assess their own learning (p. 9).
4. The type of assessment most likely to improve teaching and learning is that conducted by faculty to answer questions they themselves have formulated in response to issues or problems in their own teaching (p. 9).
5. Systematic inquiry and intellectual challenge are powerful sources of motivation, growth, and renewal for college teachers and Classroom Assessment can provide such a challenge (p. 10).
6. Classroom Assessment does not require specialized training; it can be carried out by dedicated teachers from all disciplines (p. 10).
7. By collaborating with colleagues and actively involving students in Classroom Assessment efforts, faculty (and students) enhance learning and personal satisfaction (p. 11).

**Using CATs Effectively.**    In order to use CATs most effectively, we should follow three steps. The first is to *decide* which CAT will provide the information we really need or desire because each CAT has been designed to give somewhat different information from the others. At this step, we should also think about the kinds of changes that might be implied in students' responses and be sure we are willing to consider them.

The second step is to *implement* the CAT. Angelo and Cross (1993) give clear directions for implementing each CAT, as will be seen below. Most CATs are administered in the last few minutes of each class and require note cards or half-sheets of paper.

The third step is to *respond* to the feedback collected. After collecting data from students, we should review the responses before the next class and decide what changes, if any, need to be made in the course (e.g., revisit a topic already discussed, assign a new reading, use more small group discussions, etc.). At the next session, we should share a summary of students' responses with the class and explain what changes will be made based on the students' input. Although it is not necessary to respond to every suggestion students make, it is important to follow through when an area for improvement is clearly indicated. In this way, students learn that their feedback matters.

If we do not feel changes are warranted, we should explain *why* changes will not take place as a result of the feedback. In other words, feedback received from students is matched with feedback given by the instructor and a complete feedback loop is created.

Among the most commonly used CATs are the Minute Paper and its variation, the E-mail Minute, the Muddiest Point, the One-Sentence Summary, the Word Journal, Directed Paraphrasing, and Applications Cards. The three steps for using CATs effectively should be employed with all of them.

**The Minute Paper.** This technique is sometimes referred to as the One-Minute Paper or the Half-Sheet Response because it is a quick and simple way to obtain feedback on student learning. Angelo and Cross (1993) claim that "no other Classroom Assessment Technique has been used more often or by more college teachers than the Minute Paper" (p. 148). The popularity of this CAT is attributed to its simplicity. Faculty members who use the Minute Paper regularly comment that "it is the best example of high payoff for a tiny investment.... The payoff of the reflection required of students is often as great as the payoff of information provided for the instructor" (Cross & Steadman, 1996, p. 133). For the small investment of time and energy, the feedback received from students can influence the effectiveness of the learning process.

When using this CAT, we should stop the class two or three minutes early and ask students to respond to questions like:

1. What was the most important thing you learned during this class?
2. What important question remains unanswered? (Angelo & Cross, 1993, p. 148).

Students usually write their responses on index cards or half-sheets of paper and turn them in anonymously. In large classes, it is not necessary for all students to respond each time the Minute Paper is used. Some method of sampling can be chosen. For example, the professor might say, "Today I'd like all students with birthdays in March to respond."

The purpose of the Minute Paper is to make it easy and quick for students to give feedback, as well as easy and quick for faculty members to gather it. The feedback helps instructors decide if efforts should be redirected or if changes should be made during the course. The Minute Paper is so popular that many faculty members modify the questions to fit their needs, but the goal remains the same: to have students respond to a few questions in a short period of time. Other questions that could be asked include:

- How was the pace of the class?
- Were the examples clear?
- Were the topics presented sufficiently?
- What specific questions do you have?

The Minute Paper helps us know how well our students are understanding. It makes students aware that teachers are concerned about their learning. The Minute Paper is a simple way for faculty and students to become aware of barriers to the learning process so that they can be removed or at least minimized.

**E-mail Minute.**    One modification of the Minute Paper is to combine it with electronic mail (e-mail). Using e-mail to encourage communication is well documented in the education and communication literature (Strasser, 1995).

The benefits of e-mail include allowing faculty or students to send or read messages at their convenience, a factor which is advantageous for commuting students. Basically, e-mail extends office hours by allowing more time for communication among students and instructors. Another important feature of e-mail is the ability to send one message to numerous addresses simultaneously by using a distribution list. This makes the process of communicating between faculty and students efficient.

The E-mail Minute works in one of two ways. In the first, students are asked to respond anonymously to two questions in the last two or three minutes of each class, using index cards or half-sheets of paper. Immediately after class, the professor reads through the responses looking for common themes and questions or comments that require a response. The professor sends a summary of the themes to the entire class using e-mail. Faculty members using this method report that this system opens up communication with students, and students tend to ask questions or send comments beyond the E-mail Minutes.

The other way to use this CAT is to distribute the two questions to students in class and have all or a sample of them answer the questions using e-mail. Students who prefer not to ask questions in class often feel more comfortable using e-mail which is more private.

Whatever method is used, the most important part of the process is to complete the feedback loop by discussing with students the themes that emerged in their feedback. When changes are made as a result of student feedback, students understand that the process has credibility and their input is valued.

**Muddiest Point.**    Muddiest Point is perhaps the easiest and quickest CAT since it involves asking only one question: What was the muddiest point in _____? The focus of the question may be a lecture, a discussion, an assignment, or an event. As the title suggests, the point of this CAT is to find out what was least clear or what was somewhat confusing about the class. The feedback can be used to identify the concepts that students find most difficult to understand. Responses help determine which topics need further discussion and provide guidance for allocating time among topics.

Similar to the Minute Paper, the Muddiest Point question addresses a particular aspect of one class. It is asked during the last few minutes of class, and responses are written on index cards or half-sheets of paper and collected as students leave class. Again, it is important to respond to students' feedback during the next class period or as soon as possible. Responses can be grouped into themes if themes emerge. The focus should be on clearing up any "muddy" areas before moving on and introducing new concepts, theories, and practices (Mosteller, 1989).

A business professor from Florida State uses a variation on this technique, asking three questions:

1. Did you get what you came for today?
   a. If yes, what did you get?
   b. If no, what was missing?
   c. If not sure, please explain.
2. What was the muddiest point remaining at the end of today's class?
3. What percent of mud was due to:
   a. Unclear presentation by instructor?
   b. Lack of opportunity to ask questions?
   c. Your lack of preparation?
   d. Your lack of participation in class discussion?
   e. Other? (Bateman & Roberts, 1992, p. 18).

**One-Sentence Summary.**  The One-Sentence Summary enables instructors to determine how well or whether students can summarize a large amount of information on a particular assignment. This CAT assesses comprehension by asking students to respond to the questions: Who does what to whom, when, where, how, and why (WDWWWWHW)? A particular topic or passage is the focus, and students synthesize their answers into a long summary sentence. The purpose is to find out how well students can identify critical points by focusing on these specific questions. This technique is quick and easy to administer because students are limited to one sentence. Students should be encouraged to make their sentences grammatically correct, factual, and complete. When this CAT is used consistently, it encourages students to focus on key questions when they read an assignment.

**Word Journal.**  A CAT similar to the One-Sentence Summary is the Word Journal. First, students summarize an assignment (article, reading, text) in one word. Then, students write a paragraph or two explaining why they selected that particular summary word. Like the One-Sentence Summary, this

CAT assesses how well students can condense large amounts of information by focusing on the key concept or thought in the assignment. It also encourages students to seek out the main points when reading an article.

Both the Word Journal and the One-Sentence Summary can be used to assess how well students understand the material they read and how well they can focus on the main points. It is possible to use these CATs instead of quizzes to evaluate student performance.

**Direct Paraphrasing.**    In Direct Paraphrasing, students are asked to paraphrase for a particular audience part of a topic, concept, lecture, or article. This technique assesses how well students understand what they have learned and how well they can use their own words to explain it to individuals with different perspectives. Students can be asked to role-play (Assume you are the director of marketing…Imagine you are the teacher…) in order to direct their paraphrasing to an audience other than faculty and students. Because their paraphrase is for a specific audience, this CAT is extremely practical and applicable to building skills needed for the future. Students should be told how much time will be allowed for this assessment and about how long their paraphrases should be.

Direct Paraphrasing results can be analyzed by separating the responses into categories: confused, minimal, adequate, and excellent. They should also be examined for accuracy, relevance for audience, and effectiveness in satisfying the assignment. The rubrics discussed in Chapter 6 may be useful in giving students feedback about how well they are able to accomplish this CAT.

Angelo and Cross (1993) emphasize that Direct Paraphrasing is "useful for assessing the students' understanding of important topics or concepts that they will later be expected to explain to others" (p. 232). In fields such as marketing, social work, education, law, and others, success often depends on how well people can understand specialized and complex information and then effectively communicate this information to others.

**Application Cards.**    After students have heard or read about an important principle, theory, concept, or procedure, the instructor hands out index cards and asks students to write down at least one real-world application for what they have just learned. This is an instantaneous way to determine how students have connected their new learning to prior knowledge and how well they understand how to apply the concepts. This CAT helps students to see more clearly the relevance of what they are learning.

At the beginning of class, students are asked to think about possible applications for topics as they are discussed. At the end of class, the professor selects one concept, principle, theory, or procedure and asks students to write down no more than three applications on an index card in three to five minutes. The professor collects the responses and shares a few of the applications in the next class period. Because of the simplicity and flexibility of this CAT, it can be used in almost any course of any size. Like Direct Paraphrasing, the focus is on encouraging students to think about applications of the course material. It helps students make connections between what they are learning in their course and in their experiences outside the class. It reinforces the relevance of their learning.

## Continuous Quality Improvement Techniques

Continuous quality improvement (CQI) techniques from the business management literature are being adapted to improve learning and teaching processes in education. Even though more progress has been made implementing CQI on the administrative side of institutions, interest in implementing quality principles continues to evolve on the academic side as evidenced by the growing literature (e.g., Bonstingl, 1996; Chizmar, 1994; Cornesky, 1993, 1994; Cornesky & Lazarus, 1995; Freed & Klugman, 1997; Wolverton, 1994).

The assessment and continuous quality improvement movements are both based on collecting feedback for improvement. The principles of continuous improvement parallel the themes of Classroom Assessment, and CQI techniques are very similar to CATs. Both strive to accomplish the same goal: to improve the learning of both teachers and students by collecting and sharing data.

**Two-Way Fast Feedback.**    Similar to CATs, Two-Way Fast Feedback is a process of collecting feedback and reversing the feedback so that students and professors work together in the improvement of the learning processes and environment (Luechauer & Shulman, 1996; Roberts, 1995). The name of this process emphasizes the fact that faculty members "give feedback to students on the student feedback just received, a new channel of communication opens up, hence two-way fast feedback" (Roberts, 1995, pp. 517–518). The approach is "systematic, frequent, and focused on learning about specific problems that students may be experiencing" (Bateman & Roberts, 1995, p. 250).

In two-way fast feedback, students complete a one-page questionnaire at the end of a class meeting. (See Figure 5.1 for an example.) The results are simple and easy to summarize because the students merely circle a number on five, seven, or nine point scales, and summaries require only simple calculation of average responses or the percentage that chose each response. Space is allowed for students' comments, but the questionnaire is usually a page in length. Questions refer to issues like clarity of lectures, presentation skills, and student preparation outside of class.

The essential step in this process is the reverse feedback. After collecting feedback from the students, the professor responds to the group—either orally, in writing, or both as soon as possible. This may sound time-consuming, but

**FIGURE 5.1    Sample Fast Feedback Questionnaire**

Date _____

| | Little or nothing | | A fair amount | | A great deal |
|---|---|---|---|---|---|
| Overall, how much did you get out of today's class? | 1 | 2 | 3 | 4 | 5 |

What was the most important thing you learned?

What was the muddiest point?

What single change by the instructor would have most improved this class?

Please comment briefly on the helpfulness of the advance reading assignments for today's class.

*Your Preparation for Today's Class*

| | Little or nothing | | A fair amount | | A great deal |
|---|---|---|---|---|---|
| Overall, how much did you get out of your preparation for today's class? | 1 | 2 | 3 | 4 | 5 |

What one thing can the instructor do to help you to improve your future class preparation?

What one thing can you do to help improve your future class preparation?

*Your Progress on Your Project*

| | Behind Schedule | | On Schedule | | Ahead of Schedule |
|---|---|---|---|---|---|
| On balance, how are you doing on your project? | 1 | 2 | 3 | 4 | 5 |

What one thing can the instructor do to help you make better progress on the project?

What one thing can you do to help you make better progress on the project?

General

Is there any other feedback about any aspect of this course that you would like to learn more about?

Are you having problems unrelated to this course that the instructor should be aware of?

---

(Bateman & Roberts, 1995, p. 253)

Bateman and Roberts (1995) claim from experience that the process prevents "rework" for students and instructors. Since the questionnaires are completed anonymously, students feel comfortable responding in ways that may improve the course for them while they are still enrolled.

The point of this approach is not to find out from students what content to cover—this would be inappropriate. Rather, the technique is based on the assumption that students are capable of commenting accurately on the learning process. Students know when they are confused, bored, or uncertain, all of which decrease the effectiveness of learning.

**Instantaneous Feedback.** This is a modification of Two-Way Fast Feedback. At a point late in a class session—usually when 10–15 minutes remain in the class—say to students, "Reflect upon the class. In two minutes, think of any questions you wanted to ask or comments you would have liked to make and write them down on paper." Collect the anonymous papers in the remaining minutes of class, and answer the questions orally for everyone. The exercise does not need to take more than 15 minutes, and the rewards for students are well worth the time spent. Using this process in about 75% of class meetings is enough to collect sufficient feedback and to indicate to students that you are serious about continuously improving the course (Reilly, 1995).

**Plus/Delta Feedback Tool.** This tool, sometimes referred to as Plus/ Change, is used as a feedback tool at the end of a class session to determine what processes to change and how to change them. Using an index card, ask students to divide the card into four quadrants and complete these two steps: 1) Identify the things that are working and should stay the same (Plus). 2) List the things that are not working and should be changed (Delta).

Ask students to complete these two steps both for the teacher and the course and for themselves, resulting in feedback in the four quadrants. The essential step for the Plus/Delta is that students have to reflect upon their own behavior and take ownership for their learning. Students ask themselves what they need to keep doing for the course to be successful (Plus) and what they need to change for the course to improve for them (Delta) (Helminski & Koberna, 1995). Figure 5.2 is an example of Plus/Delta.

**The LEARN Model.**   "The purpose of LEARN is to help students and faculty members work together to improve teaching and learning" (Baugher, 1995, p. 266). The model utilizes a team of students who design, administer, and evaluate feedback and then implement suggestions for improvement. The goal is similar to most classroom assessment goals: to identify areas of strength and weakness. "The difference in focus is at the heart of the LEARN process—to help students and instructors begin to focus on continuous improvement of processes rather than to seek out and solve problems" (p. 266).
     LEARN is an acronym for the steps in the process:

- Locate an opportunity for improvement.
- Establish a team to work on the process.
- Assess the current process.
- Research root causes.
- Nominate an improvement and enter the Plan-Do-Study-Act (PDSA) cycle (Baugher, 1995, p. 270).

The LEARN team works through this process several times during a course, identifying improvements and implementing suggestions.

**FIGURE 5.2   Sample Plus/Delta Feedback Form**

| THE TEACHER/COURSE— WHAT'S WORKING? | THE TEACHER/COURSE— WHAT NEEDS CHANGING? |
| --- | --- |
| *The teacher stayed focused on objectives.* | *One student dominated discussion.* |
| Class is enjoyable and the time goes fast. | We did not go over assignments. |
| Small group discussions are helpful. | The video was not helpful. |
| *The Student—What's Working?* | *The Student—What Needs Changing?* |
| I was prepared for class. | I need to participate more in class. |
| My attendance is good. | I should study more for exams. |

(Adapted from Helminski & Koberna, 1995, p. 323)

The PDSA cycle, sometimes referred to as the Plan-Do-Check-Act cycle, is a simple, effective, data-driven tool for continuous learning and improvement.

- *Planning* requires collecting the data needed to understand the process to be improved and developing a plan for improvement. In teaching, this means moving beyond the typical measures of progress such as examinations, quizzes, and summative evaluations to a much more active, ongoing data collection process. Gathering and interpreting the data drives the cycle. The importance of data as a driving force in improving the process of learning cannot be overemphasized. "Data are the foundation for understanding this process and for planning and developing changes —the doing" (Sherr & Schwoerer, 1995, p. 454).
- *Doing* represents making changes based on data collected. Alternatives are generated from the data and changes are implemented on a test basis.
- *Studying* refers to monitoring the changes by collecting more data and evaluating. This step may lead to revisions or adjustments.
- *Acting* means that an effective change is permanently implemented when it seems appropriate. The cycle continues. To continuously improve, the cycle is repeated when needed (Sherr & Schwoerer, 1995).

The LEARN team acts as a quality improvement team that focuses on process improvement rather than problem solving and implements its own improvements. But the team does *not* dictate course content to the instructor, handle student grievances, or translate improvement to mean responding to all student demands or lowering course expectations. (For additional information on implementation, refer to Baugher, 1995.)

**Critical Incident Questionnaire (CIQ).**    The CIQ is a one-page form that is handed out to students to complete during the last 10 minutes of class. Five open-ended questions on the form ask students to write down details about events that happened during the week. Rather than asking them what they liked or did not like, the focus is on specific, concrete events that were important to them. (Refer to Figure 5.3 for an example of a CIQ.)

The benefits of using CIQs include alerting professors to potential problems before they develop, encouraging students to be reflective learners, and building trust between teachers and students. As with other feedback techniques, it is important to report back to the students about the themes that emerge in the CIQs. When students witness their opinions, reactions, and feelings shared publicly and taken seriously, they know they have had some input into the process of improving the course (Brookfield, 1995).

**FIGURE 5.3    Sample Critical Incident Questionnaire (CIQ)**

**Directions**

Please take about five minutes to respond to each of the questions below about this week's class(es). Don't put your name on the form—your responses are anonymous. When you have finished writing, put…the form on the table by the door…. At the start of next week's class, I will be sharing the responses with the group. Thanks for taking the time to do this. What you write will help me make the class more responsive to your concerns.

1. At what moment in the class this week did you feel most engaged with what was happening?
2. At what moment in the class this week did you feel most distanced from what was happening?
3. What action that anyone (teacher or student) took in class this week did you find most affirming and helpful?
4. What action that anyone (teacher or student) took in class this week did you find most puzzling or confusing?
5. What about the class this week surprised you the most? (This could be something about your own reactions to what went on, or something that someone did, or anything else that occurs to you.)

(Brookfield, 1995, p. 115)

## Feedback from Teambuilding Techniques

In many disciplines, increasing importance is being placed on preparing students to interact collaboratively and cooperatively in the workplace. As a result, professors are increasingly structuring activities in which students work in teams. Training is provided in the interpersonal and problem-solving skills needed to create a successful team experience (Scholtes, 1988). Students learn about expectations, roles, and conflict resolution techniques.

Some of the techniques used to prepare students to be successful team members can also be used to generate feedback about learning. Idea-generating tools such as brainstorming and the nominal group technique are examples of techniques that can be used in this manner.

**Brainstorming.**    The team's goal in brainstorming is to generate as many ideas as possible. Members initially share ideas without judging their worth because the focus is on quantity not quality. One person acts as recorder or scribe and summarizes ideas using a flip chart. As pages are filled, they are taped in sequence to the wall or blackboard. This creates a team memory so that all ideas can be viewed simultaneously.

Professors can use this approach to gather information for course improvement. Students can work in teams to generate as many ideas as possible about changing the course to improve learning. This technique encourages creativity and provides the professor with a wide variety of suggested modifications to consider (Scholtes, 1988).

**Nominal Group Technique.**   The Nominal Group Technique (NGT) is used to make decisions in teams. It is similar to brainstorming, but it has some unique features that facilitate efficiency. In advance of the meeting at which the technique is to be used, the question to be addressed is distributed to participants. Members thus come to the meeting prepared to share their responses. In a round-robin fashion, members give one response at a time, and the ideas are recorded on a flip chart, the board, or a transparency until all ideas are given. In this way, everyone has an equal voice, and the focus is on generating a complete list of ideas rather than on advocating for certain ideas.

Once this step is finished, a second tool, N/3, is used to help teams or groups arrive at a consensus quickly. The number of ideas that has been generated is divided by three, and the resulting number determines the number of ideas each person selects from the list. For example, if 15 ideas are generated, every person selects five in a round-robin fashion. Typically two or three ideas emerge as the most popular.

This second step of coming to consensus can also be used with data collected by other methods. It allows a group to prioritize any list of data in a short period of time because ideas emerge about which there is some agreement without having to discuss every idea (Freed & Klugman, 1997). In the case of gathering data to improve learning, NGT provides a process for finding out which of many ideas for course improvement are the most important ones to students.

## Other Feedback Activities

**Turn to Your Partner (TTYP).**   Turn to Your Partner (TTYP) is a technique professors can use to enhance student learning at the same time they collect feedback about learning (Licklider, 1996). Adapted from the paired discussion activity of Johnson, Johnson, and Smith (1991), the purpose is to provide students with maximal opportunity to develop deep understanding by discussing what they're learning while they're learning it. It is a technique that can be used in large lecture classes, as well as small seminars.

In this approach, every student has a partner, typically an individual sitting beside him/her, and the partner is identified at the beginning of class. During the class session, the professor periodically asks the class questions about the topic under discussion, and then tells them to TTYP. First the members of the pair must formulate their individual answers to the question privately. Then each shares his or her answer with the partner. It is important for each student to listen carefully to the partner's answer. Then, through discussion, the pair creates a new answer to the question. The professor calls upon pairs at random, using this as an opportunity to get immediate feedback about how students are understanding the topic of the day.

Other purposes for this technique include focusing student attention at the beginning of class, regaining student attention when it appears to be waning, highlighting a key point, engaging students in open-ended thinking when it's desired, and allowing the professor to refocus him- or herself (Licklider, 1996). The technique reinforces the social skills of active listening, summarizing, paraphrasing, justifying and asking for justification, and asking good questions.

**Tools for Teaching.** Davis (1993) outlines several useful feedback activities in *Tools for Teaching*. The emphasis in all of the activities is on involving the students in improving their learning. This requires them to give input and to be engaged in the learning processes. We describe two of these tools as follows.

One tool is to ask students to give definitions, associations, and applications for complex concepts or ideas. During the last few minutes of class, distribute a short questionnaire based on the concepts covered that day. On the questionnaire, students complete the following or similar sentences:

- The main point of today's session was…
- A good example of an application of this idea is…
- I believe that the main point of today's lecture is most closely related to the following concepts, people, places, events, or things…
- I am most unclear about…

A second tool is to ask students to write a closing summary. At the end of a class session, ask students, individually or in pairs, to write a brief summary of the main ideas covered in class. Inform them that this is *not* a quiz but rather an assessment of their understanding of the material. Another approach is to ask students at the beginning of class to summarize the main ideas from the previous class and to write one question they would like to have answered. This helps students reflect on their learning and make connections between class periods.

**Redesigned Course Evaluation Forms.** Most end-of-course evaluation forms that faculty distribute to students reflect the traditional model of teaching. They focus on the professor (was he/she well-prepared, organized, etc.) and other inputs to the course (the textbook, other instructional materials, etc.). These are important aspects of the course to evaluate, but the end-of-course evaluation process could be strengthened if there were also questions that focused on student learning.

For example, students could be asked, "Which of your skills improved the most during this course?" Or, areas in which learning is expected to occur could be listed (e.g., understanding the concepts of the course, writing, critical thinking, speaking, analyzing, synthesizing) and students could rate their improvement, thus providing data to be used in making future changes in the course. By gathering data using questions that reflect each of the intended learning outcomes in the course, faculty can learn more about what they did well and what needs to be improved in their courses.

For example, the Instructor and Course Evaluation System (ICES) at the University of Illinois at Urbana–Champaign (Office of Instructional Resources, 1977) is comprised of a collection of items from which professors can select in developing a course evaluation form. The items fall into several categories (e.g., Course Management, Instructor Characteristics and Style, etc.), and one category is Student Outcomes of Instruction. Students respond on a five-point scale, and the anchors at the end of each scale have a verbal description. In the area of cognitive outcomes (p. 8), professors can select either general concept items (e.g., "How much have you learned in this course? A great deal/very little") or specific items (e.g., "Did you improve your ability to solve real problems in this field? Yes, significantly/No, not really"). Similarly, in the affective area (p. 9), one can select a general concept item ("Did this course increase your interest in the subject matter? Yes, greatly/No, not much") or a specific item ("Were you stimulated to do extra reading about the course material? Yes, very much/No, not really").

Figure 5.4 is an example of a course evaluation form that includes questions focusing on student learning. The form begins with traditional questions about the professor's characteristics (Section A). The remainder of the questions (Sections B through F) are designed to focus on learning outcomes and to encourage students to reflect upon their experiences.

---

**REFLECTIONS**

*As you create your own meaning from the ideas in this section, begin to think about...*

- Which of the feedback tools interest me the most? Why?
- Which techniques seem most conducive to my style and my students? Why?
- How can I systematically incorporate these techniques into my courses?

- How can I develop an approach for discussing assessment results with students that is comfortable for me?
- How can I ensure students that I am open to listening to their suggestions?

**FIGURE 5.4  Sample Redesigned Course Evaluation Form**

Course Title and Number _____
Instructor _____
Semester _____

A.  *For each of the five areas below, answer the question by placing a check in the appropriate column.*

| In this course, to what extent was the instructor: | Very | Somewhat | Not at all |
|---|---|---|---|
| 1. Knowledgeable about the subject? | _____ | _____ | _____ |
| 2. Able to communicate well? | _____ | _____ | _____ |
| 3. Organized? | _____ | _____ | _____ |
| 4. Courteous and respectful to students? | _____ | _____ | _____ |
| 5. Successful in bringing a variety of voices and perspectives into the course? | _____ | _____ | _____ |

   6. What would you most like to say about the instructor's effectiveness as a teacher?

B.  *Please describe the way in which this course affected your learning in each of the following areas.*
   7. Knowledge of the content of the discipline
   8. Critical thinking
   9. Writing
   10. Speaking
   11. Teamwork
   12. Other

[Note: Instructor can list other intended learning outcomes in this section.]

C.  *Please complete the following statements.*
   13. My learning in this class was helped most by...
   14. My learning in this class was hindered most by...
   15. The aspect of this class that most helped me take responsibility for my own learning was...
   16. The factor that was most important in preventing me from taking responsibility for my own learning was...
   17. As a result of this class, I now understand that the area of my development as a learner that I most need to work on is...

D.  *Please complete the following statements by checking one of the alternatives and briefly answering each related question.*
   18. In this course, I found that
      _____ many different teaching approaches were used.

      _____ some different teaching approaches were used.

      _____ very few teaching approaches were used.

      What are your feelings about the teaching approaches used?

19. In this course, I found that the instructor was responsive to students' concerns

_____ always.

_____ sometimes.

_____ rarely.

What are your feelings about this level of responsiveness?

20. In this course, I found that the teacher was successful in bringing about _____ student participation

_____ consistently.

_____ sometimes.

_____ rarely.

What are your feelings about the amount of participation by students in this course?

21. In this course, I found that I received information about my learning

_____ regularly.

_____ occasionally.

_____ rarely.

What are your feelings about the frequency with which you received information about your learning and the quality of that information?

22. In this course, I found that democratic habits of equity, inclusion, and negotiation were practiced

_____ regularly.

_____ occasionally.

_____ infrequently.

What are your feelings about the level—or lack—of democracy in this class?

E. *Please complete the following two statements.*

23. Overall, the moments in this course when I was the most engaged, excited, and involved as a learner were when...

24. Overall, the moments in this course when I was most distanced, disengaged, and uninvolved as a learner were when...

F. *Please answer the following questions.*

25. What would you most like to say about your experiences as a student in this course?

26. What piece of advice would you most like to give the instructor on how to teach the course in the future?

27. If there is anything else you would like to say about the experience of being a student in this class that you have not already said in response to previous items, please write it below.

(Adapted from Brookfield, 1995, pp. 268–270)

Course evaluation forms should be based on helping teachers gain a better understanding of how they are assisting learning and how their actions as teachers are being perceived. Too often forms continue to be used year after year without reflecting changes taking place in the field of pedagogy. Institutions and/or individual professors should regularly revise their course evaluation forms so that they accurately assess important characteristics of effective teaching.

## ENHANCING THE PROCESS OF GATHERING AND INTERPRETING FEEDBACK FROM STUDENTS

Chapter 2 began with a discussion of how people learn. The theory of constructivism suggests that all individuals actively create their own knowledge through a process of continually "making sense" of information and experiences. People create meaning by integrating new ideas with existing knowledge, and through this process, existing knowledge is reorganized and changed. The process of seeking to understand is not a choice; people are driven to create what they know and understand. Teaching and learning are two aspects of performance about which professors and students create meaning in a course.

One difficulty with creating meaning about one's own performance as a teacher or a learner is that the information on which interpretations are based is not always accurate. For example, when professors assess their effectiveness as teachers, some information is readily available to them (e.g., students' test scores) and other information is not (e.g., how students feel about a particular class experience or teaching technique). Similarly, when students assess their effectiveness as learners, some information is readily available to them (e.g., their test scores) and other information is not (e.g., specific suggestions about what and how they could improve).

Sometimes needed or helpful information comes too late (at the end of the course), and sometimes it never comes. Sometimes information is available but is too threatening to consider. For example, when information about performance is conveyed in a negative, harsh, or punitive manner, people pay less attention to it or minimize its importance. At other times, information may not be threatening, but it may be difficult to understand. For example, nonverbal reactions are often noticeable, but they may be ambiguous and thus difficult to interpret.

When clear, accurate, timely information is not available in a supportive manner that allows it to be heard, people's interpretation of their own performance suffers. As Wiggins (1993) points out, most learning situations do not provide what teachers and students need most: information designed to enable them to accurately self-assess and self-correct—so that assessment becomes a component of learning. After years of examining school systems and organizations, Gilbert (1978) observed, "I have almost never seen an ideal confirmation (feedback) system. Managers, teachers, employees, and students seldom have adequate information about how well they are performing" (p. 178). Thus, the goal of assessment should be to provide information to support learning.

Self-knowledge is empowering (Bateson, 1990) and feedback is the foundation of learning about ourselves and about the effect of our behavior on others. Christensen (1991) states it this way, "Self-knowledge is the beginning of all knowledge. I had to find the teacher in myself before I could find the teacher in my students and gain understanding of how we all taught one another" (p. 103). Ken Blanchard, author of *The One Minute Manager,* refers to feedback as the "breakfast of champions" because it is something which people need for growth and improvement and is something on which we thrive (Blanchard, 1984).

Although we may feel comfortable when we give feedback to students about their learning, we may be less comfortable when students give us feedback about our teaching. In higher education this type of communication has not been the norm. Recall from Chapters 1 and 2 that in the teacher-centered paradigm the professor is the expert information giver and the only evaluator in the course. Usually the direction of feedback during the course is from professor to student. In this environment, feedback is typically evaluative and judgmental rather than descriptive, and it may not be expressed in a manner that is constructive and helpful. Receiving feedback from students takes place only at the end of the course, and it is usually mandated by the institution.

Because of the timing, faculty members using a teacher-centered approach rarely have to face students immediately after feedback has been received. This is not the case when using CATs and CQI techniques. Fast feedback refers to faculty members quickly communicating back to the students regarding the data collected. Initially, this may not be easy to do if it has not been a common practice.

Similarly, students may be uncomfortable giving feedback to teachers. One reason may be fear of retribution. Another reason may be that they are not accustomed to being asked for their input on a regular basis. The role of giving feedback to the professor may conflict with the way they perceive their appropriate role in the course.

As professors and students shift from a teacher-centered to a learner-centered paradigm, ideas and practices will be put in place that support a comfortable view of mutual feedback. Professors will begin to view themselves more as partners in helping students learn than as expert information givers. They will welcome students' active involvement in their own learning, and students will learn new roles and take more ownership of their learning. Dialogue between professors and students will increase, and respect for students as people and as learners will be a more visible component of the course. As the course climate changes, the environment will be more supportive of a mutual feedback loop in which clear and accurate information is shared in a timely and supportive manner. There will be mutual trust, a perception that feedback is a joint effort, and the type of conversation that encourages the learner to be open and talk.

During the process of making the transformation to a learner-centered approach, however, some guidelines—presented in Figure 5.5—can be followed for facilitating the process of gathering feedback from students.

First, help students make the distinction between giving feedback to the professor and criticizing the professor. Feedback describes what took place and what did not take place in terms of the intended goal (Wiggins, 1997). Feedback is descriptive and criticism is evaluative. Useful feedback is value-neutral, without praise or blame. Praise is useful in learning because it encourages a learner (in this case, the professor) to keep going, but only feedback helps a learner improve (Wiggins, 1998). Useful feedback helps to build and maintain communication channels between students and professors.

Second, allow students to provide feedback anonymously. This will create an environment in which students feel comfortable giving feedback to professors. When students realize their input is valued, even though their suggestions may not always be feasible or realistic, their fears will be transformed into enthusiasm. When that happens, it is not unusual to find them signing their names to their suggestions. This level of comfort leads to more open channels of communication and increased dialogue in class discussions.

Third, focus questions—and encourage students to focus responses—on behaviors and processes instead of personalities. This makes the activity less personally threatening, and typically makes the recipient of the feedback more receptive.

**FIGURE 5.5   Guidelines for Gathering Feedback from Students**

1. Help students make the distinction between feedback and criticism.
2. Allow students to provide feedback anonymously.
3. Focus questions–and encourage students to focus responses–on specific behaviors and processes instead of on personalities.
4. Maintain a focus on using data for improvement.
5. Learn to practice active listening skills:
   - Listen to the message.
   - Summarize your understanding of the message.
   - In the next class session, share your summary with students to be sure that the message heard is the message sent.
6. Identify changes you will make in the course and share them with students.
7. Reinforce an atmosphere of mutual respect by thanking students for their feedback.

Fourth, maintain a focus on using data for improvement. When students see that the information they share leads to discussions about improving learning, rather than to arguments about whether their perceptions are "right" or "wrong," they become more comfortable participating and sharing. Furthermore, an emphasis on improvement puts the process in perspective for professors. They seek out common themes and patterns in student responses instead of reacting to every variation in the system. As the old adage says, "You can't please all of the people all of the time." Therefore, the goal should be to address issues of concern to most students and to stay in touch with their progress in order to determine if additional adjustments are necessary.

Fifth, learn to practice active listening skills. In the traditional paradigm professors are information givers, but as the paradigm shifts, teaching becomes not only the art of thinking and speaking, it is also the art of listening and understanding. But listening is not just keeping still; effective listening is an art that must be practiced (Gragg, 1940).

Not surprisingly, one aspect of effective listening is to listen to the message. According to Covey (1989), "Seek first to understand, then to be understood" (p. 237). By this, he means that listening is a more important skill than speaking. It is important to be receptive to the idea of listening for input for the purpose of improvement. Because we are accustomed to being the primary speakers when we teach, actively listening to students may present a challenge.

Figure 5.6 points out that active listening requires us to be open to suggestions, interpreting student feedback by viewing the course through students' eyes. When students point out aspects of the course that may be interfering with learning, we should accept responsibility for our actions and avoid being defensive or rationalizing what we have done. We should explore and reflect on the feedback, resisting the temptation to brush it off or minimize it. Continuous improvement principles advocate that it is important to explore the feedback, listening for recurring themes. It is not wise to

**FIGURE 5.6   Guidelines for Interpreting Feedback from Students**

1. Try to view the situation through students' eyes.
2. Avoid acting defensively.
3. Avoid rationalizing any undesirable behaviors/processes students identify.
4. Accept responsibility for your actions.
5. Explore the feedback; look for recurring themes.
6. Avoid brushing off the feedback with misplaced humor or sarcasm.
7. Avoid putting yourself down, assuming that students are correct in all respects.
8. Identify constructive ways to use the feedback.

(Adapted from Stewart, 1997)

react to every comment, complaint, or suggestion, or to put ourselves down, assuming the need for improvement is a sign of failure. Use student suggestions as a springboard for creative modifications in the course.

It is also important to develop a summary of the feedback, focusing on positive as well as negative feedback. Students' suggestions for improvement can be grouped into categories such as

- those you can change this semester (i.e., decreasing the turnaround time for assignments);
- those that must wait until the next time the course is offered (i.e., the textbook);
- those that you either cannot or will not change for pedagogical or philosophical reasons (i.e., number of tests or assignments) (Davis, 1993, p. 349).

Another aspect of active listening is to be sure that the message heard is the one that was sent. Share summaries with students to ensure that their opinions were properly understood. It is critical that students believe their input was taken seriously, and it is important to convey this as soon as possible after the assessment was used, typically at the next class meeting. Keep the tone and attitude neutral, and avoid being defensive or unnecessarily apologetic. Ask questions to clarify or to receive more information.

Sixth, respond to students with proposed changes in the course. As mentioned several times in this chapter, this step convinces students that their input is valued and helps build trust in the learning environment. When students witness faculty members responding to their input, they interpret these actions as a serious commitment to continuous improvement. Students understand their feedback is important and they tend to increase the amount of feedback given. When systems are in place so that students can anticipate being asked for feedback on a regular basis, they typically become more engaged in the learning process, and they are able to shift more easily to a learner-centered paradigm.

Seventh, reinforce the atmosphere of mutual respect by thanking students for their feedback. Because feedback is not always easy to give, be appreciative of the time and effort students are taking to improve their learning processes and environment. Invite their continued participation in improving the course.

Giving feedback fosters self-responsibility, encouraging students to take more ownership in their learning. As partners in the learning process, students can help professors make changes so that learning is enhanced for everyone involved. As students begin to perceive that the course has improved as a result of their input, their expectations may rise. This should not be interpreted as dissatisfaction with the course or instructor, but rather as a sincere effort to continue to make the course better for this particular set of learners.

Continuous improvement practices focus on striving to satisfy or exceed customer expectations. However, because it may be difficult to view students as stakeholders or customers, we have not typically asked for student feedback on a regular basis in higher education. Nevertheless,

> in many ways, college students are customers. They are customers because they have engaged in an economic agreement, a contract for goods and services and an opportunity to learn in an organization that is in the business of selling opportunities to learn. As a result, students should be given an opportunity to voice their needs, desires, and satisfaction with their learning environment and their voices should be heard (Groccia, 1997, p. 31).

However, "students are learners as well as customers" (Groccia, 1997, p. 31) and the growth process does not mean that professors should simply give them what they want. Rather, the purpose of collecting student feedback through CATs, CQI techniques, and other activities is to engage the students in their learning, to encourage them to take more ownership of their learning, and to remove any unnecessary barriers to the learning processes.

Based on extensive experience and research on teaching as a profession, Brookfield (1995) makes these observations and challenges us to practice what we teach.

> The most important thing I have learned from reading years of learning journals, portfolios, and classroom critical incident responses is that what we do as teachers has enormous significance in the eyes of our students. The degree to which you are prepared to take the risks you ask students to take and the extent to which you are genuinely open to new ways of thinking about teaching and learning will determine how far students are prepared to do these things themselves…How you model in your own life a continuous engagement in learning determines very significantly the extent to which students take learning seriously. And the only way you'll know how well you're modeling these values and processes is by seeing your actions through students' eyes (pp. 112–113).

Finally, even though the feedback methods discussed in this chapter take class time, faculty members who systematically practice them report that the time is well spent. They reap rewards such as more class cohesion, increased class discussion, and enhanced learning because barriers to learning have been removed along the way (Roberts, 1995). Feedback becomes "the breakfast of champions" (Blanchard, 1984), and it is difficult to get enough because there is a desire for more. As faculty and student expectations go up, so does the quantity and quality of learning.

REFLECTIONS

*As you create your own meaning from the ideas in this section, begin to think about...*

- How do I feel about accepting suggestions for change from students?

- How do I typically react when students propose changes?
- How can I apply the guidelines suggested in this section to make the feedback process more useful?

## LOOKING AHEAD

This chapter described techniques we can use to *solicit* feedback from our students about how well a course is meeting their needs as learners. Chapter 6 is also about feedback, but the focus of that chapter switches to techniques and issues associated with the process of *giving* feedback to learners about their learning.

## TRY SOMETHING NEW

1. Select from this chapter at least one feedback technique you have never used and implement it sometime in the next few weeks. Make sure that you share with students the themes that emerged from the data.
2. Review your approach to gathering and interpreting student feedback. How could you improve it to create a climate even more conducive to student learning?
3. Examine the guidelines for gathering and interpreting student feedback in Figures 5–5 and 5–6. Select one from each list that represents an area in which you would like to improve. Decide what you need to do to begin the improvement process.

## REFERENCES

Angelo, T. A., & Cross, K. P. (1993). *Classroom assessment techniques: A handbook for college teachers.* San Francisco: Jossey-Bass.

Bateman, G. R., & Roberts, H. V. (1992). *Total quality management for professors and students.* Unpublished paper, the Graduate School of Business, University of Chicago.

Bateman, G. R., & Roberts, H. V. (1995). Total quality for professors and students. In H. V. Roberts (Ed.), *Academic initiatives in total quality for higher education* (pp. 241–264). Milwaukee, WI: ASQC Quality Press.

Bateson, M. C. (1990). *Composing a life.* New York: The Atlantic Monthly Press.

Baugher, K. H. (1995). Listening to our coworkers: Using the LEARN process to improve teaching and learning. In H. V. Roberts (Ed.), *Academic initiatives in total quality for higher education* (pp. 265–278). Milwaukee, WI: ASQC Quality Press.

Blanchard, K. (1984). *The one minute manager.* London: Fontana.

Bonstingl, J. J. (1996). *Schools of quality.* Alexandria, VA: Association for Supervision and Curriculum Development.

Brookfield, S. (1995). *Becoming a critically reflective teacher.* San Francisco: Jossey-Bass.

Chaffee, E. E. (1997). Listening to the people you serve. In *Assessing impact: Evidence and action* (pp. 41–50). Washington, DC: American Association for Higher Education.

Chizmar, J. (1994). Total quality management (TQM) of teaching and learning. *Journal of Economic Education, 25* (2),

Christensen, C. R. (1991). Every student teaches and every teacher learns: The reciprocal gift of discussion teaching. In C. R. Christensen, D. A. Garvin, & A. Sweet (Eds.), *Education for judgment: The artistry of discussion leadership* (pp. 99–119). Boston: Harvard Business School Press.

Cornesky, R. (1993). *The quality professor: Implementing TQM in the classroom.* Madison, WI: Magna Publications.

Cornesky, R. (1994). *Quality classroom practices for professors.* Port Orange, FL: Cornesky & Associates.

Cornesky, R., & Lazarus, W. (1995). *Continuous quality improvement in the classroom: A collaborative approach.* Port Orange, FL: Cornesky & Associates.

Covey, S. R. (1989). *The 7 habits of highly effective people.* New York: Simon and Schuster.

Cross, K. P. (1993, February–March). Involving faculty in TQM. *AACC Journal, 15–20.*

Cross, K. P., & Steadman, M. H. (1996). *Classroom research: Implementing the scholarship of teaching.* San Francisco: Jossey-Bass.

Davis, B. G. (1993). *Tools for teaching.* San Francisco: Jossey-Bass.

Freed, J. E., & Klugman, M. R. (1997). *Quality principles and practices in higher education: Different questions for different times.* Phoenix, AZ: American Council on Education and The Oryx Press.

Gilbert, T. F. (1978). *Human Competence.* New York: McGraw-Hill.

Gragg, C. (1940). Teachers also must learn. *Harvard Educational Review, 10,* 30–47.

Groccia, J. E. (1997, May–June). The student as customer versus the student as learner. *About Campus,* 31–32.

Helminski, L., & Koberna, S. (1995). Total quality in instruction: A systems approach. In H. V. Roberts (Ed.), *Academic initiatives in total quality for higher education* (pp. 309–326). Milwaukee, WI: ASQC Quality Press.

Johnson, D. W., Johnson, R. T., & Smith, K. A. (1991). *Active learning: Cooperation in the college classroom.* Edina, MN: Interaction Book Company.

Licklider, B. (1996). *Project LEA/RN training manual.* Unpublished document. Ames, IA: Iowa State University.

Luechauer, D. L., & Shulman, G. M. (1996). Fast feedback permits students to assess faculty performance. In T. W. Banta, J. P. Lund, K. E. Black, & F. W. Oblander (Eds.), *Assessment in practice: Putting principles to work on college campuses* (pp. 288–291). San Francisco: Jossey-Bass.

Marchese, T. J. (1991). TQM reaches the academy. *AAHE Bulletin, 44* (3), 3–9.

Mosteller, F. (1989). The 'Muddiest Point in the Lecture' as a feedback device. *On Teaching and Learning, 3,* 10–21.

Office of Instructional Resources. (1977). *Instructor and course evaluation system (ICES).* Urbana–Champaign: University of Illinois at Urbana–Champaign, Division of Measurement and Evaluation.

Reilly, T. (1995). Instantaneous feedback. In H. V. Roberts (Ed.), *Academic initiatives in total quality for higher education* (pp. 333–334). Milwaukee, WI: ASQC Quality Press.

Roberts, H. V. (1995). Introduction. In H. V. Roberts (Ed.), *Academic initiatives in total quality for higher education* (pp. 1–16). Milwaukee, WI: ASQC Quality Press.

Scholtes, P. R. (1988). *The team handbook: How to use teams to improve quality*. Madison, WI: Joiner Associates.

Sherr, L. A., & Schwoerer, C. E. (1995). Continuous improvement in education: The process of learning in an introductory statistics class. In H. V. Roberts (Ed.), *Academic initiatives in total quality for higher education* (pp. 453–470). Milwaukee, WI: ASQC Quality Press.

Stewart, W. (1997). *An A–Z of counselling theory and practice* (2nd ed.). Cheltenham, UK: Stanley Thornes (Publishers) Ltd.

Strasser, S. E. (1995). E-Mail Minutes: The marriage of e-mail and the One-Minute Paper. In H. V. Roberts (Ed.), *Academic initiatives in total quality for higher education* (pp. 359–366). Milwaukee, WI: ASQC Quality Press.

Study Group on the Conditions of Excellence in American Higher Education. (1984). *Involvement in learning: Realizing the potential of American higher education*. Washington, DC: National Institute of Education.

Wiggins, G. P. (1993). *Assessing student performance: Exploring the purpose and limits of testing*. San Francisco: Jossey-Bass.

Wiggins, G. (1997). Feedback: How learning occurs. In *Assessing Impact: Evidence and Action* (pp. 31–39). Washington, DC: American Association of Higher Education.

Wiggins, G. (1998). *Educative assessment: Designing assessments to inform and improve student performance*. San Francisco: Jossey-Bass.

Wolverton, M. (1994). *A new alliance: Continuous quality and classroom effectiveness*. (ASHE-ERIC Higher Education Report No. 6). Washington, DC: The George Washington University, School of Education and Human Development.

# CHAPTER 9

# THE ELEMENTS OF EFFECTIVE ONLINE TEACHING

## OVERCOMING THE BARRIERS TO SUCCESS

Written by Anita Bischoff of the University of Phoenix, this chapter from *The Online Teaching Guide* provides novice online instructors a highly effective introduction, or, to those more experienced in online teaching, a highly useful assessment device. Interestingly, it emphasizes "high touch " techniques and tools for the professor to employ in facilitating more effective online learning experiences. Among the most significant of these are strategies for providing timely, effective feedback to "students at a distance," to maximize student retention and program completion—an increasing concern of administrators at all colleges and universities.

Chapter passages focused on evaluation, selection, and organization of online teaching and learning materials are especially useful. Whether online teaching is in your immediate plans or not, this succinctly written chapter will provide nuggets of insight into an increasingly significant instructional delivery method.

# THE ELEMENTS OF EFFECTIVE ONLINE TEACHING

## OVERCOMING THE BARRIERS TO SUCCESS

ANITA BISCHOFF

Chapter 6 from *The Online Teaching Guide*
Ken N. White & Bob H. Weight
Allyn & Bacon, © 2000

Students often choose a group-based online learning environment because they enjoy learning from other working adults. Their interest in learning is maintained when the instructor and other students share in their journey toward greater understanding of course topics.

As part of the learning model at the University of Phoenix (UOP), online students learn not only from their instructors, who provide content expertise and feedback to each individual, but also from other adult learners in the classroom. Instructors expertly facilitate discussions that help working adults apply the lessons from their texts and the instructors' lectures to their work lives.

When I speak at conferences on distance learning, academics often approach me afterward with some variation of "Sounds intriguing, but does it really work?" In fact, many express an interest in being trained to teach online so that they can see for themselves whether it works. Fortunately, my experience with the University of Phoenix Online Campus and research on online learning leads me to believe that asynchronous group-based conferencing is a highly effective tool for learning.

Recent research by the University of Phoenix's Institutional Research office indicates that online instruction is "every bit as effective as regular classrooms in serving working adult students in business and management programs" (Kauffman, 1996). Further, many University of Phoenix instructors of both onsite and online students argue that online students interact and learn at least as much, if not more, than other UOP students. They attribute this to the highly interactive online learning model, which encourages more regular communication with the online instructors and other students than usually experienced in onsite classrooms.

The key to online education's effectiveness lies in large part with the facilitator. While serving as director of Academic Affairs at the University of Phoenix Online since 1995, I identified certain competencies that directly enhance teaching and learning in a discussion-based online medium. By reading student end-of-course surveys each week, speaking with academic counselors, and talking to students at graduation each year, I found that an instructor's performance in the following areas seems to tie closely to perceptions of their effectiveness: (1) *visibility,* (2) *feedback,* (3) *materials,* and (4) *retention.*

Not coincidentally, the UOP training program focuses largely on these areas. Specifically, online instructors are taught to (1) maintain visibility, (2) give regular feedback, (3) provide high-quality materials, and (4) remove obstacles to student retention.

Even experienced onsite instructors need training, coaching, and mentoring in these areas to translate their effectiveness from the actual to the virtual classroom. Having seen how important these skills are, I am convinced that prospective online instructors should receive extensive training and mentoring in these areas before "flying solo." This training will prevent them from making avoidable mistakes that detract from their effectiveness as online facilitators.

As an added bonus, instructors who attain proficiency in the preceding four areas tend to receive the most positive feedback from their students and colleagues. They also enjoy the gratification and intrinsic rewards of helping students fully grasp the class objectives and progress toward degree attainment.

This chapter will focus on each of the topics mentioned, providing prospective, new, and experienced online instructors with a thorough understanding of the importance of each aspect of online teaching and how to attain proficiency in each area. In each of the following four sections, I will share a vignette or two to illustrate the significance of the topic, then generally discuss the components of each instructional competency. Finally, I will provide more specific examples and further explore the components that make up each of the four main areas of online instruction.

## THE ROLE OF VISIBILITY IN ONLINE TEACHING

About a year ago, a new online teacher received negative feedback due to students' perceptions of his "low participation" in the class discussion. Students complained to an academic counselor that they only heard from the instructor at the end of each week's discussion. Since previous instructors had been more involved in class discussions, they wondered if their current instructor was lazy or uninterested. When their counselor suggested that they ask the instructor about their perceptions, the students did so with great trepidation, for fear of offending the instructor.

While taken aback at their criticisms, the instructor explained that he was trying to avoid dominating the discussion; thus, he read each day's notes with interest, but saved his own remarks until the end of the week. He further described how he summarized the discussion, analyzed it in light of his experience and the readings, and extended on the discussion to foreshadow the next week's lecture. The students agreed that his input was valuable, but pointed out that the relative sparseness of the input was discouraging to them, since they were used to more regular messages from their instructor.

The instructor finally realized what the problem was. The students could not "see" him reading notes and nodding his head encouragingly, or were not aware of his presence on days when he did not write to the class. When the instructor fully understood the dilemma, he agreed to write more notes to the discussion meeting during the week. Soon, the students perceived that he was "visible," and his consistent presence reassured them that they were progressing appropriately. The students felt gratified that their feedback had been taken seriously and that it resulted in a positive resolution, since the instructor's accommodation to their needs as learners made their class more interactive and rewarding.

Consider another example: During an online mentorship, an instructor-in-training with full responsibility for an online class suddenly disappeared for a few days. His mentor tried to reach him by computer and phone yet was unable to get any information other than that the trainee was out of town on vacation. By the time the trainee finally resurfaced days later, his mentor had already stepped in and saved the class from derailing. When asked for an explanation, the trainee described how he had gone on vacation to another city, expecting to load the conferencing software onto his host's computer. However, the host happened to have a Macintosh, so his Windows-based software was not compatible. Even after he officially failed mentorship and was denied admission to the online faculty, the disgruntled trainee could not understand why being offline and out of communication for a total of six days out of a five-week class was such a concern.

Lack of visibility and desertion of a class without communication to the administration does not bode well for an online instructor's willingness to put the students' needs first. Every online instructor needs to be aware of the various ways they can increase their visibility in their classes.

## Online Visibility and Public Messages

The preceding vignettes point out that public messages are key to the perceptions of an instructor's presence. Similarly, since no one can sense someone's presence in an online environment, written messages from the instructor to students in the online class are necessary for students to feel connected in the online classroom environment.

On a related note, online instructors often do not realize that sending personal correspondence via the online medium does not substantially enhance their visibility. Namely, if instructors answer individual questions by replying to personal mailboxes, other students fail to see the interaction; that is why conducting as much class business as possible in the open forum is recommended.

What kind of messages does a visible instructor send? A sampling of the variety available and examples of each include the following:

- Content-related messages (lectures, handouts, clarification of points in the text, discussion questions, synthesis of discussion)
- Process-related messages (order of assignments, directions for sending assignments, description of the flow of the class, guidance when students become confused)
- Technical tips (software tips, information about how to send attachments, discussion of how to format notes, URLs)
- Protocol guidelines (code of conduct, plagiarism statement, netiquette, online tone)
- Responses (answers to student questions, feedback on work submitted to the meeting)

If students benefit from visibly seeing the instructors' notes in the online classroom, which messages are particularly effective in establishing visibility? Messages demonstrating that the instructor is actively reading the discussion often prove effective. ("Canned" messages, although at times necessary, are somewhat less effective in establishing visibility because they do not represent individualized responses, nor clearly reflect that the instructor is involved in reading and responding to this particular class.)

As one technique that enhances the instructor's visibility while adding content-related value, some instructors remove the name from a question addressed to the instructor's personal mailbox, share the question in the main forum, and answer it publicly to benefit others in the class who may have the same question. In fact, the question may be from a student in another class being taught concurrently or even from a student in a previous class. The origin of the question does not matter, as long as the sender's anonymity is protected and students benefit from the instructor's response.

## Online Visibility and Modeling

Another benefit of instructor visibility is that the visible instructor is modeling how the discussion-based instructional model works. If students are required to write to class meetings a certain number of times each week, for example, I would argue that online instructors should maintain at least the same level of participation as the students.

Another key to setting a positive example is that an instructor modeling a high level of participation often motivates students to enhance their own participation. They know that the instructor demands their participation by observing the instructor's high participation level. On the other hand, when an instructor does not maintain an adequate level of participation, students may assume they have been given tacit permission to reduce their own levels of participation. They assume that their instructor will not feel comfortable confronting them or grading them down for the same behavior that the teacher is exhibiting.

## Online Visibility and Reducing Isolation

A final reason that visibility is critical is to prevent a sense of isolation that distant students often encounter. If the students connect to the classroom once or twice a day, finding a number of new messages in the open forum each time, they feel reassured to be working collaboratively with their instructor as well as other students. If they fail to see a note that they expected (e.g., a weekly lecture), they learn to react and ask the instructor directly for the materials that are missing. The comfort felt by students whose instructors are visible cannot be underestimated in the distance education environment, where students do not have the trappings of the traditional university (e.g., familiar faces, student unions, and student activities) to provide a sense of belonging.

Ultimately, taking responsibility for being "visible" means that it is the instructor's responsibility to alert necessary personnel if anything occurs that would prevent the individual from fulfilling his or her contractual obligation. If an emergency arises, the instructor should follow the university's procedures in order to ensure that the students' learning will not be interrupted. Often, a substitute teacher is essential, due to the high need for instructors to be visible in the online classroom.

## THE ROLE OF FEEDBACK IN ONLINE TEACHING

One neophyte online instructor whom I observed felt strongly that the university's focus on regular feedback, particularly evaluative feedback, was exaggerated and that it distracted from the learning process. He told students that they would hear from him only if they were "heading for trouble." Otherwise, they should assume that they were doing fine. Only when he received several furious student end-of-course surveys after his class did he realize that his practice, while understandable and consistent with his teaching style, was neither appropriate nor effective from the perspective of his online students. Students stressed that they needed regular feedback to know how their performance was judged, how they could improve, and how their final grade was calculated. The instructor discussed this situation with more experienced online facilitators and, with their assistance, adapted to his students' demands for substantive and frequent feedback.

## Frequent and Consistent Online Feedback

Effective online instructors not only write to class meetings regularly but they also provide frequent and consistent feedback to the class as well as to individual students. Frequent and consistent feedback in the online classroom can stimulate active engagement by techniques such as questioning assumptions, disagreeing with certain points, and pointing out well-analyzed points.

Of course, these facilitation skills are not dissimilar to those of an instructor in a face-to-face classroom; yet, the frequency and consistency of feedback are even more necessary in an online classroom. Why? Online students cannot see their instructors or other students nod their heads, frown, look quizzically, or smile encouragingly. What is usually nonverbal feedback must occur through written messages, which makes online feedback particularly critical.

Giving feedback in the main meeting includes asking questions, suggesting alternative perspectives to consider, and extending on students' ideas. Feedback also includes answering questions in the main forum whenever possible, since many times the answer to one student's question may prove useful to the entire class.

## Timely Online Feedback

Providing timely feedback within the class forum is important. Since an online class moves quickly, timeliness is essential to give students guidance and teach them the material in depth. Further, when guiding asynchronous discussions, the instructor needs to facilitate and foreshadow, instead of "catching up" with the discussions that have already been written and digested. Less timely feedback may lead to a perception that the instructor is not fully involved in the class, whereas timely feedback reassures students that the instructor is focusing on them and on their learning. Furthermore, feedback that is timely is far more motivational and beneficial to performance improvement than delayed feedback. Thus, online feedback is best when it is prompt.

## Diplomatic Online Feedback

When feedback is provided to students in the main class meeting, diplomacy is essential. Since student motivation is closely linked to self-efficacy, well-worded feedback will encourage learners to continue in their programs and feel confident that they will succeed online.

Well-worded suggestions from the instructor are valuable not only for the student's learning process but they may also provide learning opportunities for the entire class. For example, gently pointing out the need to explore a theory underlying an opinion more fully may lead to the class's understanding that "gut feelings" are not convincing within the context of an academic discourse. The point can generally be made without undue embarrassment to the student who shared the gut feeling.

Occasionally, an instructor requests that students critique each other's assignments in the online classroom, usually providing guidelines for effective analysis to make the criticism constructive as opposed to personal or negative. When diplomatically worded, this type of feedback may also enhance the learning experience, since students practice the skill of receiving peer feedback as well as the skill of providing critiques to their peers in a written forum. I am convinced that setting the correct guidelines to ensure that students are supportive, as opposed to attacking, is essential to the success of this technique.

When the instructor needs to provide critical feedback to individual students, the feedback should be couched in a way that maintains the learner's dignity. If a student is exhibiting behaviors that are disrupting the learning process, for example, he or she will need to receive positive but clear feedback that the conduct is not appropriate. The wording (and private transmission) of such a message will help to avoid further disruption in the learning environment by reducing the chance of the situation escalating. A critical message may need to be rewritten several times before the correct tone and wording are achieved; however, this attention to diplomacy is far more likely to bring about the desired outcome than sending a less reflective message.

## Evaluative Online Feedback

One online instructor whom I coached became increasingly frustrated when students asked how she calculated grades for the course. Having worked with elementary school students for years, she was not used to being challenged about her grading policies and procedures by students. Fortunately, through our discussions she realized that grading was part of teaching, and that doing it well would lead to more effective student learning. Further, by scoring students' work and tying it to the grading guidelines shared in her syllabus, she removed some of the ambiguity in her grading procedure and demonstrated to her adult learners that their performances matched the grades they earned. Additionally, after teaching more courses, she recognized that her students needed regular, detailed feedback during the course, not just a grade at the end. Fortunately, she no longer needed to answer frequent questions about grading, since her new procedures and guidelines were clear and consistent, thereby allowing relatively little ambiguity.

Evaluating students (covered more completely in Chapter 14) is an important part of providing effective feedback. As at any university campus, learning to grade fairly and effectively is a teaching skill that must be mastered by all online instructors.

Why should an instructor invest the time to provide detailed evaluative feedback to online students? Online students tend to have high standards for their own performances, especially if they are adult learners who have returned to school after succeeding in their work lives. Like any learners, they need to know where they stand in order to gauge how best to improve. Substantive feedback helps them perform at higher levels and thereby earn higher scores in subsequent courses.

Students in an online forum, perhaps because it is a relatively young learning medium, may resist accepting a grade given by an instructor, more than students faced with a similar situation in a regular classroom. This is even more likely due to the ease with which a student can send a quick electronic message, as opposed to the possible intimidation factor when addressing an instructor in person. Although often the most uncomfortable aspect of teaching, grading effectively is critical to student learning and effective online teaching.

What should an online instructor do to encourage students to understand the need for and utility of grades? When his students balk at his (particularly rigorous) grading practices, Douglas Beckwith, curriculum supervisor and faculty member for UOP Online Campus, compares the process of grading to that of evaluating employees. Discussing grading in this context seems to help set the right expectations and attitudes when students fail to recognize that grading is unavoidable in most programs, not to mention that the instructor is the authority when grading disagreements arise.

Completing a weekly grading summary with point values helps both the instructor and student recognize when a student needs help to succeed. If a student does poorly in a class and fails to improve with constructive weekly feedback, some advising may be necessary, such as a suggestion that the student consult an academic counselor.

## Templates and Online Feedback

How is evaluative feedback delivered in an online setting? Universities establish their own guidelines and often articulate these in the instructor's contractual agreement. As an example, at the University of Phoenix Online Campus, specific feedback on assignments (including grades) must be provided within a week of the assignment's receipt. This specific evaluative feedback, as well as the use of weekly templates, helps students to understand how their grades are earned and to avoid surprises at the end of the course.

Experienced UOP online instructors have often attested to the value of using templates when providing weekly feedback to students' personal mailboxes. Each individual student receives a completed template that articulates the points they earned on assignments (out of total possible points), as well as points for each week's participation. A few sentences highlighting the student's performance, such as encouraging him or her to try harder the next week, are also highly recommended. Here is an example of a typical week's template:

Dear Jim:

Your point totals for this week are as follows:

    __06__  of 6 possible points for discussion

    __10__  of 10 possible points for participation

    __17__  of 20 possible points for the week's essay

    __06__  of 6 points for weekly summary

Your total is 39 out of 42 points. (Please use the past week's grading summary if you wish to compare your total points so far with the points possible and look up your grade so far in the course.) Also, let me know if you did not receive any of your assignments this week, as I returned them earlier this week with specific feedback and suggestions.

Jim, you showed a great deal of improvement in your participation levels this week, sending quality messages 6 out of 7 days this week, as contrasted with 4 out of 7 days last week. I particularly enjoyed message #57, in which you outlined a situation at work and tied it to the theories in Chapter 4 of your text. I hope that next week you will continue to participate actively, since your well-considered questions bring up important points and add to your peers' learning experience at this online university.

Warmly,

Jill B. (Instructor)

## THE ROLE OF INSTRUCTIONAL MATERIALS IN ONLINE TEACHING

A seasoned instructor, hurrying to upload the syllabus and the first week's lecture, failed to proofread online materials that she had used many times to teach the same course. The due dates for assignments within the syllabus included various dates in April, although the class was running in June. After asking the appropriate questions to correct the situation, her students still expressed a high level of frustration with the instructor, having perceived (correctly) that she did not take the necessary time to customize her materials for the current class. The embarrassment that resulted made such an impression on the instructor that she warned other instructors to revise their materials carefully, which likely saved others from similar mistakes.

### Content-Driven Online Materials

Instructional materials include syllabi, mini-lectures, handouts, references to URLs and readings on the topic, assignments, discussion questions, examples, answers to assignments, and other materials that are either prewritten before the class begins or added during the class to enrich the content of the course.

Messages that are not content driven should be minimized, since discussions need to be focused on the class and noncontent messages may prove distracting to the topics being explored. Although an instructor's role is to facilitate, it is also to provide supplemental material that enhances the text and thereby helps students to attain a deeper understanding of the course and to meet the stated learning objectives.

## Carefully Edited Online Materials

The content expertise that is infused into a written online lecture, along with the chance to see examples of other's materials, can lead to a higher-quality presentation than typically seen in traditional classrooms. If, however, the instructor does not edit the materials carefully, the result may be an embarrassing situation, as shared in the preceding vignette.

The ability to polish and improve class materials each time a class is taught is a huge advantage of online teaching over onsite. Of course, refining class materials demands that an instructor remembers to record when an assignment needs clarification or when a point demands more elaboration next time. For future classes, the ensuing modifications directly benefit students, who are the recipients of increasingly polished materials (often worthy of publication).

If the university uses modules or course materials that are appropriate for a regular classroom, the instructor may be called on to adapt the course to an online format. In cases like this, all of the oral presentations should be removed and group projects should take into account the time involved in coordinating group projects within an asynchronous medium. Modifications to an onsite module must be carefully communicated to online students in a timely fashion to avoid confusion.

Speaking with a colleague who teaches for another well-known online university, I asked how and when their curriculum developers adapted syllabi from the regular to online versions. She explained that the developers usually provided an online-specific version *after* publishing the onsite version. She also noted that the curriculum adaptations were not always successful, since the adapters were usually not online teachers, but editors. Once, in fact, the editors had missed something significant—proficiency in oral presentations was listed as a learning objective of a text-based online course. Even more tellingly, four group projects were due in a five-week online course. She and the other online instructors were forced to reedit the curriculum so that it would work online. As a result, they suggested to the administration that future syllabi be adapted solely by experienced online instructors.

An instructor teaching a course for the first time, whether onsite or online, may wish to contact previous teachers with curriculum questions or suggestions. At some universities, instructors are encouraged to share online syllabi and/or lectures as examples, although instructors usually develop their own lectures. This helps to personalize them and infuse them with their own content expertise.

Online lectures need to be concisely written, since they are not mere transcripts of oral lectures. Drawing on text readings, work experience, and outside sources, the online instructor crafts a thought-provoking and polished piece based on the theories covered in the assigned readings. Further, online lectures may conclude with two or three well-placed discussion questions designed specifically to promote critical thinking and stimulate the week's discussion in the class forum.

Last, since Web addresses (or URLs) change frequently, a careful instructor always checks the URLs thoroughly before sending up a lecture that includes Web addresses. (The rationale for the use of URLs will be more thoroughly covered in the next section.)

## Copyrighted Online Materials

Instructors may be tempted to send full-text articles from newspapers or the Internet to their classes, particularly if they are accustomed to handing out copies of articles in traditional classrooms. However, the practice of sending full-text articles without permission from the publisher is legally prohibited except for rare instances.

When speaking at academic conferences, I encourage current and aspiring online instructors to share up-to-date and relevant materials by providing students with URLs instead of sending full-text articles to the online classrooms. This practice protects them and their universities from copyright issues.

Not only is the practice of providing URLs effective from a legal standing but it also encourages students to explore the Web. Students may be compelled to do further Web-crawling during or after looking up the cited articles, so the extra effort may prove helpful to their researching abilities.

As in regular classrooms, instructors may highlight and attribute short excerpts from published materials according to copyright laws. The 1997 booklet, *Questions and Answers on Copyright for the Campus Community*, by the Association of American Publishers, is an excellent resource for educators determining whether to cite a passage or refer students to URLs.

## Orderly Online Materials

Posting materials on set dates helps students get into the flow of an online course and program. If the university prescribes these dates, the students move forward in their programs without needing to readjust to each new instructor's timing. For example, students may learn to expect a weekly lecture, depending on what the university requires. Similarly, they may anticipate that certain assignments, such as weekly assignments, are due on certain dates from course to course.

Other materials, such as handouts, need to be clearly highlighted by the instructor for maximum clarity and usefulness. Besides highlighting these materials, instructors may use branch meetings or otherwise distinguish the readings for clarity's sake. Further, students should be clearly informed whether reading each handout is mandatory or discretionary. This will enable the students to focus, organize, and manage their time and will support their success as learners.

## THE ROLE OF THE ONLINE INSTRUCTOR IN STUDENT RETENTION

A student whose personal and professional life hit rough patches at about the same time felt depressed and generally pessimistic about her online studies. While she had been doing well and making solid progress toward obtaining a diploma within a year, she felt that her focus was scattered and that she should "stop out" for a few months before returning to the university. She mentioned this to the instructor from whom she had taken her first online class. The instructor, who had been honored in the past for her teaching skills and commitment, spoke for half an hour on the phone with the discouraged student. Actively listening to the student's story, she asked questions such as, "How would you know whether the time was right to return?" She also asked about the student's online cohort, whom she might miss at graduation if she walked across the stage at a later date.

Upon reflection, the student decided that she wanted a predictable goal in her life, something that at times brought a sense of mastery, so she returned to complete her program. When she met her instructor in person for the first time at graduation, they hugged each other, and the teacher, seeing the fierce pride and joy of the graduating student, felt a renewed determination to support other students in deciding whether to continue in their degree programs.

As mentioned earlier, online students may more easily feel isolated, since they are not getting the immediate feedback that their onsite counterparts enjoy. Instructors who help students to succeed are the best online teachers, particularly for teaching the first courses in each program. When students stumble, these instructors often reach out to encourage them and inspire them to continue with renewed confidence.

In my experience at UOP, online students who take a break during their programs, a phenomenon known as *stopping out,* may never return to achieve their educational objectives. That is why instructors who truly believe in education wish to help their students overcome obstacles to educational success and attain the goal they set out to achieve, which is an undergraduate or graduate degree from UOP.

Distance education traditionally poses a particular challenge to student retention. Researching why online students leave is even more difficult, since locating out-of-attendance students and then getting accurate answers about why they left are challenging obstacles to valid research on this topic. Yet, from my discussions and reading, the following factors appear to contribute to online attrition:

- Students leave because of isolation.
- Students leave because of the accelerated pace.
- Students leave because of competing responsibilities.
- Students leave because of technical issues.

## Isolation and Online Retention

When a student is alone at a terminal, no matter how many messages that student is seeing on the screen, he or she may still feel alone. Why? A student may find it more difficult to develop the same informal relationships in an online environment that arise onsite. However, mechanisms such as a student chat room and posting online biographies at the beginning of each class may help facilitate camaraderie and student bonding. Further, a student might miss seeing nonverbal communications from others. When a student feels stressed, he or she might pull back from the group more easily, since he or she will not "lose face" as openly as in an onsite classroom. This, in turn, may cause the sense of isolation to worsen.

The instructor should monitor all his or her students' participation and contact those who are not participating. Depending on the situation, a phone call may prove more timely and effective in reaching a student who appears to be nonresponsive to overtures from the instructor. Continued nonresponsiveness may demand that the instructor involve the university's staff, depending on the university's guidelines.

## Accelerated Pace and Online Retention

Many online programs model the University of Phoenix's accelerated learning pace so adult learners can earn a bachelor's or master's degree while continuing to work full time. When the pace is grueling, students may leave for what they think is a few months' break, and then lose the momentum to return to school. Since students report that life never seems to slow down, the accelerated pace of an online program may be far more challenging than they initially anticipated.

Burnout is also possible, depending on whether a student can cope with the demanding pace of reading texts, discussing online, researching, writing lengthy papers, and completing study group projects. Particularly when time management is a challenge, students may procrastinate, being to accumulate "incomplete" grades, and then feel overwhelmed at the prospect of making up the uncompleted coursework.

Sharing time-management skills in the class, along with setting the evaluative criteria, providing regular encouragement, and giving clear feedback about students' progress will help keep students encouraged through long nights of studying at a distance. Occasionally, I have found it helps to focus the student on the pride he or she will feel on the day of graduation, and then move the discussion to his or her "to do" lists and small accomplishments.

## Competing Responsibilities and Online Retention

Most students who choose an online program do so at least in part for the flexibility offered by a distance education program. Not having to be online at a specific time is attractive to busy working professionals. Some students, however, confuse flexibility with lack of rigor.

For whatever reason, it may be easy for a student to underestimate the commitment required to complete the challenging coursework of an accredited online program. This commitment often involves delaying gratification in other areas of life in order to succeed in the degree program. Turning on the computer after an exhausting day of work and family responsibilities may prove daunting, particularly if a student overestimated the time commitment involved in participating actively online as well as working on research papers and projects.

Even for students who knew what to expect when deciding to return to school, life might intervene and demand another analysis of school as a priority. For example, working adults are in the age range where they often face unanticipated work pressures (e.g., a downsizing or a promotion) as well as the dual demands of children and elderly parents. Any of these, particularly when a student is in an accelerated online program, may compete for attention with schoolwork and attainment of educational goals.

Students may consider withdrawing from a program due to feeling overwhelmed by work, home, or other responsibilities. Discussing with students the value of attaining their educational goals and helping them to prioritize will assist them in juggling their responsibilities while continuing to progress toward their educational objectives. Being flexible with deadlines is also an effective strategy. (For example, instructors often require that students must communicate with them before a deadline to arrange a postponement; those who do not do so are docked for lateness.)

## Technical Issues and Online Retention

Occasionally, students encounter technical issues related to hardware, software, and their levels of proficiency with either. If the students are relatively nontechnical, the mystery involved in solving technical issues may seem overwhelming. Students may become so annoyed at their inability to set up an Internet service provider (ISP) connection, for example, that they get discouraged and frustrated instead of reaching out for technical assistance.

An online student prevented from logging on to the classroom is comparable to a onsite student driving up to an educational facility to find the doors locked. Being unable to reach an online classroom, for whatever reason, rates as an emergency that must be resolved quickly.

In the online classroom, issues related to software or hardware will likely arise. User issues can often be resolved by the online instructor or by other students in the class. Other issues may involve calling technical staff at the university or the software vendor. In emergencies, instructors often help students obtain the appropriate technical support, which is essential to the students' retention and success. For example, if the online university has a help desk that serves students and instructors with technical questions, calling the line for a student may help him or her receive more prompt attention and thereby decrease the probability of the student leaving the program.

## CONCLUSION

Mastering the skills described in this chapter will bring online instructors the satisfaction of knowing that they can motivate, educate, and retain adult learners earning their university degrees through the online medium. With practice and commitment, they will be gratified to find that their efforts increasingly prove effective in producing the desired learning outcomes of the courses that they teach.

As educators expand and polish their teaching repertoires in the online medium, experienced online facilitators will help lead new instructors to adapt successfully to this flexible yet demanding and dynamic learning environment. As part of this adaptation, online instructors should build on the four areas of proficiency (visibility, feedback, materials, and retention) with fresh perspectives and innovative instructional strategies.

**REFERENCE**

Kauffman, R. (1996, Summer). Assessing the virtual university. *Adult Assessment Forum,* 13–16.

# CHAPTER 10

# THIRD GENERATION WEB SITES AND LEARNING

Writing for educators more than hardcore "techies," William B. Sanders carefully weaves together the importance of basic design principles and the features of current website development technology, with the contemporary learning theory espoused in previous chapters of this book. From analysis of the learning context, through fundamental decision considerations, to actual development of the site, this chapter addresses each issue thoroughly, yet succinctly.

Third generation websites have great potential for gaining the student's attention and maintaining engagement, and therefore achieving a wide variety of learning goals. By informing ourselves more fully on this key issue, we increase our chances to meet students when and where they are most available, retain and expedite them through their instructional programs, and achieve "win-win" long-range outcomes.

# THIRD GENERATION WEB SITES AND LEARNING

Chapter 3 from *Creating Learning-Centered Courses for the World Wide Web*
**William B. Sanders**
**Allyn & Bacon, © 2001**

This chapter examines design models for communicating over the Web. When all is said and done, the purpose of a Web page is to invite learning, and to do that, there must be good communication. For good communication to exist there must be good design. In the same way that an instructor must organize a presentation or lecture, a Web site must be designed to convey the information and engage the audience—the learner, a term that focuses on the centrality of who's getting the message. If it does not communicate, we cannot expect much learning to take place. The same is true for a poor classroom learning environment.

As we saw in Chapter 2, the basic learning environment we are creating is one that uses text, graphics, and links. This simple set is expanding rapidly into full-blown multimedia where sound, video, animation, and fuller interactivity are possible. However, by getting the text, graphics, and links right first, we establish a starting point from which to move into more sophisticated multimedia and improved learning environments.

## THE LEARNING CONTEXT

In thinking about creating a Web page, it must be envisioned in a learning context. As we saw in Chapter 1, the idea of distributed learning means that learning is going to occur in more places than just the classroom. The same is true with Web pages. Students will learn from the Web page, but that will be only one of the places that will be the source of learning. Clearly it can be a central locus of learning, but it may be a sidebar—a review session, extra help, or adjunct to the book or classroom presentation. Virtual realities, such as flight simulators, have been around for a long time. However, they are only part of the learning that pilots go through. There are classroom meetings, lots of books and readings, maps, flight computers, and actual flying. The flight simulator is only part of the overall design for learning to fly. Web pages must be considered in the same light. What role are they expected to play in the overall course design? In this section, we will consider some roles that a Web page may have, and some design features of a page.

## Adjunct to Reading

If a Web site is an adjunct to reading a book, the pages should do something that was not done, could not be done at all, or could not be done as well as on a printed page. For example, if the reading is about certain math problems, the Web page might be sample problems the students can solve and assess. A literature assignment in a book might be supplemented by Web pages that show maps and pictures depicting the time and place of the novel. However, if there are only to be textual comments the instructor wants students to read, a printed handout might do just as well if not better.

## Adjunct to Classroom or Lab Meeting

One thing that a Web page can do that cannot be done easily in a class or lab is to be available at all times. Often students just begin to get something in class, and then the hour is up and everyone is off, sometimes in the middle of a thought. Web pages with interactive elements or with email links to the professor can help out with key points that need further explanation or student involvement not available in class. Instructors need to think of what the Web site can add, if anything, to the classroom experience. This requires global consideration for the entire course as well as for individual classes. Review sessions are great on Web sites so that students can spend more time on them than in class. Pre-class Web site reviews generate questions to be asked and answered in class.

For faculty who have large classes, email links in Web pages, either through forms or through browser email, do a lot to help shy students. This is especially true for shy students in large classes. Attempting to respond to hundreds of emails each day can be daunting, but it helps students. Some faculty overcome having to send hundreds of individual emails by grouping answers to questions using LISTSERV® or some other distributed email list.

## Replacing a Classroom/Lab Meeting

The most thorough replacement demanded by Web pages is that of a traditional classroom or lab. Full distance learning occurs when electronic meetings replace all face-to-face meetings. If that is the goal, then a learning-centered approach is essential to the success of a Web-based design. As we discussed in Chapter 1, the instructors can improve their overall teaching effectiveness by taking a learning-centered approach. If a learning-centered approach is being used in the classroom, the change is a matter of transferring the learning-centered experiences from the classroom to the Web. In some cases this may be relatively easy, and in others extremely difficult or even impossible. Effective interactive Web-based biology labs have been created that simulate work in the lab. Students learn by going through the process that they would otherwise go through in an actual lab. Classroom designs involving high student-instructor interaction, immediate feedback, and abstract concept applications, on the other hand, may be more difficult. Replacing a talking head in a classroom by videotape, CD-ROM, or eventually streamed video over the Internet is very simple. However, learning is less likely to take place if a talking head in the classroom is replaced by a talking head on a Web page. Moreover, straight information that students passively receive can be handled better and more effectively with a printed page. The remainder of this chapter will present a model of a Web site to capture the essence of what best can be done with sites that fully replace the face-to-face meeting in a classroom. At the same time, it will be important to discuss design lessons, mostly applied to printed pages, which may be usefully incorporated in Web pages. This is not to suggest the student be a passive actor, but rather this chapter will explore connections between page design per se and page design on the Web.

## Light and Heavy Solutions

In bringing together design and technology, especially technology on the Web, *weight* is an important consideration. By "weight" I am referring to the amount of time it takes to create a page, the size and load time of the page, and the amount of software running in your computer's memory. This is important because while the computer used to develop lessons may be fast enough and big enough to handle everything you put in a Web lesson, the learner's may not be. This is especially true in considering bandwidth and the speed of Internet service. Educational institutions, especially colleges and universities, are likely to have T1 lines or faster. These lines may be running data in the megabit (millions of bits per second) range, while the home user receiving Web pages over a modem may be getting only kilobit speeds (thousands of bits per second).

You may have seen a dazzling page with wonderful animated graphics, lots of interaction, and full sound. Such pages are likely to have been the result of several thousand dollars in investment, sophisticated development tools and developers, talented designers, and months in planning and execution. These are very *heavy* pages. Besides taking up a lot of memory resources on your computer, they take up a lot of bandwidth. On the other hand, pages with gray backgrounds and nothing but text are relatively *light* in terms of everything from development time to the amount of memory they take up. Pages that have lots of graphics, animation, and other associated files take up more memory. These are very heavy pages. Besides taking up a lot of memory on your computer, they take up a lot of bandwidth on the Internet. On the other hand, pages with gray backgrounds and nothing but text are relatively light in terms of everything from the time it takes to create them to the time it takes to load them on your computer over the Internet.

With the development of new tools, more and more can be added. Web page designers must be cognizant of a page's weight. Therefore, in discussing design, weight is a constraint in the technological context.

## FUNDAMENTAL DESIGN CONSIDERATIONS

In 1997, David Siegel wrote *Creating Killer Web Sites: The Art of Third Generation Site Design.* At the time the book was published, the level of the design capability of HTML was relatively primitive, and by the book's second edition, Cascading Style Sheets were just becoming available. The third generation Web site is one that invites the viewer into the site with lures and metaphors. They are nonlinear and alluring. They should be attractive and interesting to get the viewer's attention. Siegel contrasted his concept with what he defined as first and second generation sites which were, at best, technologically interesting, but tended to be linear and based on simile rather than metaphor. Concepts built around similes treat Web sites *like* some other kind of communication device—such as a book or some other familiar communication source. However, a metaphor assumes that the Web site *is* a virtual representation of the metaphorical entity. For example, a cave may be a metaphor for a Web site that is to be explored. All of a cave's characteristics can be brought to bear and provide the same sense of exploration that a real cave would. (By the way, third generation design has nothing to do with the version of Web browser being used. One could use a Version 5 browser to create a first generation Web site.) What is important for Siegel and other designers is this:

> No matter how important and content rich your message, if no one is going to look at it, they're not going to get the message.

This message is especially important to those of us trying to generate a learning-rich environment on the Web. It's hard enough keeping a group of students in the same room interested in the class. How can we expect to do it on the Web unless we pay attention to designers who have spent a lot of time developing principles and techniques to get the viewer to do exactly that? We probably can't very well, and so we need to consider carefully what they have to say and use their wisdom where possible.

Another important designer is Edward Tufte from Yale University. In 1983, Tufte published a remarkable book entitled *The Visual Display of Quantitative Information.* This book took on the challenge of explaining how to best take rich and complex sets of data and display them in a manner that was clear. Using the history of design as a backdrop, Tufte examined and explained the nature of communicating quantitative multivariate relationships.

Tufte's insights, along with those of David Siegel and other designers, are employed in this chapter to provide the larger context of what it means to design a meaningful Web page.

## THE SINS ARE MANY AND VARIED

Sometimes avoiding doing wrong will better inform us of how to do it right. Siegel (1997) listed "Seven Deadly Sins" of Web page design, as did interface designer Jakob Nielsen (1998, 74). However, both Nielsen and Siegel went on to describe a good deal more than seven sins. Likewise, Tufte enumerated a number of design flaws that are relevant to Web and non-Web pages. Drawing on these and other designers, this section represents my own list of sins that I have found to most get in the way of good Web page design.

> **All Caps:** One of the best ways to call attention to one's design ineptness is to use all caps in the body text. Even headings with all caps can be difficult to read, and there are better ways to bring headings to the attention of the reader. It's best to avoid all caps until your design skills are high. Good designers know how to use all caps effectively, but they tend to use them sparingly as well.

> **Interference from Background Graphics:** One of the fun additions to Web pages was the background graphic. Unfortunately, many who created Web pages felt obliged to include cluttered designs in their background, making it very difficult to read the text. Edward Tufte (1997, 74) talks of "chartjunk" as unnecessary graphics that get in the way of the message being delivered, and bad backgrounds certainly qualify as "chartjunk." Often one will see backgrounds causing a moiré effect—a vibration to the eye. Other times the background will effectively camouflage whatever message or other graphics are on the page. Careful use of certain backgrounds can enhance a page's appearance, but for the most part I avoid using them altogether.

> **The Long Load:** For a Web page designer, the greatest fear is that her page will be ignored. If the page is a long time in loading, the user might hit the back button and zip off to the next page that requires a short attention span. For designing learning pages, the threat is not quite as great, but a long load time for a Web page means that it is taking up a lot of memory. By taking memory size into account, using tricks to reduce file size, and remembering that added material can be placed on another page, good and rich designs are possible without a long load.

> **Dancing Baloney:** In an early version of HTML, the <BLINK> tag was introduced, causing text to blink incessantly. (This too can be classified as "chartjunk.") It was used to draw the viewer's attention to some

aspect of the page, but its major achievement was distracting the viewer. Since then, animated GIFs and other forms of "dancing baloney" have found homes on Web pages with a similarly distracting characteristic. There are very few applications where the same jumping or blinking item on a page serves much purpose after the initial blink or bounce. Slowly moving objects and gradual changes are far more effective and less distracting.

**The Long, Long Page:** How long should a page be? Loading up a long page with lots of text invites the user to print out the page. Loading up a long page with lots of text, graphics, and other heavy extras invites the user to leave and jog around the block while the page gets squared away. It's better to concentrate on a good system of navigation than to have the seemingly endless scroll.

**Broken and Missing Links and Graphics:** Jakob Nielsen suggests hiring a "Web gardener" to keep outdated information off your page. The same gardener needs to keep a page's links current as well. In creating learning pages, instructors need to keep checking to be sure that a valuable educational link is still around when the new term begins. The target page may be long gone and the same or newer information is elsewhere. Sometimes graphics become corrupted on a server and need to be replaced so that they'll load as well.

**No Real Paragraphs:** David Siegel went to great lengths to lambaste those who did not use indented paragraphs on their Web pages. With CSS, this is not a difficult matter, but many page designers use either big blank lines or (worse) horizontal rules to separate paragraphs. The nonbreaking space [ ] should be used, even if it requires hand coding to create a proper indent. Using indents for paragraphs not only gives the page a better flow and unity; it follows good rules of punctuation.

**Random Style:** In designing a Web site, remember that a consistent style is a unifying force. Imagine reading a book with different typefaces and spacing for every page. Quickly, the attention would be drawn from the content to the design. Even a relatively bad design that is consistent is better than several different designs that keep pulling the viewer's attention away from the content.

**Clutter:** Edward Tufte (1990, 53) noted that "Confusion and clutter are failures of design, not attributes of information." As a designer's knowledge of Web page capability increases, she often adds all the new technology she can on a page. The content is smothered in a train wreck of techno-pieces happily added by the Web page designer. It is reminiscent of the early days of desktop publishing. The desktop publisher, in a rush to use *all* of her new fonts, ended up with a page that looked like a ransom note. A clear page does a better job.

## DEVELOPING THE THIRD GENERATION
## LEARNING SITE

In discussing third generation sites, the concept is one that emphasizes designs that are engaging, active, interesting, and well ordered. Third generation design is not a technological development so much as taking the technology and applying good design principles to it. Wedding learning-centered educational practices to a third generation concept is a dynamic one meant to be a starting point and a point of reference. The concept is offered as a guide and not a straitjacket.

In the remainder of this chapter, I provide one of David Siegel's third generation models and transform that into a learning-centered model. Then I want to show some examples of how that model was actually applied. There are many parts to the process, and one of the most important is working with others who have talents and skills that educators may not. Most important of those skills include those of basic artistic design and the technology of page development. In working with my own pages and helping faculty work on their pages, the concentration needed to be on the content and ways that content could communicate in a pedagogically sound manner. On the following pages is the tip of the developmental iceberg.

### The Basic Model

Beginning with the idea of a "core page" replacing a "home page" Siegel argues that the viewer needs to be provided a clear and intuitive yet alluring experience. Rather than beginning with a "home page" up front, the viewer begins with an "entry page" that gives a quick look at what's available and invites her to see more. The entry page is bait to attract the viewer to look beyond the entry. An "entry tunnel" pulls the viewer into the site, providing more information as she enters the tunnel. Once "inside," the viewer encounters the "core page," a menu and map that reveal and guide the viewer. Throughout, there are clearly marked exits and guidance back to the core page. Likewise, clear guideposts show the way to the exit, and like the entrance tunnel, an exit tunnel escorts the viewer out of the site.

### THE THIRD GENERATION LEARNING SITE

Adopting Siegel's model to a learning-centered one is relatively straightforward. However, instead of beginning within the site, the starting point is the *syllabus.* In one sense the syllabus is the core of the course, but in the model presented next, the syllabus is more of a launching pad—perhaps an index. Each lesson constitutes a third generation site, and so the *lesson* is the focal point.

**Entry:** Entry to the lesson is from the syllabus. The *entry page* is one that tells the student what the lesson is about. It begins with something interesting and appealing, and gives the student a hook of interest. Following the entry page are two *entry tunnel pages.* The first page lays out the lesson's *objectives.* This page tells the student what she can expect to get from the site. Second is a *pre-test or pre-assessment page.* A lot can be done with this page. It can be treated as a challenge, an impetus of interest, or simply a set of questions that will alert the viewer to what he can expect to learn.

**Core:** The *core page* is something like a mini-syllabus. It shows the student the title of all of the pages so that she knows where the lesson is headed. This is where contextual material needs to be included to set the stage for the entire lesson. Depending on the topic and nature of the material, linear or nonlinear courses can be charted. To some extent most material is linear, either developmentally or due to the necessity of having a sequence of topics to cover in a limited time period. However, a page within the linear series can and should have many nonlinear features.

**Exit:** The *exit tunnel* is made up of a review of key concepts and a quiz prior to the exit page itself. The *key concept* page is an opportunity for the student to review the essential concepts presented in the lesson. Next a *quiz page* gives the student immediate feedback to how well he understood the materials. Finally, the *exit page* offers a return to the core page or syllabus. It also is a good place to include recommended reading or off-site links for a student interested in further exploring the topic.

Permeating the site are good practices for learning-centered understanding. The design lends itself to incorporating these practices. Figure 3.1 shows one way to design a learning site using third generation design.

## SYLLABUS AND COURSE CONTENT

### Deciding on Content and Creating a Syllabus

This first step in developing a course is deciding on what content should be included. This is no different from deciding what material would be covered in a traditional course. The scheduling of content along with all assignments are put into a syllabus. Because the course material is online, the first Web page to be developed is an online syllabus. If the course meets in a classroom as well, the online syllabus serves as a resource for updating a syllabus, adding material, and alerting students to exams or due dates for events occurring in the classroom. An online course syllabus template should have all the materials a traditional syllabus does as well as email and URL links. For example, a faculty member may want to have an email link to herself, links

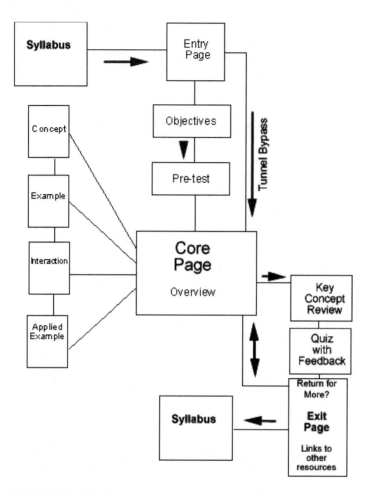

**FIGURE 3.1    Third generation site developed for lessons in a course.**

to online discussion groups, and links to individual students or groups of students on a syllabus. Good navigation is essential to an online syllabus because the students will be using it often. It should be easy to update so the faculty member can add reminders, extra-credit assignments, or study guides to the syllabus. Figure 3.2 shows a syllabus with navigation and several links for increasing class communication.

## Preparing Content for Transfer to Web Pages

To help faculty organize the content into the format of the Web site, a word processor template was developed. Faculty can follow the template so that

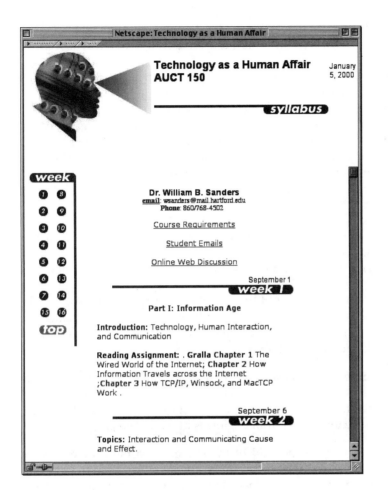

FIGURE 3.2    A good online syllabus provides more ways
for students and faculty to engage one another.

each element of the lesson design is incorporated. Reminders of what should
be included are built into the form. Faculty write the content and describe
graphics, links, and any other instructions in arrowhead < > brackets. All
phases of the course are discussed with the student assistant (if available) at
different stages to ensure the pages meet faculty standards.

TEMPLATE WORD PROCESSOR FORM

1. **Entrance Page:** Tell something interesting about material. Including a
   graphic is a good idea.
2. **Objectives:** List what student is expected to learn, understand, appreciate, and accomplish.

3. **Pre-Test:** Pose several questions to let student determine how much he understands. If interesting questions are posed, student will want to learn more.
4. **Core with Overview:** Provide a thesis paragraph or two to set the stage for what will come.
5. **Lesson Pages:** This is where the content goes.
   - Page 1 <Describe graphics between pointed brackets> E.g. <Create a collage of text and graphics that show different political beliefs—maybe a donkey and an elephant with words like Liberal and Conservative and issues such as taxes, abortion, education.> Text content follows....
   - Page 2
   - Page 3
   - Etc.
6. **Review Key Concepts:** List all of the key concepts, ideas, and major points in lesson.
7. **Assessment:** Provide an online self-grading quiz based on material in lesson.
8. **Exit Page:** This page should be a gracious exit with appropriate links back to the core page in case the students want to review materials. This also is a good place to include links to other interesting or related sites, books, articles, or other references.

**Schedule.**   During the initial stages of preparing materials for the Web, the faculty and student assistant need to meet and work out a schedule. Without experience, initial trial and error helps to get an idea of what it takes to get the content into the forms and from the forms into the Web pages.

**Training.**   Depending on the skill of the student assistant, there may be need for training in working with various software tools and Web page languages. Faculty may also want to learn to work with the graphic and page-design software and languages for better understanding of what can be done with the software and hardware.

**On Your Own.**   Many faculty will be on their own with no help from student assistants. In this case, it is even more important to get a template, a faculty-development schedule, and the organization to get everything where it belongs in a timely manner. For wholly online courses, all of this needs to be worked out ahead of time because getting a complex lesson together at the last minute and winging it is not much of an option.

## CREATING LESSONS

### Preparing Content for Web Pages

With a standard Web Site Template, the student assistant's job is much simplified. The student assistant knows what to look for, what to expect, and what needs to be done. Since the faculty member provides the content in a word-processed format, the student's main job is taking the material from the word processor and transferring it to the pages. The entry page requires a graphic along with a little textual material to interest the student in the lesson. The graphic here is important because it provides a visual context for the entire lesson. Experimentation has shown that the entry page graphic repeated on the core page provides a good link from the introduction to the heart of the lesson. Figure 3.3 shows a typical entry page.

## Consistent Elements

In setting up pages, consistent elements aid in navigation and communication. In the example, a green right-pointing arrow indicated a link to the next page and black right-pointing arrows indicated links to other forward pages. Left-pointing arrows linked to the previous pages, an "X" marked the current page relative to the other pages in the lesson, and a special core page button linked to the core page. (They were intuitive enough so that no students asked for instructions on how to use them.) By placing identical sets of navigation buttons at the top and bottom of the lesson pages, navigation was convenient as well. Figures 3.4 and 3.5 show two entry tunnel pages with objectives and a pre-test. Note the little arrow in the lower left of the page for one-way navigation through the tunnel.

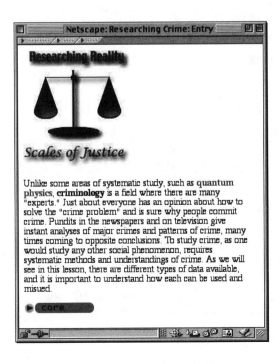

FIGURE 3.3   An entry page should have something that will pique the student's interest. The "core" page icon is a jump around the entry tunnel.

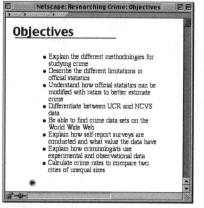

FIGURE 3.4  Objectives are part of the entry tunnel.

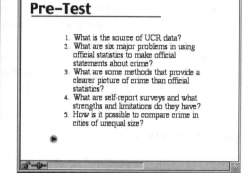

FIGURE 3.5  Pre-test questions can pique students' interest.

## CORE PAGE

The core page sets the context for general navigation because it provides an overview of what is in store for the viewer. From the core page, students can go to any place in the lesson except back through the entry tunnel. Figure 3.6

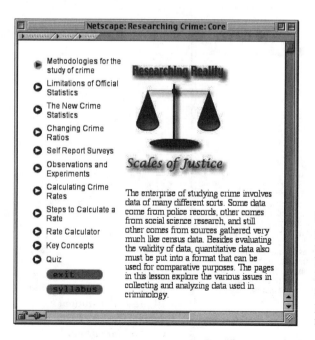

FIGURE 3.6  The core page is a center from which students can see both the sequence of the lesson and yet have the ability to jump to any part they may want to review.

shows a sample core page that provides links to the lesson, to the exit, or even back to the syllabus—just in case they got the wrong lesson.

## LESSON PAGES

### General Page Elements

Most pages consist of text, the navigation buttons, and a graphic relating to the text. These pages can be very much like a book page except that the navigation system is nonlinear. It is very important that a simple, effective, and clear navigation system be used consistently throughout the lesson and the course. Haphazard or inconsistent navigation can be confusing and wastes time.

## INTERACTIVE PAGES

Some pages require the student to provide feedback to the professor using email links or email forms. Feedback can also be built-in using JavaScript or links to feedback pages. This may be done over several pages or on a single page. Figures 3.7 and 3.8 show a set of pages that first shows a student how to accomplish a task and then sends the student off to gather information and perform the task himself.

**Test Pages.**    Each lesson has self-scoring quizzes in the exit tunnel once the lesson is completed. Faculty members provide quiz questions and answers, and the student assistant creates JavaScript quizzes using software designed specifically for generating short-answer and multiple-choice questions. Faculty or student assistants would most likely use a program such as *Dreamweaver*

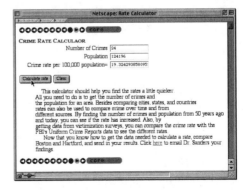

FIGURE 3.7   Links on pages provide students with sources of data.

FIGURE 3.8   Web pages with forms can be used as ways to actively involve students.

*Attain* so that all he would have to do is provide questions and answer selections. After completing the test, students are scored and given the list of incorrect answers.

**Projects.**   Interactive projects can be handled using either email or email forms. Figure 3.7 provides the student with several links to look up information that would be calculated into a rate. The results would then be emailed to the professor.

**Forms for Pages.**   Another way of communicating directly with students is through email forms. Essentially, the student writes the requested information in a form, then clicks a **Submit** button that sends the data to the instructor. This method can be used to direct the student to a number of more structured interactions. Using forms allows a closer connection between the task and the student's behavior. However, in creating forms, care is necessary with the coding of the HTML. Sometimes there is cross-browser incompatibility. Specifically, Netscape Navigator and Microsoft Internet Explorer sometimes behave differently with forms.

## EXIT TUNNEL

At the end of the lesson, rather than drop the student off when the last content has been presented, several pages ease the student into several options and a review of what has passed. First, a simple listing of key concepts gives the learner a quick overview of what major points were made in the lesson. This is a simple and short page that can be reviewed in a glance. Figure 3.9 shows a Web page that begins the exit tunnel with a set of key concepts.

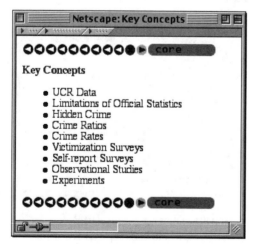

FIGURE 3.9   An exit tunnel should have a review of the key concepts the lesson covered.

There are opportunities in the exit tunnel to bring in many different pages that help the learner better understand the content. For example, the instructor may wish to have pages that ask the student to apply what he has learned, solve a problem with the knowledge, or take a simple quiz. Whatever the option, though, this site design concept discourages ending when the last page of content has been offered.

## Self-Assessment

One of the important principles of learning-centered education is prompt feedback. One way to achieve that feedback is through self-assessments. Figure 3.10 shows a typical online quiz students use to receive immediate feedback. A combination of multiple-choice and short-answer quizzes are self-scored by a quiz program written in JavaScript. Faculty simply enters their questions and answers and the quiz-making program does the rest.

**Professor Feedback.**   Another type of assessment may involve the instructor responding to a student email. This helps ensure the student has covered the material and understands it and provides the instructor a chance to respond directly to the student. A good deal of clarification, explanation, and instruction takes place when professors deal directly with student queries through email.

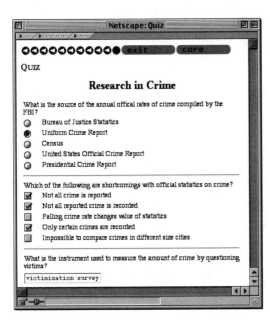

FIGURE 3.10   Online quizzes provide immediate feedback to students.

**Exit Page.** The exit page serves as a capstone for an online lesson and should not be overlooked. It provides both a way back and a way out for the student. Also, the professor can use it for links to other sites or paper references the student may need to review. Figure 3.11 is a typical exit page.

## SUMMARY AND REVIEW

The most important lesson to take from this chapter is to learn something about design. If possible, use the services of a good designer. In my own experience, I hired a student with design skills and no Web technology skills at all. In a short period of time, he mastered the tools needed to create Web pages and enough HTML and JavaScript to make first-rate pages. If you cannot hire someone with designing skills, at a bare minimum, avoid the most glaring design sins. Half the battle is avoiding ugly and distracting Web pages. Better yet, read some books on design, especially those that discuss the connection between design and communication. Edward Tufte and David Siegel have excellent works cited in this chapter. Again, both are highly recommended. Another book that bears a recommendation for those who have never read a design book is *The Non-Designer's Web Book: An Easy Guide to Creating, Designing, and Posting Your Own Web Site* by Robin Williams and John Tollett.

Because learning is about paying attention, and design is about getting attention, the connection between learning and design is fundamental. This

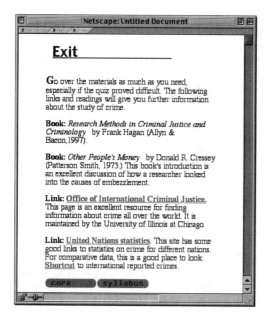

FIGURE 3.11 The exit page provides a last opportunity to provide links and references as well as a way out of the site.

is especially true when there is no face-to-face contact between instructor and student as is the case with full distance learning. The idea behind a third generation Web site is to gain the viewer's attention and keep it. Learning basic concepts and many of the facts and figures needed to understand a course requires the learner to pay attention to what is on the Web page. Encouraging and enhancing that attention by engaging the viewer goes far to achieve the learning goal. Ignoring design altogether is both naive and counterproductive. Transferring the third generation Web site concepts to learning is a means of easing the work of creating lessons on the Web and encouraging learning there.

## GLOSSARY OF TERMS

*Core page*    Different from a home page, a core page is a true overview of a Web site. It puts the viewer into a position where she can see the site, its logic, and its context.

*Entry page*    The entry page in a Web site is an invitation to a viewer to enter the site. Often with little content and a lot of enticement, the entry page tweaks the viewer's interest.

*Entry tunnel*    As an enticement to enter a Web site, third generation sites often employ a series of Web pages to lure the viewer into the site.

*Exit page*    The last page in a third generation site provides an exit for the viewer along with an opportunity to return to the site. It is the door out of the site.

*Exit tunnel*    As an aid to navigation, a clear exit, and an opportunity for the viewer to review a Web site, the exit tunnel guides a viewer through a series of pages that escort him out of a site.

*Third generation Web site*    Web sites that employ nonlinear design and metaphor in their creation. Use of intuitive navigation and a core allow users to easily explore this kind of site.

## REFERENCES

Nielsen, Jakob. "Seven Deadly Sins of Web Design." *Technology Review* (Cambridge, MA: MIT Press, September/October 1998), p. 74.

Siegel, David. *Creating Killer Web Sites: The Art of Third Generation Site Design* 2nd ed. (Indianapolis, IN: Hayden Books, 1997).

Tufte, Edward. *The Visual Display of Quantitative Information* (Graphics Press: Cheshire, CT: 1983).

Tufte, Edward. *Envisioning Information* (Graphics Press: Cheshire, CT: 1990).

Tufte, Edward. *Visual Explanations* (Graphics Press: Cheshire, CT: 1997).

Williams, Robin and John Tollett. *The Non-Designer's Web Book: An Easy Guide to Creating, Designing, and Posting Your Own Web Site* (Berkeley, CA: Peachpit Press, 1997).

# CHAPTER 11

# QUESTIONS WRITERS ASK

Following his very well written foundational chapters on writing for publication, Kenneth T. Henson provides this highly useful opportunity to have many of our most frequent questions answered. From the volatile issue of simultaneous submission of articles to multiple publications, to the nuances of collaborating, this chapter conveys the grounded wisdom accumulated by this author of twenty books and two hundred published articles.

Among the most valuable of insights provided, Henson addresses how to deal with the rejection experienced by so many writers. Dr. Henson's response draws upon his experiences, as well as those of the editor of a periodical and another writer, providing perspective that would otherwise be extremely difficult for the reader to access.

# QUESTIONS WRITERS ASK

**Chapter 9 from** *Writing for Professional Publication*
**Kenneth T. Henson**
**Allyn & Bacon,** © **1999**

All beginning writers can be put into two categories: those who ask questions and those who want to ask questions, if only they were brave enough to do so. All writers—beginners and experienced writers alike—have questions to ask. *Successful writers are bold.* This does not imply that they are pompous, arrogant, or egotistical. Boldness in successful writers means that they are confident, determined, and persistent. Those who ask questions are likely to grow much faster than those who have questions to ask, but wait, hoping that someone else will ask their questions for them.

In previous chapters we have addressed some of the most frequently asked questions: How do you find the time to write? What tools do writers use? Should I use query letters? When is the best time to write? Where is the best place to write? and How do you identify topics? In this chapter, I will ask—and answer—some of the remaining questions you may have.

## WHY DO YOU WRITE?

All writers have their own reasons for writing. Many successful writers offer two reasons for writing. First, they are compelled to write. Apart from any tangible benefits—and far more important—they have a personal need to write. A psychology professor and practicing psychologist told the following story to impress on his students the importance of an individual's perceptions and the way these perceptions determine the individual's world.

> I walked into the private ward of the hospital to see a patient. Mr. Jones was screaming at the top of his lungs. I asked him what was wrong.
> He shouted, "They're killing me! They're killing me!"
> I said, "Mr. Jones, who's killing you?"
> "Those little devils on my chest! They're stabbing me with pitch forks! Can't you see them?"
> I responded, "No, but I can see that they are hurting you."

As workshop participants talk about their reasons for writing, sometimes their reasons sound so bizarre that they are almost unbelievable; then I remember the patient and the pitch forks. To him the devils were real. *People have different reasons for writing, and they have a right to these reasons—whatever they are.* Some people write only because their job requires them to publish; these people may never understand how others could ever feel compelled to write. The fact remains that this compulsion is the major force that motivates many people to write.

Most successful writers also say that they write because they immensely enjoy writing. Given the choice between writing or watching television or going to a movie, they will take writing every time. Perhaps it's a combination of creating something, completing a task, and knowing that someday it will be read by others.

Recently, I was attending a workshop conducted by Kurt Vonnegut, and someone asked him: Why do you write? Vonnegut answered that there is only one justifiable reason to write. He said that some people have a burning desire to be published, and, although this is getting close, this is not an acceptable reason for writing. Vonnegut said the only justifiable reason for writing is because you have something that is so compelling that it must be said. Certainly, such passion provides the internal motivation that writers must have to hone their manuscripts while honing their writing skills.

## WHAT SUGGESTIONS CAN YOU GIVE TO ASPIRING WRITERS?

First, write. If you want to become a *successful* writer you must become a *good* writer. The best way to do this is to write. Write often and much. Make mistakes. Don't worry about it. First, get your ideas on paper. That's what counts. Then edit your work, and rewrite it. Set some goals; then set yourself a schedule. Give your goals some deadlines. Then watch your writing activities move forward.

Second, if for some reason you forget or choose to ignore all that you have read in this book, remember this one thing: you can succeed as a writer *only* if you think you can. I have yet to hear anyone say that for years they have really tried to learn how to write well but have failed to reach any of their writing goals, but I do receive many letters containing passages like this one:

> I can't believe it. Once I finally took that first bold step and learned a few basic techniques, then I learned how easy it really is. I've had an article accepted in that journal that I always wanted to have publish my material. Not only have I had one article published in it, I've since had others accepted and it's easy.

One way to learn the basics and then continue to expand your ability is to attend writing workshops. Appendix K contains detailed information about workshops.

## HAVE YOU A FAVORITE SUCCESS STORY?

Yes. My favorite story happened to a friend. It's full of coincidences. In fact, it has all the earmarks of a fisherman's lie; I can understand if you don't believe it.

I walked into a trophy store in a large mall. There on display was a desktop nameplate with the name of an old army buddy. Let's call him Rey (Wayne) Washam. It is such an unusual name that I decided to check the phone directory to verify my discovery. I found the number and dialed it. For the first time in 25 years, I heard my friend's voice. I asked him to have lunch with me at a local club. We set a date. As I drove up to the club, I noticed that my friend (who hails from a background that rivals my own for being humble and unknown) stepped out of a new limousine. As we ate, we reminisced about our experiences as enlisted men in Uncle Sam's army. Wayne was the outdoors person who actually enjoyed bivouacking and sleeping on the ground, eating K-rations, and, in short, roughing it. In school Wayne was never considered a star pupil. By his own admission, he was lucky to get through freshman English composition. Although he did well in his major (wildlife), his writing skills were so limited that he had to repeat freshman composition. Twice!

As we ate, Wayne told me that he was sitting at home one day bored because the rain was keeping him inside. To cope with his boredom, he decided to write an article to share some of his personal experiences in the out-of-doors. He modeled his article after those in a leading national wildlife journal. To his utter amazement, the journal accepted his article, and with his letter of acceptance he received a substantial check. This whetted his appetite; so he wrote a second article, then a third, and fourth. In summary, this person who, in his own words, was lucky to ever pass freshman composition wrote a string of 15 articles for wildlife magazines—and, with the acceptance of the 15 articles, he had never received a rejection!

Equally amazing, Wayne began to write books, experiencing the same degree of success. He disclosed that he had just signed a contract for his eleventh book, a cookbook for campers, for which he received an advance of $85,000. He and his wife had been conducting writing workshops, but even for an enormous fee he could no longer afford to take time from his writing to conduct the workshops. With their writing and workshop earnings, Wayne and his wife had purchased their own publishing company and two hunting and fishing lodges. They had recently bought a summer house in Montana and a winter house in Georgia.

Several lessons can be learned from the experiences of this writer. Even with his bleak school record, Wayne was able to succeed; nevertheless, Wayne would be the first to agree that better composition skills would have made his writing much easier. What contributed most to his success? Wayne loved the out-of-doors. Since childhood, he nurtured a passion for hunting, fishing, and trapping. As he grew older, this passion gradually shifted from killing animals to preservation and conservation. He even took a job as a wildlife ranger on a national game reserve, a job which he loved from the first moment and grew to love even more.

Wayne was fortunate in that he was a modest person who was able to see his weaknesses and even admit them to others. He explained that he was astonished by the acceptance of his articles. "I just wrote about what I enjoyed doing. My articles were nonfiction, focusing on my own experiences." *A key to success for many writers is writing about a subject for which they care passionately.*

## HOW DO YOU HANDLE REJECTION?

As an experienced writer and teacher of writing, I always want to respond to this question with fatherly advice and say something like, "I view rejections as evidence of growth." But to the novice, such fatherly advice may sound like "Eat your spinach; it's good for you." Well, as many parents will attest, spinach is good for you—but only if it doesn't cause you to throw up. Similarly, getting rejections may be good for you, but only if they don't cause you to give up. Greg Daugherty, editor of *Money* magazine (1996, p. 28), says that if you haven't been rejected lately, it may mean "you simply aren't trying hard enough."

Perhaps a better response is that *all successful authors get rejections.* Successful writers grow as a result of rejections because they learn from experience. Some aggressive novices ask the editors for advice. They ask the editors of referred journals for copies of the reviewers' evaluations of their manuscript. With this feedback in hand, rejections can become painful blessings.

Perhaps the best advice for dealing with rejections is to *study the rejections immediately, make the necessary improvements, and promptly send the manuscript to another publisher.* If no feedback is received, either ask for it, or quickly examine your returned manuscript for editorial marks. Then make the needed corrections, put the manuscript and a self-addressed stamped envelope in an envelope, and send it to another publisher. Remember, *sometimes the reasons behind rejections are unrelated to the quality of the manuscript.*

There are two reasons for handling rejections hastily. If you leave the rejection on your desk, you will dwell on it—even if only in your subconscious—and it seems to grow. Second, by promptly sending the manuscript out again, you decrease the time between acceptances, and this increases your number of publications. If your manuscript has any value at all, there is likely to be some correlation between your number of acceptances and the time that your manuscript spends on an editor's desk.

After twenty years of writing, I still get rejections, and each one has a little sting. But each rejection brings a smile as I think, "That's O.K. I've been rejected before, and I can take pride in knowing that I've been rejected by the very best."

Experienced authors know that some of their time is better spent planning to avoid rejections. Jesus Garcia uses an approach that is both preventive and objective. He has worked out a method to reduce rejections and a method to deal with rejections objectively.

> Rejection should not be the most difficult part of writing, but it is. I suspect potential authors do not write for publication because they do not wish to deal with rejection. I learned early in my writing career that I would need to develop my own mechanism for addressing rejection. After a few rejections, I sat down and developed a process.
>
> **First,** I always attempt to develop quality manuscripts. Usually, when I have a manuscript rejected, it is not because it is poorly written or poorly put together. Nor is it because my idea was not well thought out.
>
> **Second,** I target the manuscript for at least two journals. If one rejects it, I send it to the other.
>
> **Third,** when I receive a rejection I read the cover letter and file the manuscript for a week.
>
> **Fourth,** after the hurt has subsided, I return to the manuscript and read the cover letter and the constructive criticism provided on a rating sheet or on the manuscript. (If no constructive comments are provided, I send the manuscript to the second journal).
>
> **Fifth,** when constructive criticism is provided, I weigh the comments and make those changes I feel are warranted. I then send the manuscript to the second journal.
>
> Individuals wishing to write for publication should not copy my approach but develop a mechanism that is reflective of their own personalities.

Garcia's effort to develop a quality manuscript before sending it to an editor saves time and disappointment. His process of carefully scrutinizing and using criticisms to improve the manuscript is wise. This may be difficult when readers are unkind, but remember that, left unchanged, the manuscript might affect others in equally negative ways. Garcia's concluding advice is the voice of experience, individual authors must develop their own systems for dealing with rejection.

## WHAT DISTINGUISHES HIGHLY SUCCESSFUL WRITERS FROM LESS SUCCESSFUL WRITERS?

Apart from their degree of commitment to learning the basics of good writing and applying them with diligence, *highly successful writers usually have several projects going simultaneously.* At any time, highly successful writers have a couple of investigations under way, two or more manuscripts partially completed, and several manuscripts being considered by editors. In contrast, the novice writer often uses a linear approach to writing, writing one draft, then correcting and revising the draft, then polishing it, then sending a query letter, then waiting for a response, then sending the manuscript, and then waiting for months or years for a response. For this type of writer, the highest success rate possible is one or two acceptances a year.

## IS IT O.K. TO SEND A MANUSCRIPT TO MULTIPLE PUBLISHERS?

Simultaneous submission of article manuscripts to multiple publishers is nothing short of Russian roulette. The desperate writer who plays this game never considers the possible adverse consequences. Put simply, multiple submissions can produce multiple acceptances. Then, the writer must decide which journal to reject. Editors like rejections even less than writers do—for editors invest not only their own time but also their reviewers' time evaluating manuscripts. Editors also plan issues so that manuscripts complement each other. When one of these manuscripts is abruptly withdrawn, a unique piece of the jigsaw puzzle is missing. Because most journals operate on a tight schedule and may operate behind schedule, there simply isn't time to locate a satisfactory replacement for a withdrawn manuscript.

Despite the problems created, multiple submissions is a frequent occurrence. It has caused such a problem that some publishers and societies have written codes forbidding this practice. For example, the American Sociological Society has a written policy published in its journals to remedy the situation (see Figure 9.1).

An author who refuses to let a publisher print an accepted manuscript should be prepared to have this door of opportunity closed in the future, and no serious writers can afford to shut out any possible markets for their manuscripts. The alternative is even worse; allowing different publishers to publish the same manuscript would be professional suicide. The bottom line for writers is: *don't make simultaneous submissions to journals.*

This advice applies to journal manuscripts only. For books, multiple submissions are acceptable and they are recommended but only when used according to the process described in Chapter 10.

**FIGURE 9.1    Statement of ASA policy on multiple submission.**

Submission of manuscripts to a professional journal clearly implies commitment to publish in that journal. The competition for journal space requires a great deal of time and effort on the part of editorial readers whose main compensation for this service is the opportunity to read papers prior to publication and the gratification associated with discharge of professional obligations. For these reasons the ASA regards submission of a manuscript to a professional journal while that paper is under review by another journal as unacceptable.

Section 11, B4, ASA Code of Ethics

## ARE THERE ADVANTAGES IN COLLABORATING?

If you find the right partner, collaborating can offer several advantages. *The most important quality to seek in a partnership is similar personality.* For example, if you have a Type-A personality and feel compelled to get your work done on time, you should never work with a Type-B who thinks a deadline is the sign that it's time to start working on the job. Such an arrangement is equally painful for both partners.

When personalities are compatible, collaborating can bring out the best in all. Each partner stimulates the other. The unique expertise of each writer complements that of the others. For academicians who are required to publish, collaborating can accelerate the rate of publishing of all partners. But, even under the best of circumstances, all writers should go solo part of the time; otherwise, they become vulnerable to the criticism that they let others write for them. A few articles of your own can nullify such a charge.

Should you decide to collaborate, you will need to produce a product that is consistent and coherent. A good method to achieve these goals is to have each collaborator edit the entire manuscript. Each edit will remove some incoherence and inconsistency.

I asked Tom Good if he would share some of his insights on collaborating. Here is his response:

> I have had the pleasure of publishing a lot of my work with coauthors. This experience, although sometimes awkward (why must my coauthor be in Tibet or at the condo when page proofs arrive?) has provided an important context for learning. Differences of opinion (theoretical values; what constitutes a good example; what represents valid evidence) have to be seriously confronted and negotiated successfully. Hence, issues one might "conveniently avoid" become opportunities for new learning. For example, I have learned much about Piagetian theory from Jere Brophy, my long-time coauthor who teaches at Michigan State University, and I have learned much about socially situated learning and Vygotskian theory from Mary McCaslin, who teaches at Arizona University.

## SHOULD I COLLABORATE LONG DISTANCE?

Some special advantages and limitations can be realized when authors collaborate over long distances. Perhaps the limitations are more obvious. For example, there is the delay in sending manuscripts through the mail. Facsimile machines and electronic mail are improving these conditions and making long distance collaboration more feasible. But in some fashion collaborators should read, edit, and rewrite their partners' work. Otherwise, the manuscript is likely to lack a uniform tone and consistent style.

A second limitation of collaborating long distance is the increased likelihood of miscommunication. As an author who has collaborated long distance on about a dozen books, I will share an example of this limitation. On one of my book projects, one of the coauthors wrote a chapter and sent it to the others as a model. Receiving the chapter, one of the authors took great care to ensure that his drafted chapters had the same pedagogical subheadings. Later, when we met to go over their chapters, the coauthor who sent the sample chapter explained that the subheadings were optional and perhaps should differ according to content. His purpose for sending the sample chapter had been to show the other authors the length that his chapter set for certain parts—a feature that some authors had not thought important.

But, with care, these difficulties can be handled. An advantage of collaborating long distance is that it brings to the work a broader range of perspectives, which improves the product and allows each collaborator to develop awareness and insight that can only be gained through long-distance collaboration. Whether the advantages outweigh the disadvantages depends on the collaborators, their differences in expertise, and the topic of the book. A look at the number of textbook authors who collaborate over a long distance is testimony that for many the process does work, and for many it works extremely well.

## SHOULD I WRITE ARTICLES BEFORE WRITING SHORT STORIES OR BOOKS?

The best answer to this question is probably "yes." Article writing is excellent preparation for writing nonfiction books, and writing short stories is good preparation for writing fiction books. Article writing provides the opportunity to develop important writing skills. For those who wish to strengthen their ability to get a new job and for those who need to fill their résumés to earn merit pay, promotion, or tenure, article writing is usually a far better investment of their time than book writing.

## WHAT IS A REFEREED JOURNAL?

At institutions of higher education, no term is more common among faculty members than "refereed journal." The extent of its use is exceeded, however, only by the degree to which it is misunderstood. Although to everyone the word *refereed* reflects scholarship, when cornered, even among those who so readily use the term, few could accurately define it.

Although the academic world disagrees on the many definitions of *refereed journal*, most academicians would readily agree that journal refereeing has three common characteristics: *where, how* and *by whom* the refereeing occurs.

Generally, the jurors or referees are considered to be peers in the profession (see Figure 9.2.) At some journals, referees are carefully chosen for their reputations and because they are recognized throughout their field as experts.

FIGURE 9.2   Refereeing occurs in degrees.

| | Criteria |
|---|---|
| Third Degree meets all three criteria | Is refereed by experts throughout the country. Editor provides a rating instrument. Referee process is conducted anonymously. |
| Second Degree meets two of the three criteria | Is refereed by experts throughout the country. Editor provides a rating instrument. Referee process is conducted anonymously. |
| First Degree meets only one of the criteria | Is refereed by experts throughout the country. Editor provides a rating instrument. Referee process is conducted anonymously. |

Some journal editors who claim refereed status for their journals would argue that they themselves are qualified referees. Another aspect of refereeing is location. Some people think that all refereed processes must be nationwide because it ensures a national viewpoint as opposed to a provincial perspective; others consider the location of little consequence. Many professional journals are published on large university campuses. Some of the editors of these journals send each manuscript to a colleague in the appropriate department on their campus. Others would even argue that refereeing can and does occur in the editor's office.

Perhaps a more important criterion than either *who* evaluates the manuscripts or *where* the manuscripts are reviewed is *how* the manuscripts are evaluated. The most loosely conducted evaluations consist merely of the reviewers' subjective opinions. Some evaluators use rating scales to make their judgments. The most rigid evaluators provide evaluation instruments to referees across the country and conduct the reviews anonymously.

## IS IT WISE TO USE VANITY PUBLISHERS?

Vanity publishers are those who require their authors to pay all or part of the publishing costs. Sometimes this type of publisher may be a good choice; usually it is not. Suppose you have something important to say in a book, and you have tried several commercial publishers but all of these publishers have declined to publish your work. Suppose the content is accurate but the market for the book is too small to make it profitable. So, you cannot get a contract from a commercial publisher. One alternative is to turn to a vanity publisher. (You could also choose to publish it yourself). But suppose you don't have the money that is required to pay for the printing and materials;

and suppose the vanity press requires only that you use the book in your classes. Vanity publishing might provide your only option.

Under most circumstances a vanity publisher would be a poor choice. For example, suppose your main motive for having a book published is to accrue academic prestige or academic rewards. Most academic institutions place far less value on works that are published by vanity presses. Some colleges even refuse to recognize vanity publications. The reason is clear; unlike other publishers, vanity publishers seldom send the manuscript off to be evaluated anonymously by experts, and, for a fee, some vanity publishers will publish almost anything. Likewise, if your goal is to produce a very successful book, one that is recognized as a leading textbook or a leading professional book, many vanity publishers would not have the marketing capabilities needed to make their books highly competitive with those published by other publishers. Indeed, most vanity presses provide very little marketing support for their authors' books.

## WHAT ABOUT SELF-PUBLISHING?

Like vanity publishing, the self-published author must bear the expenses—and like vanity books they seldom prove to be a route to professional recognition, fortune, or fame.

Some authors, however, have been successful at self-publishing. Hanoch McCarty is one such author with extensive experience in this method, and he gives the following advice:

Self-publishing has some big advantages and some very big disadvantages. On the positive side:

- Your potential profit on book sales is much larger. My first book was a college text published by a major house. With three authors dividing the royalties, my per-copy earnings were about $.55. Each of my current self-published books earns me about $4.00 per copy. Sounds great, doesn't it? The real question is: Who is likely to sell more, you or the publisher? If you believe that your platform and other sales will be substantial, then self-publish. After all, you eliminate the middleman.
- No compromise. You decide everything. No one intervenes in your creation. This is delightful for an independent soul such as I. Yet, those times that I've had an editor, I've gained far more than I've lost. A good editor brings fresh insight, new ideas, courageous feedback for improvement (which your best friends may not have the courage to tell you).

The negatives are very significant. As I indicated, you'll miss the feedback and fresh ideas an editor brings. In addition:

- You must find the printer, graphic designer, photographer, etc., yourself. We publish a number of my books, and we get competitive price quotes from at least six printers every time we have a print run. Prices vary widely, and you save big if you shop. This is very time consuming. You also have to do all the other details such as copyright, photo and quote clearances, etc.

- You don't have the distribution network that a decent publisher will have. (Note: if you're choosing a publisher, this is one of the most important questions you should explore!)
- You must take a large financial risk in the initial publication and may be left with hundreds or thousands of unsold copies.
- You have to spend much time marketing and promoting the book. You must store a large inventory, become familiar with UPS, parcel post, Federal Express, and collection agencies (for customers who don't pay).
- Academic institutions don't give much credence to self-published material. Therefore, if publication is important for promotion and tenure, don't self-publish.
- Finally, you must do all the record keeping for tax purposes.

In spite of all this, I self-published six of my own books, tapes and video programs. In addition, I write under contract to several publishers. My contract with them allows me to buy large quantities of my own books for platform and catalog sales. (This is a very good idea. It allows me to gain larger profit than a royalty alone would, but I don't have to worry about all the other details I've discussed). I have also produced a video program as a partner with a small video production company which gave me some relief from the financial risk and from all the many headaches and details necessary to complete that project.

One of my most valued colleagues has written books comparable to mine. She has a contract with a publisher. They send her books ahead to her speaking engagements for platform sales and take care of all the details. The company does all the artwork and design. She simply flies from place to place and gives her speeches. The publisher does all the rest. While she makes much less per copy than I do, she has much more time to devote to her next project than I have. With the wisdom of hindsight, I'd advise most people not to self-publish.

The self-published author is always subject to suspicion. This suspicion may or may not be warranted. For example, suppose Professor Jones writes a book and later discovers that she cannot find a recognized publisher who is willing to publish it. Many colleagues will conclude that it is because the book is shallow or that it is full of errors. This could be true, but there are other reasons for rejections. For example, the decision to reject a book proposal is often based solely on the publisher's perception of the market size. Sometimes the publisher knows that the market for the book is so small that, even if the book were bought and used by *everyone* in this specialized field, the sales of the book would not be large enough to make it profitable for the publisher. This introduces my second favorite story.

In the late 1960s two professors at a Midwestern university developed a prospectus for a book aimed at a new market. They contacted several publishers and were consistently told that such a market did not exist. Convinced otherwise, these authors went to a local press, designed a layout, and paid to have 2,000 copies of this new book printed. Using a small mailer which they also designed and paid a printer to produce, they quickly sold the 2,000 copies and immediately printed a second 2,000 copies. The success of the book prompted the authors to write and self-publish a second edition. The second edition was more successful than the first. As you might guess, the second edition led to a third edition. The book is now in its eighth edition and its sales have exceeded 40,000 copies, all mailed directly from the home of one of the authors. Obviously, these authors are pleased with their decision to self-publish. Such success stories make self-publishing sound attractive, yet such success may be more a product of the authors' own capabilities and commitment than of the merits of the self-publishing process itself.

The odds against a self-published book reaching this level of success are gigantic though there are always a few Davids with slingshots who are willing to tackle such giants. If you have a book inside you that must come out at any expense, self-publishing may be a viable option for you to consider.

Clearly, self-publishing provides an opportunity to get a book into print that otherwise might never be published. *What Color Is Your Parachute?*, a guide for job seekers, by Richard N. Bolles was first self-published and later turned over to Ten Speed Press. This book has been on the *New York Times* Best-Seller List consistently for over a decade and has sold well over 3 million copies.

Peter McWilliams and John-Roger's *You Can't Afford the Luxury of a Negative Thought* has sold over a quarter of a million copies and still sells several thousand copies a month. McWilliams, a phenomenon in self-publishing, has been doing it for 20 years. He estimates that the sales of his books (including *Life 101* and *Do It: Let's Get Off Our Buts*, both coauthored with John-Roger) have now passed 7 million copies. His book on self-publishing, *Self-Publishing, Self-Taught* was published by Prelude Press (which McWilliams named after his car). He spends about $1 a copy to advertise, another $1 a copy to promote through giveaways and press releases. Modern technology has made self-publishing affordable. Printing and binding 3,000 to 5,000 copies costs about $1.50 a book. The laser printer, personal computer, and software required to turn out a quality, camera-ready product cost about $5,000.

## IF ASKED, SHOULD I PAY A JOURNAL PUBLISHING EXPENSES?

For decades journals in some disciplines, particularly some of the sciences, have required their contributing authors to pay for certain publishing expenses such as the costs of graphs, charts, and page proofs. In recent years, additional disciplines (such as education) have begun charging such costs to their contributors. Because some professional journals do not sell advertisements, charging expenses to contributors is often considered acceptable—but as an incentive to get faculty members to publish, many colleges and departments pay part or all of these expenses.

A few journals charge their contributors a reading fee. Many professionals find this practice unacceptable, unprofessional, and a contrivance to make money.

## SHOULD I BE A SPECIALIST OR A GENERALIST?

As many aspiring authors think about their futures, they are uncertain whether they will benefit more from becoming a specialist or generalist. This decision is tough. It depends on the author's writing goals. If your purpose is to earn recognition in a particular field, the nature of the subject may restrict you to publishing in only one or two specific journals. If your field of expertise does not restrict your publishing so severely, there may be much benefit in your writing for a wide array of journals. The wider the range of your topics and audiences, the greater the number of outlets you will have for your manuscripts. Writing for a wide range of journals also enables you to reach more varied audiences and to indulge in different kinds of writing. You may have knowledge that can benefit groups outside your own academic major, and because they do not read your journals, the only way to reach them is through publishing in their journals.

Still another benefit of being a generalist is the opportunity it gives you to learn about the knowledge bases in other fields. This is important in that you can enrich your own knowledge base by studying several fields. For example, all administrators need to understand principles of leadership, and all fields have studies that contribute significantly to the understanding of leadership theory. Those who write for publication on this topic should at least review the leadership literature in other disciplines.

## QUESTIONS ABOUT COPYRIGHT

   1. **Exactly what is meant by copyright?**  Copyright is the legal right that all authors and other artists have to prohibit others from copying their work. Some of the copyright laws have changed, making the author's job of keeping up with them challenging.

   2. **How long is the copyright valid?**  The time of endurance of copyright has changed. The length of coverage depends on the date of the copyright. To determine whether a work is still under copyright protection, first check the date to see if it is before 1950. If so, the work will be under protection for 75 years beyond the copyright date.

For works published between 1950 and 1977, the copyright will endure for 56 years. For works published since 1978, the copyright extends throughout the life of the author plus 50 years.

**3. Are all published works subject to copyright laws?** No. Works such as government documents are under public domain. This means that you can use them as you wish, but to help the reader locate these works and to show professional courtesy to their authors, you should always cite the source.

**4. Can I ever quote copyrighted works without securing permission?** Yes. Fair-use guidelines permit you to quote up to 300 words from a book. You can also quote up to 10 percent of an article. But should you wish to quote from a poem or song, be careful; the laws are more restrictive for these works. Diagrams, charts, and photos also require permission, regardless how small or how few you are using. Photos also require signed releases or permission from each recognizable person. Children's photos require signatures of the child's parent or guardian. At best, most of the copyright laws are "fuzzy," leaving you the responsibility to use your own judgment to determine what is honest and fair.

**5. Does this mean that I should avoid using ideas and facts that I have discovered in books and journals?** No. Facts and ideas themselves are not copyrighted. Many beginning authors limit themselves unnecessarily because they are afraid to use ideas that they may have read in a book, magazine, or other printed material.

For example, suppose you are writing about the water cycle: Rain turns into runoff, which eventually evaporates, later condensing to form clouds, which in turn condense to form rain. This is a well-known process, and you need not quote any source or ask for permission to use it. But if you wish to lift a description of the process verbatim from a book or magazine, this would require permission.

You could also draw a graphic representation of the water cycle without seeking permission, but if you want to copy an existing diagram, you will need to seek permission.

**6. To whom should I write for permission?** First, notice who holds the copyright. If you can tell that it is the publisher, write the publisher. If it is the author, you still may need to write to the publisher to secure the author's address.

**7. How Can I Get My Works Copyrighted?** There are three ways a writer can get copyright protection. You could write the copyright office at:

Register of Copyrights
Copyright Office
Library of Congress
Washington, DC 20559

A second way to get copyright protection is to put a small c inside a circle, followed by the date on your new work.
*Example:* © 1994 by Hilda Monza

A third way to get copyright protection is just to write down your ideas and then do nothing. As soon as you put your ideas into writing, the writing itself automatically becomes subject to copyright laws.

## HOW CAN AUTHORS LEARN TO USE THE
## LIBRARY MORE EFFECTIVELY?

Because I am no expert in this field, I turned to someone who is, Dr. Toby Graham, who offers the following help:

> Efficient use of the research library requires a basic knowledge of the information sources and services an institution provides that are relevant to the users' scholarly interests. The most valuable of these resources are the librarians, themselves. Librarians are trained information professionals with accredited higher degrees in information studies. Authors should take time to become acquainted with the librarians or archivists in the repositories they consult. Whether in the form of a formal reference interview or in an informal conversation, it is to the researchers' advantage to talk to librarians about their topics, providing enough detail that they can offer suitable advice.
>
> Researchers should identify the reference materials most appropriate to their interests. To make the most efficient use of the library catalog, they should familiarize themselves with the Library of Congress subject headings used to provide subject access to the topics under investigation. Besides a public access catalog, research libraries provide print indices and electronic bibliographic databases that index the literature of discrete scholarly areas. For example, ERIC covers the literature on Education and America: History & Life does the same for American History. The electronic versions of these sources save time and provide comparable results to the print alternatives; some provide full-text versions or abstracts of the materials indexed. Academic libraries will not own all of the material cited in an index, but in most cases, the libraries can borrow the requested material from the collections of other institutions within a reasonable amount of time. The Internet, the World Wide Web in particular, is another important source of information research libraries provide. The uncontrolled nature of this vast resource requires that Web researchers become careful and critical consumers of online information, however.
>
> Successful academic writing is a product of effective research and the starting point for scholarly research is the library. Information needs are unique to individual writers, but common to all is the need for a working relationship with information professionals and a familiarity with the print and online library resources relevant to researchers' specific information requirements.

## ARE COLLOQUIALISMS
## AND CLICHÉS ACCEPTABLE?

Colloquialisms offer skilled fiction authors a way to provide authentic descriptions of their characters. But for nonfiction authors, colloquialisms are like inside jokes. They invite miscommunication, leaving the outsider feeling estranged. A good rule for nonfiction writers is to avoid using colloquialisms.

Clichés seldom offer anything that brings quality to a manuscript. They are popular because they are convenient. Frequently, authors use clichés as substitutes when they cannot find the appropriate words to express their ideas. Because of their overuse, clichés soon become objects of boredom. They may identify you as a weak writer.

## WHAT SHOULD I DO WHEN AN EDITOR KEEPS HOLDING MY MANUSCRIPT?

At one workshop I was conducting a participant said, "This editor has promised to give my coauthor and me a decision several times but always misses the deadlines. My coauthor wants to choke him. What should we do?"

My first advice was "Don't choke the editor." I realize that this editor has been unfair, and fairness is definitely a two-way street; yet, nothing would be gained from squaring off against the editor. On the contrary, something would be lost; you would eliminate one target journal for your future manuscripts. Perhaps one thing would be gained; you would have your manuscript back and would be free to go to another publisher. But you can do that without shutting off this one.

Calmly write a letter saying something like, "If I haven't heard from you by (include month and day), I will assume that you are no longer interested in this manuscript and will pursue this project with other publishers. Thank you for your continuing interest in this manuscript." This course of action should reclaim your manuscript and leave you on good terms with the editor. Should the editor fail to respond, soon after the designated deadline, go ahead and resubmit the manuscript to another publisher. Be careful to file a copy of this correspondence with your manuscript to be used as evidence of your innocence, should you end up with two acceptances.

## WHOSE NAME COMES FIRST?

If your collaborators are colleagues, the person who initiated the manuscript should have the privilege of being listed first. If I asked you to join me in writing a manuscript, I would probably generate the first draft or at least an outline, and I would probably specify exactly what I considered your work role in this project. With your approval, I would even set deadline dates for the completion of the various stages of the project. These actions would make me the originator, organizer, and manager—and would entitle me to the placement as first author.

I have developed a system of collaboration that eliminates the possibility of conflict—I do not ask anyone to collaborate with me on just one article. When I initiate one idea, I make it clear that I expect the collaborator(s) to come up with an idea for a second article. For that article, the originator would be the first author. Remember, the sooner you specify what's expected of all parties, the fewer misunderstandings you will have.

## WHO IS LISTED FIRST IF THE COLLABORATORS ARE PROFESSORS AND GRADUATE STUDENTS?

Some graduate advisors encourage their students to write for publication. Even more admirable, some professors collaborate with students. If an article reports a student's research performed in support of the thesis or dissertation (which of course, belongs to the student), fairness dictates that the first article generated from the study also belongs to the student. Therefore, I would insist that the student be listed as first author.

Many theses and dissertations have enough data for more than one article. Should the professor collaborate with this student on a second article, the professor would usually take the lead in writing the second article and should be listed as the first author.

## IF I FURNISH MY DISSERTATION OR THESIS FOR A COLLABORATOR TO SHAPE INTO A MANUSCRIPT, IS THAT AN EQUITABLE EXCHANGE?

I don't believe I know anyone who would be willing to undertake the interpretation of someone else's work. I wouldn't feel competent to do the job unless perhaps I had served as the committee chair for the study. The first article from a study should be drafted by the student who conducted the study.

As to the question of equity, beginning authors often perceive the difference between a dissertation and an article to be small, only requiring a few adjustments here and there. I know this because as a guest editor I have received theses that have had only minor tinkering. But, these papers seldom, if ever, are accepted for publication. Actually, the task of converting a thesis into an article is tantamount to writing an article from scratch. The study provides the data; that's a lot, but it isn't enough to justify getting your name on an article.

## IF I SHARE A BOOK IDEA WITH A PUBLISHER, HOW CAN I BE SURE IT WON'T BE TURNED OVER TO A MORE EXPERIENCED AUTHOR?

This suspicion raises its head in almost every workshop I teach. My first response is to share my own personal perception which is based on 20 years of submitting book prospectuses. Most editors are too honest to try such a stunt. Publishing houses need to retain credibility with authors, and the potential gain in such shady dealings would be outweighed over the long haul by loss of reputation with potential authors. Most publishing companies are in business for the long run.

But as I give this response I see that worried look on the questioner's face, and I remember how important this question is to an individual who wants to protect a really great idea, so I offer the following advice. If you are still worried that the editor might give your idea to an experienced author, before sharing your idea, go ahead and develop it. Begin working on some of the chapters so that when you do approach an editor you are far enough ahead in the project that you can finish it long before anyone else could write it.

## WHAT DOES IT MEAN WHEN AN EDITOR ASKS THE AUTHOR TO REWRITE AND RESUBMIT A MANUSCRIPT? SHOULD I DO THAT?

Occasionally editors neither accept nor reject a manuscript. Instead, they write or phone the authors and ask them to revise the manuscript. Sometimes authors ask me how they should respond to such a request. I tell them: First, let's determine what this request means, or what it tells us about the editor's view of the manuscript; then, let's consider how rewriting and resubmitting a manuscript affects its chances of being accepted.

According to my latest questionnaire returns, professional journal editors receive about five times as many manuscripts as they have undesignated space in their journal. This means that most editors probably have enough good manuscripts to fill the next several issues of their journal. If that's so, why don't they just reject your manuscript instead of asking you to rewrite it? The answer is probably one of the following:

1. They see a good "fit" between the manuscript topic and the journal (which is to say that your topic is of interest to their readers).
2. The editor believes that your manuscript offers a worthwhile contribution (which is to say that the editor believes that you have something important to contribute).

The next essential consideration is how a resubmitted manuscript's chance for acceptance compares to that of an original submission. For that information let's consult the survey responses.

Contrary to some people's suspicions that a resubmitted manuscript will automatically be accepted, most editors indicate that they send the resubmitted manuscripts for review. Sometimes the author is asked to rewrite the manuscript a second or third time. But the good news is that 75 percent of all resubmitted manuscripts are eventually accepted, compared to a 15 percent acceptance rate for original submissions. This means that rewriting a manuscript to meet the requests of the editor improves its chances for acceptance by 500 percent. For me, the answer is clear; I usually honor the editor's request by making as many of the requested changes as I find comfortable.

So my advice is: gladly accept this offer and give the rewrite close attention to meet all of the editor's requests.

One editor responding to the survey (Henson, 1993) said, "A revise and resubmit recommendation indicates interest in eventual publication. If possible, look at recommended revisions as positive attempts to improve the manuscript. The most successful authors are those who revise well."

## SHOULD I USE A COMPUTER?

This is a question that must be answered by each writer. Since I cannot think as freely and clearly with typing as I can while writing, I prefer to put the first draft in script. But, I have known individuals who, I am convinced, can think more clearly when they have their fingers on the keyboard. I suggest that you decide which system affords you the opportunity to think clearly, and then use that system.

I asked a couple of authors for their views on using computers. Robert Maddox, Associate Professor of Business at the University of Tennessee, says:

> There is, I believe, no way to write except by using a computer. Legal pad and pencil or typewriter just do not work. The ability to load tons of files of notes in the computer, to move around in these notes, and to switch from these notes to the document on which you are working (carrying some of the material with you) is invaluable as a time saver. I think that using a computer also helps me overcome the problem of having to discipline myself to write. I used to find it difficult to put words on paper when they had that permanent quality of going on paper. However, using a computer, I feel freer to get words down, knowing that poorly thought out or stated ideas can easily be deleted or changed.

## PROFILE

Vance Wisenbaker earned bachelor's and master's degrees at Florida State University and a Ph.D. from the University of Georgia. All three degrees are in sociology.

For the past eleven years, he has served as Dean of Social and Behavioral Sciences and Professor of Sociology at Eastern Kentucky University where he served as chair of the Department of Anthropology, Sociology, and Social Work for 10 years before becoming dean.

His book, *Programming with Macintosh Pascal*, 2nd ed. (co-authored by Richard Rink and Richard Vance) was published in 1994 by Prentice Hall.

There are many small technical advantages to using a computer with word processing software to write. I could easily prepare an entire chapter for this book listing and explaining these individual advantages. The truth, however, is that the computer simply allows me to concentrate on the content and flow of my writing and forget the appearance and style. I need not worry about misspelled words or margins or formatting page numbers and footnotes. The computer can do all of these things later, after the rough draft has been committed to paper. Not only can it easily make such changes and corrections, it can do so swiftly and with a consistency that I otherwise could never achieve.

I have one bit of advice for anyone just getting started in the use of a word processor. Start out simple and let the word processor help with only a few things. Do not try to master its full features with your first book or article. Learn to do essential and simple things like margins, fonts, tabs, headings, and the spelling checker. Save some of the more difficult features for later projects. Some of us will use this software for years and never master its full range of features. It may be that you will never have an urgent need to do drop caps or circular text (to mention a few). Finally, do not hesitate to ask an experienced friend when you need help. Most computer "experts" are more than glad to share their knowledge with their friends.

## WHAT SHOULD I LIST ON MY RÉSUMÉ AS PUBLICATIONS?

Academic writers have a difficult job deciding what to list in their résumés under the heading "Publications." Obviously, some find this decision very easy; they use the same process that many academicians use when applying for promotion or tenure. The rule seems to be, if it fits in a pickup truck, include it.

For those who are a bit more selective, several questions arise. A common question concerns "in press" publications. This is a great camouflage term. Some evaluators are willing to believe that "in press" means the manuscript has been accepted and is sitting suspended on a launching pad about to blast off. But others are more skeptical. Professor Allen Berger (1985) of Miami University teaches Writing for Publication courses, and he says that to him "in press" means only that the person knows his way to the post office and is able to buy stamps.

Writers also ask if they should list meeting proceedings. The answer depends on the discipline. Some disciplines place considerable weight on meeting proceedings, but others do not. For example, in education, meeting proceedings have little meaning as evidence of scholarly achievement because usually they are not evaluated and therefore are not weighted heavily as evidence of scholarship.

My advice is, unless you know that it can significantly add to your credits, do not list it. By including questionable evidence, candidates run the risk of discrediting their complete résumé.

## A FEW OF MY COLLEAGUES AND I HAVE BEEN TALKING ABOUT GETTING TOGETHER ON A REGULAR BASIS TO DISCUSS OUR WRITING. DO YOU RECOMMEND THIS AND, IF SO, CAN YOU GIVE US SOME ADVICE?

I like this idea. In fact, when giving writing workshops on college campuses, I always recommend this to the audience. I call such a group of writers a "support group" because I believe that beginning writers need support, which is unlikely to come from outside. If conducted properly, other benefits can come from such an organization. Consider the following guidelines:

First, be systematic and set aside the same day(s) for such meetings, say the first Monday in every month. Second, keep the meetings short. Brown bag luncheons work well for most groups. Third, have a designated speaker and topic for each meeting. Some speakers can be members of the group but invited guests can also contribute significantly. For suggested topics, check the chapters of this book. You might ask a successful author from any department on campus to give a 20- to 30-minute presentation on "Why I write for publication" or "How I find topics" or "How I choose my target journals." Or you might ask a researcher to speak on developing and using questionnaires. A prolific English professor might be willing to speak for 20 to 30 minutes on "Writing lead sentences" or "Getting the reader's attention." Also, other departments on campus have some book authors. I would hold an occasional meeting aimed at motivating and reinforcing the desire to write.

## RECAPPING THE MAJOR POINTS

Most questions that plague writers are perennial. For years these questions have baffled and impeded the success of writers, and they will continue to present problems for writers. Simply try to remember:

- Most successful writers immensely enjoy writing; they are compelled to write by a need to say something that they feel must be said.
- To become a successful writer, you must believe in your abilities, and you must write often.

- The best way to handle rejections is to repair the rejected manuscript and immediately send it to another publisher.
- Highly successful writers have two or three manuscripts under way while two or three others are being considered.
- Authors should never simultaneously submit a manuscript to multiple journals.
- Collaborating on writing projects with colleagues can provide needed motivation and opportunities to learn from your colleagues, while expediting your writing program. Such success depends on finding partners with similar personalities and work habits.
- Tables and graphs are more expensive to print than words and, therefore, should be used only when the journals to which you submit manuscripts use them and only when they communicate messages clearer than written comments.
- For the beginner, time is best invested in writing for national journals.
- There are several definitions of *refereed journals*. To make your writing program pay off, learn how your institution defines "refereed," and act accordingly.
- Vanity publishing is seldom a good choice for authors.
- Self-publishing is usually a better choice than vanity publishing—but only if you can both afford it and tolerate the risk involved.

---

**REFERENCES**

Berger, A. (1985, April 3). Perish the thought. *Baltimore (Maryland) Sun.*
Daugherty, G. (1996, January). Get motivated…and stay motivated. *Money Magazine,* pp. 28–29.

■ ■ ■ ■ ■ ▬▬▬▬▬▬▬▬▬▬▬▬▬▬▬▬▬▬▬▬▬▬▬▬

# CHAPTER 12

# TEACHING AND THE TENURE TRACK

Having provided a philosophical base and having fostered teaching and learning skills required for success in today's higher education environment, *New Strategies for College Teaching* looks forward and concludes with David Royse's excellently written chapter on managing the cultural assimilation and tenuring processes. His practical tips on managing multiple academic tasks, avoiding political mistakes, and an array of other critical issues are invaluable.

Senior faculty members who read this chapter will confirm especially the section on developing the professional portfolio. To the junior faculty member, each recommendation should be embraced completely and immediately, ensuring the saving of countless hours and emotional energy, and certainly enhancing the attainment of long-term professional goals.

# TEACHING AND
# THE TENURE TRACK

Chapter 15 from *Teaching Tips for College and University Instructors*
David Royse
Allyn & Bacon, © 2001

*Overview: In his book* The New Faculty Member, *Boice (1992) has claimed that there are three obstacles facing most new faculty: teaching, writing, and collegiality. Thus far, this book has already covered many of the potential classroom problems. This chapter will be addressing issues and problems often occurring outside the classroom. Using Boice's scheme, these can be roughly categorized as those associated with writing and publishing, and the academic pitfalls found in most institutions of higher learning sometimes thought of as "office politics" and requiring one to be "politically savvy." To achieve tenure—to make a career out of teaching—one must be at least an acceptable instructor, must not alienate colleagues, and must create a portfolio of published papers that cannot be easily dismissed. How are you going to find time to do all of that? That topic is addressed in these pages.*

## JUGGLING RESEARCH, PUBLICATIONS, AND TEACHING

Like it or not, this is a competitive world. Most research universities have the expectation that you will not only teach but publish. At many universities new faculty are commonly instructed that they should seek to publish at least "two solid pieces" of research per year, and this is the advice of Weaver (1992), too. However, the number of required publications varies quite a bit. At smaller colleges and even some regional universities, it may be possible to get tenure without publishing in a refereed journal. The publishing demands are often inversely proportional to the number of courses you teach. If your normal teaching load is four or five courses per semester, then it is unlikely that you'll have to do much professional writing. If, on the other hand, your teaching load is one or two courses a semester, then there is probably the expectation that you should be publishing somewhere on the order of two or more articles per year—and this may be in addition to securing external grant funding.

Most new faculty do not have the option of choosing, say, between teaching and researching in order to publish—they have to do both. The good news is that it is possible to be a good teacher *and* a fine researcher. These two activities do not detract from each other; rather, they complement each other. Reading articles for a literature review, for instance, will turn up wonderful examples of research and hypotheses, even flaws in methodologies or logic that can be used in the classroom. Sometimes it is possible to give students assignments where they not only are able to learn how to do conduct research but also to participate in a way that assists you. For example, students could help you interview subjects or collect surveys from a sample of adults. If you share with them the hypotheses and problems you are working on, a student may find an especially relevant study that you didn't know about. And although you shouldn't give assignments designed only to further your own research efforts—such as requiring your students to conduct exhaustive literature reviews on the topic you'll be writing about next—there is a strong tradition in academia of using students as subjects and research participants. (More about this later in this chapter.)

Besides working smart, which we'll talk about next, making the best use of your time is a critical key to successfully managing the demands of teaching and publishing. Start by finding a quiet place where you can work undisturbed. If that place is your office, so much the better. If it is your home, that's okay, too. But neither of these places count if the phone rings three or four times an hour or if there is always someone stopping by to chat.

Insofar as possible, schedule your social contacts. When there are people you need to talk with or who need to see you, do it when you would normally be stopping for lunch, anyway. Try to find blocks of times (three or four hours at a stretch) when you can work without interruption. Take the phone off the hook if you have to; schedule at least two "writing days" a week when you don't have to teach; let it be known that you won't answer the door even if someone knocks loudly. Plan how much time you will need to develop a lecture, grade papers, and so on, and then stay within that time frame. Boice (1992) found that the most effective new faculty members prepared no more than 1.5 hours per each classroom hour. If you, like many assistant professors, are expected to be engaged in research about half of your time and in activities associated with teaching about half of the time, then schedule your research days or hours and don't let committee work or teaching responsibilities steal that time.

New faculty who love teaching often find it much to their secret liking that students call with personal problems or drop in unannounced to make small talk, to show off a new engagement ring, or to ask for advice about a job interview. If you find yourself truly enjoying these contacts, then you must be vigilant in keeping nonproductive activities from taking over your whole work week. We all tend to engage proportionately more in those activities that are fun and less in those that aren't. So, if you aren't spending at least half of your time involved in research or writing and that's the expectation of your department head, then you are going to be in trouble later when your lack of productivity become obvious.

## TIME MANAGEMENT TIPS

In addition to the suggestions just provided, here are a few others suggested by Parks (1998):

- Identify the "time robber" tasks that waste or are an inefficient use of your time.
- Once your "time robbers" are identified, create a plan to eliminate them. (For instance, are there tasks that you can delegate to a research assistant or a work/study student to do?)
- If you have too much to do, learn to say "no" nicely when new requests are made of your time.
- Break large tasks into small, manageable segments. Procrastination is not uncommon when one feels overwhelmed with the enormity of a task. Dawdling is minimized when only a small amount of time (e.g., 15 minutes or so) is need to complete a chore.

Some efficiency experts recommend that instead of trying to make major adjustments in one's schedule to create large blocks of time, it is often easier to make better use of small parcels. Get to work 15 minutes earlier, stay 15 minutes later. Know when you are most productive and protect that time for your most important projects. Other jobs that don't require as much concentration can be done when you normally get more interruptions or are less productive.

Boice (1992) has urged new faculty to establish a *writing regimen*. His research (1987) found that new faculty who find only an hour per weekday to write generally manage to submit about 1.5 manuscripts per year. Sorcinelli (1992) has recommended drawing up a daily "to do" list, using an appointment book, setting realistic goals, prioritizing projects, and initiating relaxation exercises to restore energy.

Last, keep your eye on the prize. You *can* find the time for the things you *really* want to accomplish. Along this line, here's a great story from novelist Sharyn McCrumb (1998):

> Procrastinators get no sympathy from me. In 1986 when a publishing company accepted my four-page book proposal, the catch was this: In order to meet their spring deadline, the editor would need the completed novel in six weeks. I did not have six weeks to devote to writing a novel. I was working full time at the university. I was teaching a night class in fiction. I was taking two graduate En-

glish courses that semester, both requiring research papers. I had an 8-year-old daughter, and a husband balancing a job with his own graduate course work. I was six weeks pregnant, and I felt awful.... I wrote the book in six weeks. It won the Edgar Allan Poe Award for Best Paperback Novel in 1987. It's still in print. (p. 19)

## WORKING SMART

Working smart means that you must ask for help when you need it. An example comes to mind: Before the advent of the Internet, a student complained to me because she had to spend so many hours in the library—the most of one whole weekend, as I recall. What she had been looking for had been an article that had appeared in the *New York Times.* Beginning with the month and year she thought the article had appeared, she began working her way backward, using the cumbersome microfilm reader. For 14 or more hours she labored, although had she asked the librarian a few feet away, she could have found the piece she wanted in a few minutes by looking in the reference book, *Index to the New York Times.*

Working smart means that as a junior faculty member or teaching assistant, you should ask lots of questions of those who are in a position to help you. Senior professors will probably be more than willing to recommend texts or supplements, and more than likely will be, if not glad to share, at least willing to share examples of tests and homework assignments they've used in the past. It also means that if you have very limited experience writing for professional journals and yet you are expected to do this, you ask for consultation. Go to one or more faculty members who have proven track records and ask for a consultation if you need it. Better yet, ask them to review your rough draft. Be open to suggestions and don't get defensive.

Working smart means that you try to recruit students to help with your research projects. There are different ways to do this, from independent studies to class assignments, to even including students as coauthors. If you are hard-pressed for time and don't have institutional support in the form of a graduate or research assistant, then hire a student to run to the library and do photocopying for you, or word processing, or whatever. Sure, you could conceivably spend a few hundred dollars, but on the other hand, how much is your time worth? It's probably worth a lot more than you would pay some undergraduate to photocopy articles.

Working smart also means that you consider teaming up with other faculty and work as coauthors on some writing projects. If this partnership works well, you could have twice as many publications as you would have if you worked by yourself. Of course, working with another person does have its frustrations at time: Your colleague may slip the deadline you both set, may not write well, or may be less informed or capable than you had thought. Obviously, it pays to choose well. The rule here is that someone who already has publications (and preferably a lot of them) is a safer bet for a good writing partner than someone with no publications. Look for a mentor or a coauthor capable of pulling his or her own weight and who is excited about the prospect of writing on the topic and working with you. If you do more than one project together, alternate authorship so that you and your co-author will both be first authors. Negotiate the order of authorship at the beginning of your endeavor so that there will be no hard feelings later on.

Finally, working smart means that you don't forget about your dissertation. Although you may be so sick of it that you want to bury it in a deep hole somewhere, a well-done dissertation ought to get you at least one and maybe two publications. And the best part is that you know the literature, forward and backward, and have already analyzed the data just about every way imaginable. Cut it down to a findings article where you highlight the most important results. Then, take a look to see if you can get a review of the literature article out of it.

## SUGGESTIONS FOR INCREASING THE ODDS OF GETTING PUBLISHED

Getting published in respected journals is neither difficult nor as easy as some would have you believe. Above all, you must be disciplined and approach the task logically. Make publishing a priority and give it the time it deserves—don't wait for an opportune moment or push it to the side until everything else is done. Once you've protected some part of your busy schedule just for writing and the preparation it requires, then the following suggestions may help you to think about the component tasks in the writing process:

1. Find a topic, problem, or hypothesis that is interesting and timely. What is hot and possibly controversial in your field? Where is an area with little scholarship? Plow new ground if you can, or put a new spin on a perennial problem.
2. Find a mentor or a colleague interested in the same topics as you. If possible, join or form a support group of assistant professors who are writing and researching.
3. Familiarize yourself with the journals interested in your topic. (It does you no good to draft a dazzling manuscript if you don't have an appropriate journal in mind.)
4. Study articles in the journal you have selected for length, writing style, the audience, the number and type of references they tend to carry, and so on.
5. After you have written a rough draft, set it aside for two or three days and then revise the draft again.

6. Repeat this process (reading and revising) about six times, until you can make no further refinements.

7. Let a colleague with expertise in the area read your manuscript. If you don't have a mentor, then seek out a kindly soul from another department who writes well. If one is not available and you are particularly inexperienced or if English is your second language, you might even want to hire someone to do line-editing. Sometimes such a small investment pays large dividends in terms of learning how to write professionally. (*Note:* A mentor can be very helpful with many other issues besides editing and writing. They are sources of information [e.g., more suitable journals] as well as intellectual guides and sources of emotional support when things have taken a turn for the worst. See Bode [1999] for a discussion on mentoring and collegiality.)

8. Revise again.

9. Submit to the professional journal.

10. If the manuscript is rejected, carefully weigh each of the reviewers' comments and then revise again. Don't categorically reject or accept each recommendation. Try to read the reviewers' comments objectively; if the comments make you angry, put them aside until you can read them more dispassionately. Don't throw the manuscript in the mail the same day to another journal. Although reviewers don't always understand what you were trying to accomplish and reject your manuscript, oftentimes they have good suggestions for improving it and making the paper more appealing.

11. Revise the piece by making the modifications that seem to have the most merit.

12. Submit the revised manuscript to a different journal if you were flatly rejected the first time. If the journal receiving your initial manuscript encouraged you to resubmit, then, by all means, do so. Call or e-mail the editor if you need clarification about the extent of the revision necessary.

13. If rejected once again, study the comments, revise still again, and resubmit to a different journal.

14. Consult some of the guides to publishing and writing (e.g., Thyer, 1994; Henson, 1995; Beebe, 1993). Join a writing group; start a writing support group. Sign up for a writing workshop.

15. Salvage what you can of any manuscript rejected umpteen times. Slant it, if possible, in a slightly different direction. For instance, if it reported findings, consider making it a review of the literature piece only. If it reviewed the literature, think of a way to gather some data to put with it. Alternatively, downsize the article and make it a "brief note"—something less than a full-sized article—maybe you'll have better luck with that.

A useful rule of thumb is three submissions. If you submit to three different journals and not one is interested in the paper, then something may be seriously wrong with it—there also may be no problem other than you haven't sent it to the most appropriate journals. Before you give up, take it to a colleague who has had more success publishing and ask for a consultation. Even if a journal isn't interested in your manuscript, you might look around for a conference where it could be entered as a paper, part of a panel discussion, or poster session.

Meanwhile, don't sit around waiting for the letter of acceptance to arrive. As soon as you mail off one manuscript, start immediately working on another. Because projects move at different speeds (e.g., you may have to wait for a book to arrive from Interlibrary Loan before completing your literature review section, or you may have to wait on the Institutional Review Board to grant permission before you can start data collection on another), you may be able to handle two or three projects more or less simultaneously.

## POLITICAL MISTAKES

If you've gone to the trouble of getting into graduate school, making it through most of your classes, preparing for your qualifying exam and dissertation, and then finally securing a position teaching at the college or university level, it stands to reason that you wouldn't want to just throw it away. And yet, it is possible to start off on the wrong foot and you can do this quite unintentionally. Here is some practical advice that will help you stay out of trouble with your colleagues in the department:

*1. Do not criticize your colleagues or speak ill of them:* Although the chair of the department might be an arrogant and pompous blockhead, you do not want him or her to find out that is what you think. The more people who have heard you find fault with the chair, the more avenues that are created for this information to get back to him or her. Even a trusted colleague might, after a couple of glasses of wine at a party, let some comment slip about what you "really think about ol' Harley." Faculty members enjoy juicy gossip the same as anyone else. If you let it be known that some tenured faculty member is incompetent (even if he or she is), you should assume that sooner or later, that unflattering remark will get back to the individual. Similarly, when you are the "new kid on the block," it is not wise to be critical of the program as a whole, or of admission policies or practices that have well-entrenched faculty advocates. This is not to say that you should have no opinion—only that you should always be tactful and recognize that those who've been at the institution a long time are likely to have strong feelings about leaving things the way they are. Someone on the faculty for 30 years may feel quite a lot of ownership of the program, certain courses, and so forth. These individuals may take criticism of a program personally. Particularly in small colleges, also be cautious about criticizing administrators or faculty in other departments who, unbeknown to you, may be spouses or relatives of key persons that you do not want to offend.

**2.** *Do not engage in sexual activities with a student, staff member, or other faculty at the same institution* (unless you are married to him or her):   When relationships break up, there's always the potential for the aggrieved party to want revenge in some way or another.

**3.** *Try to maintain a spirit of cooperativeness and helpfulness:* Although you may feel quite overwhelmed with duties and responsibilities, try to help your colleagues when they make a request. This doesn't mean you have to say yes to every new task group or ad hoc committee, but don't be known as someone who *isn't* a team-player, someone who automatically says no to every request. Try not to whine if you get an 8:00 A.M. class or if the spring schedule is not to your liking. Complaining about a real hardship is one matter; sounding off if you have three more students in your section than another faculty member or because your office wasn't dusted properly will really make it difficult for administrators to warm up to you.

**4.** *If there are pronounced factions within the faculty, try not to get caught up into the political fray your first year or two:*   Gently deflect attempts to pull you into one camp or the other by saying something like, "I'm still pretty new here. I don't know all the issues or have enough information to decide one way or the other. Maybe we can have a conversation about this later." It is important that you listen and observe which players are on which teams. If you have a mentor on the faculty, find out what you can about the history of the split and about the nature of the most sensitive issues. Speak to everyone. Try not to show that you favor one faction over the other. Try to be on good terms with every faculty member, even if you must keep some conversations superficial and avoid certain topics.

**5.** *Take care of business:*   Be well prepared for each class. Return papers promptly. Keep your office hours. Don't be the "office gossip" or spend much time with those who are. If others are going to discuss you, let them talk about what a fine job you are doing. In Sawyer, Prichard, and Hostetler's words, "Your most immediate priority on the job is teaching" (1992, p. 151). Abbott (1992) has expanded upon this somewhat:

> Small liberal arts colleges are deep wells. They expect scholarly achievement, excellent classroom teaching, loyalty to and love of the institution, good counseling skills, energy, imagination, collegiality, understanding of the values of the college and community, patience, hard work, personality, and tact. (p. 27)

The good news in terms of the alliances and caucuses in academia is that making it through a Ph.D. program has been a good preparation for the politics that you will encounter as a new faculty member. You already have acquired a lot of learning in this domain. You know, for instance, that there are faculty who swing a lot of clout and that there are faculty who are very territorial about their courses or programs. Faculty are not always open minded but sometimes downright opinionated and inflexible when it comes to *their* courses and *their* students. In the years that it's taken you to obtain that Ph.D., you've already overcome a lot of obstacles and learned a great deal about handling sensitive issues and difficult people. This is valuable and irreplaceable learning that will serve you well in the years ahead. Don't forget your lessons.

## THE RULES FOR SURVIVING

New faculty often feel like they have to do everything well: They have to be popular with students, entertaining and yet informative in the classroom, productive scholars, hard-working committee members, stimulating conversationalists, and altruistic givers of their time to community service projects. There's a lot of truth to these broad expectations. However, in every institution there are also informal rules. Your department might not really care, for instance, whether you get good teaching evaluations as long as you have a strong publishing record or bring in a sizeable chunk of external funding. In the most competitive of academic environments, it is not just getting published, but publishing in the "right" journals that really matters. Sometimes there is the expectation that you should have a book published before tenure; in other locations, a book of readings might be viewed as being of less consequence than two peer-reviewed journal articles. Collaborative work with others may be encouraged or frowned upon. For example, if too much of your work is done with students, one criticism might be that you exploit students. If too much of your work is done with other faculty, you might be criticized for not being the lead author often enough.

No matter how much you accomplish, there may be faculty who will not like you or your work. Of course, you can't help the way you look, the fact that you were someone's else graduate student, or that your research contradicts that of a senior faculty member. There's nothing you can do about these things. What you *can* do is be unfailingly polite and respectful to those with whom you may not agree or care for. You should go about your business of teaching or researching and work diligently at these pursuits. Don't be the loner and avoid faculty social gatherings. Don't get the reputation as being one who is always stirring up trouble. In faculty meetings the first year, listen much more than you speak. Insofar as possible, be pleasant and positive—not moody and temperamental. Don't always insist on your own way. Find out what the informal rules are for grading: Don't give all As and don't fail everyone either.

# SEEKING OR HIDING
# FROM COMMITTEE ASSIGNMENTS

Participating on committees within your academic unit and university is the proverbial double-edged sword. On one hand, it is often to your advantage as a new faculty member, because working together is a good way for you to learn more about your colleagues and for them to get to know you better. Some committees may meet only once or twice a year and require little work. On the other hand, some committees (e.g., admissions, curriculum revision, and possibly, faculty search committees) may meet frequently and can eat up several days a month when you can least afford the time (like right before the end of the semester).

Before you agree to serve on a particular committee, consider the following:

**1.** *The amount of your time this committee will need:* Although at the beginning of the semester you may have the euphoric feeling that "all things are possible," by midterm, however—when you are frantically trying to prepare for the next lecture, grade a stack of papers, and send off an abstract with a deadline 48 hours away—you may come to resent two meetings scheduled for tomorrow that will demand substantial blocks of your time. This is not to say that it is in your best interest to refuse all committee work—it isn't. Faculty colleagues will expect you to be a team-player and to carry your fair share of committee work, too. The caution here is to be careful about agreeing to serve on so many committees that your own work and well-being suffers. This advice particularly applies to persons of color and women who are joining departments where they are clearly in the minority. You will need to learn, if you don't already know, how to say "no" nicely when overextended. Ultimately, your publications and productivity will be much more important in your quest for tenure than the number of committees on which you serve.

**2.** *Relative risk to untenured faculty:* One of the great things about democracy and voting in committees is that everyone's vote counts the same, whether they are a full professor or a mere instructor. Your vote may be the one that breaks the tie or kills some ill-conceived proposal. The downside of this is that some issues before committees are politically charged and therefore place you in a position where you might have to vote against the pet proposal of a faculty member who is powerful and known to hold grudges. Before deciding to serve on a committee, it would be in your best interest to assess the possible political risk. Although it is not always possible to ascertain the potential for controversy that exists within each committee, those with chairs who are known for charging boldly ahead and those with members who have loudly professed their interest in making drastic changes to existing policies could be committees to avoid. There are usually safer committees, such as student recruitment, that won't get you into political hot water.

**3.** *Visibility:*    Although they can consume your time, one advantage of serving on committees is that they may give you greater visibility within the department or larger university. This can be a real plus if you are a very large department (e.g., 50 faculty). And even if you aren't, serving with colleagues from various disciplines across the college or university will put you into contact with talented and creative colleagues who may become your friends or mentors. Your valuable contributions to one committee could lead to an appointment to an even more prestigious committee. At a minimum, colleagues from other areas are resources—individuals who may have knowledge or skills that could some day be useful to you or your students. Serving on a committee with prominent department heads or university officials can provide an informal access to them and can open doors later when you need help navigating through university bureaucracy. Volunteering to serve on committees associated with national associations and organizations can similarly work to your advantage, particularly if you want to make cross-institutional research connections (Sawyer, Prichard, & Hostetler, 1992).

**4.** *Personal contribution:*    Given your background or personal experience, you may be a "natural" for some committees. For instance, if you are the only one in your department with a law degree, it is very likely you'll be recommended for or elected to the committee that deals with student terminations and appeals. You should probably accept this role, as to decline it might give the wrong impression to your colleagues. Along this line, knowing how you might contribute to a committee may make the prospect of your participation more enjoyable and fruitful than working on a committee with an unclear mission or charge.

## ACADEMIC ADVISING

If you love teaching, you probably won't mind advising students. And if you are really good at it, students will pass the word and you will have even more students to advise because you'll hear these lines:

"My adviser is never in."

"My adviser forgot our appointment and I have to register today."

"My adviser doesn't know what he's talking about, and made me take a course last semester that I don't need."

"I don't know what to take, because I just transferred a bunch of credits in from Upper Frozen University."

Almost every faculty member gets students to advise. Depending on your institution, you may inherit a gaggle of students to advise your first semester or you may be given a period of grace (e.g., one semester or a year) in which to learn the curriculum first. The smaller your college or program, the more importance faculty advising will be given. In larger universities, there may be numerous advising resources; in small institutions, students will complain and word will travel if you don't do an adequate job.

If you are not provided an orientation about how to advise your students, then set one up for yourself by meeting with one of the more experienced faculty or staff who can tell you things such as which courses substitute for others, which courses must be taken in the fall semester because they aren't offered in spring, which courses every major must have to graduate, and so forth. Make yourself a file and write down the things you need to remember. Does your department have a checklist for graduating seniors or department majors? If so, get a copy and study it. If not, then create one for yourself.

Should you encounter a situation where you don't have an answer, then make a phone call and try to find the answer while the student is still there. Learning the answers to these questions early on will make for shorter advising sessions later. And even though advising may strike you as an odorous task, realize that students will be looking to you to be the expert and will be righteously indignant if you are not helpful. Being known as an uncaring, uninformed, or unhelpful adviser will not work to your advantage.

Some faculty try to minimize the amount of time required for advising by scheduling set appointment hours; others have "open-door" policies, allowing students to drop by at their convenience. Both of these approaches have strengths and weaknesses; decide which one works best for you. Particularly if you have a lot of advisees and a large enough office, you might try scheduling group advising sessions where four or five students can be advised simultaneously. If you plan well, say, by scheduling all the first-year students for one day, sophomores or juniors for different days, then there is some efficiency of effort in that your answering of one question will be applicable to others, as well.

You'll find it helpful to post some "rules" for your advisees. For instance, Rule 1, might be for them to verify that all the paperwork needed to establish them as a major in your department or graduate student in good standing has been completed.

Rule 2 might be for them to study the requirements needed for graduation (e.g., the number of English, math, and social science courses). Rule 3 could require that they examine the schedule of courses to be offered and do some prior planning before meeting with you. There's nothing wrong with expecting students to take a good deal of the responsibility here. The most time-consuming and frustrating advising sessions are always those where the student has not done any initial preparation and then discovers, in your office, that Math for Poets is offered only on Tuesdays and Thursdays, which conflicts with Chemistry for Chefs. When you point out an alternate schedule, the student doesn't want an 8:00 A.M. or a 4:00 P.M. class that meets the same time as her tennis lesson. You are quite within your rights to send these students out to the lounge, waiting area, or coffee shop to work out a schedule without wasting your time.

## HARASSMENT

We are living in an age where the rights of the individual are supreme. The particular danger for educators is that if we talk enough and give impromptu examples, it is not at all difficult to say something that may be experienced as offensive by someone in the class. Even as I am writing this, a local teacher has been suspended for 10 days from his high school because he used the word *penis*. His "crime" was preparing his class to view some classic works of art involving nudity (e.g., Michelangelo's *David*). In a human behavior course I once taught, a female student complained because I made mention of Desmond Morris's *(The Human Animal)* theorizing about the evolutionary value of female breasts as a mechanism to encourage pair-bonding. The point here is that even though you don't think of yourself as harassing students, there is no guarantee that one or more students won't take exception if you use sexual language, imagery, or examples.

As a new instructor, it is sometimes easy to fall into the trap of wanting to say something provocative or controversial to "stir up" the class, to bring the students to life, to generate some discussion. As a new educator, it might be tempting to want to show the class (particularly undergraduates) how "cool" you are by using street jargon or making humorous comments with an "edge" to them. Be careful. Although your intentions might be honorable and you didn't intend to single out any one individual or group, certain language (i.e., calling young adult women "girls," referring to "you people") can stir up a lot of trouble. Just remember that your job is not to be cool or to entertain, but to educate.

You may make a slip at some time and say something politically incorrect. When you do, simply say, "I'm sorry; I didn't mean to say that" or simply admit, "I spoke without thinking; I made a mistake." Most people forgive the contrite offender. Inadvertent misstatements do not usually end one's career. Most of us, at one time or another, have been guilty of this sort of thing—and such lapses are not generally considered harassment unless they are repetitive and severe.

Sexual harassment is often described in terms of being of two types: *quid pro quo*, which might involve something like trading grades for sexual favors, and *hostile environment*, which is conduct that intimidates or is so offensive that it interferes with an individual's work performance. Isolated incidents of misconduct generally will not create a "hostile work environment," although a single severe incident may give rise to a claim (e.g., the Paula Jones case) (Mallery, 1997; Fuertes, 1998).

Harassment consists of *unwanted* and *unwelcome* conduct of a sexual nature and can include jokes with suggestive themes, compliments of a personal or sexual nature, sexist slurs, visual images (e.g., sexually explicit posters, cartoons, or drawings), public humiliation, slander, pressuring someone for a date or sexual contact, sexual gestures, unwelcome notes, or such physical activities as brushing against someone, touching, unsolicited back rubs, or blocking a doorway with one's body. To support charges of harassment, courts are generally looking for "severe and pervasive" actions—behavior so offensive that any reasonable person would agree that it should be illegal (Risser, 1999). Victims of harassment feel threatened or assaulted—there is no reciprocity involved. An isolated joke or use of endearments generally would be viewed by courts as trivial—not harassment.

Faculty need to be especially careful in relationships with students, because one aspect of harassment is that the offender has a certain clout or power of position. In other words, students can argue that they felt pressured to comply with certain requests (e.g., repeated requests to go to dinner) due to the unequal power balance that existed—they didn't want to lose their grade of A or their research assistantship, for example.

Sexual harassment is also something you can experience from another faculty member or a peer, as well as from a student. Direct confrontation is often the best strategy: Tell the individual that you are not attracted to him or her, not interested in his or her notes or back rubs or whatever, and then instruct the person to respect your wishes. If this course of action does not work, then you need to go to your program chair or your dean and make a complaint. Do not be silent just because you are still a doctoral student or because you are new to the job. If you are being mistreated, there is a strong possibility that others have been, too. Courts are sympathetic to individuals who claim "hostile work environments" where it can be shown that pervasive and severe discrimination, intimidation, ridicule, or insult existed because of sexual orientation or gender, race, religion, national origin, age, disability, veteran status, pregnancy, or marital status. Most universities are concerned about discrimination in any form and will move relatively quickly to investigate and solve these situations.

## STUDENTS AS RESEARCH SUBJECTS

In most, if not all, social science disciplines, it is quite acceptable to use one's students as research subjects—providing, of course, that it is voluntary on their part, that there is no harm or risk of harm, and that this activity does not detract from the educational instruction that ought to be occurring in the course. Always keep in mind that students (or their parents) generally do not pay tuition in order to advance your research.

The ethical principle of voluntary participation means that students cannot be coerced to complete survey forms, complete batteries of tests, reveal personal or sensitive information (e.g., about their experience with taking illegal drugs), or gather certain data against their will (particularly that from which you stand to benefit). Every student must have the right to decide whether to participate or not, without there being any penalty or repercussions for nonparticipation. Generally, this means providing (student) research participants with a written consent form that briefly explains the project, the extent of their involvement, and any benefits or risks. As a first step, you should discuss your research protocol with the Institutional Review Board (IRB) at your college or university. You will probably need to complete a form (e.g., Exemption Certification Form) identifying your research objectives and procedures to be used as well as how you plan to recruit your subjects. This somewhat formal process doesn't mean, however, that you shouldn't consider gathering data from or about your students. The classroom is a natural laboratory that has many advantages (convenience being perhaps the main one) to recommend it.

Sometimes instructors encourage students to participate in their research projects by awarding extra credit. This is generally well received in that students can look at what is being asked of them and then weigh whether they want to participate. Even when the research activity can be easily defended as a required assignment on pedagogical grounds, students should be given an option of working on another activity of similar importance or value if the student-produced data directly benefit the researcher. Students sometimes object to specific questions or sections of a questionnaire because of the fear that their data might not remain confidential or they may have religious objections to the project. In such cases, students who wish to receive extra credit without being research subjects should have other alternate projects or exercises available to them.

That engaging in a research project should not have any adverse effects on the participants seems straightforward enough. Ethically, your responsibility is to do no harm. The problem is that it is not always possible to anticipate how certain questions or activities may influence others. Interviewing students who have been victims of child abuse or domestic violence may provide much useful data but could, conceivably, impinge negatively on their self-esteem, leave them feeling depressed or in need of counseling to resolve painful issues that have been dredged up again. Studies where deception is used could leave participants feeling that they are naive or gullible, with a result that they become less likely to trust others. Punch (1986) has described a situation where a project designed to study the reactions of the police to reports of rape was scrapped because fabricated stories were going to be used and the fear was that the research might lead police to become skeptical of the real accounts of women who were sexually assaulted. Students might be willing to volunteer in such a project, particularly if there was a perception within a community that the police were insensitive to the claims of rape victims, but there would be legal repercussions for filing false police reports and the benefits might not outweigh the risks and potential harm that could result. Benefits should always clearly outweigh the potential for harm.

The third guideline is balance of the educational mission. It is one thing to take 15 minutes of class time to ask students to voluntarily fill out a questionnaire on their television viewing habits, but it is altogether another matter to ask students to give up every third class period to fill out questionnaires. If you are paid to be the instructor of a course, that must remain your paramount concern. The use of your students to supply data for your own research ought to be in a distant second or third place. In-class participation in research projects should not short-change or educationally impoverish your students. If you can't, with a clear conscience, easily defend what you are planning on having them do from an educational perspective, then you probably shouldn't involve them—even if it means you will have to conduct all of the interviews yourself or pay someone to help you.

## BUILDING A PROFESSIONAL PORTFOLIO

One thing you can be sure of—you *will* need to present documentation of your competence and contributions at some point in your teaching career. Typically, these professional portfolios contain data such as:

1. Teaching evaluations from students, syllabi prepared, new courses created, workshops or special seminars conducted, invitational lectures given, and so on
2. Scholarship: publications authored, grants obtained, and the like
3. Professional service to the community, department, or college (e.g., committee appointments or elections, number of students advised)
4. Letters from reviewers of your portfolio
5. Unsolicited letters from students and former students

Create a filing system using the evaluation scheme or categories employed at your college university and begin it your first academic term. You might want to start one manilla folder for publications submitted, another for any unsolicited letters from students, a third for thank-you letters from organizations where you've provided consultation or volunteered, and so on. Update your vita whenever something significant occurs—keep track of all the different courses you've taught, the new courses you designed or created, the overloads you have carried, as well as any special honors or recognitions. Don't assume that you will remember everything four or five years in the future—it's better and easier to keep the vita current as things occur. If you have not been given a set of the guidelines that your department or college will use in determining your status relative to tenure, then by all means ask for a copy so that you can start preparing your portfolio.

Periodically browse through your materials. If your institution values teaching more highly than publishing, your teaching folder should be "fatter" than, say, your community service folder. Similarly, at a research university your scholarship folder would likely be thicker than your teaching folder. It may be useful to talk to colleagues to see what kinds of things they file and keep for their portfolios.

## PROMOTION AND TENURE

As alluded to previously, there is a tremendous amount of variation both in terms of the tenure review process, when it begins (e.g., the fourth year, fifth year, or sixth year), and what is expected and required of assistant professors in colleges and universities across the country. These expectations should be discussed during your job interview or soon afterwards, but, in any event, should be clear to you prior to signing your contract. Even so, it's a good idea early in your first year to confirm your understanding of the requirements with the head of your department or college. Ask colleagues who've recently been promoted about their experiences and for their advice. You may also want to read such books as those by Tierney and Bensimon (1996) and relevant chapters from Sawyer, Prichard, and Hostetler (1992) and Boice (1992).

## A MODEL FOR DEVELOPING TEACHING ASSISTANTS (BY LINDA WORLEY)

A colleague tells this story about the "training" he had before becoming a teaching assistant: "The composition director happened to see me on campus late in the summer and asked me to come to his office. This was in 1972. I was scheduled to begin graduate school in English in a month. 'How would you like to be a teaching assistant?' he asked. He told me I'd teach three sections of comp and told me the salary. 'Here's the text for the course,' he said, and handed me a copy. 'Good luck.'"

"Here's the text—good luck": That was the entire training program for a soon-to-be teaching assistant who would in a few weeks find himself under the spotlight in a classroom full of undergraduates. And for many of these undergraduates, this would be their first experience with university-level teaching and academic life.

Happily, things are changing. Teaching assistants around the country are increasingly being given thorough orientations and ongoing training for their instructional roles. This increased focus on the development of teaching assistants is linked to calls for improvement in undergraduate education, especially as it affects first-year students.

Teaching assistants play many roles in the life of undergraduates. In addition to interaction in the classroom, where the teaching assistant is the sole instructor for a section of a composition, communication, or foreign language course, an undergraduate's first-year course schedule may bring a teaching assistant into contact with the students as a tutor, grader, or recitation or lab instructor. The teaching assistant may well be the most personal academic contact an undergraduate has with the institution and thus can help foster a sense of belonging to the academic enterprise and influence the success of the undergraduate's college career.

Besides their involvement in undergraduate education, it is vital to recognize the role that a teaching assistantship can play in the career of graduate students who wish to become members of the professoriate. The pedagogical knowledge base gained during the course of the teaching assistantship can become a solid foundation for the teaching functions all faculty members fulfill. In an increasingly competitive academic arena, the teaching assistant experience needs to be seen as an essential part of graduate education.

These factors underscore the necessity for a well thought-out, cohesive teaching assistant experience. How should this experience be structured? What kinds of activities should be included in a teaching assistant program? When and where should they occur? To answer these questions, we can turn to the literature on teaching assistant development. A particularly useful conceptual model sketches the changes in a novice teacher's concern vis-à-vis students over time (Sprague & Nyquist, 1991).

Preservice and first-year teaching assistants are likely concerned with issues that can best be described as interpersonal "self-concerns." Teaching assistants tend to hold "a highly engaged view toward students that is characterized by a sense of vulnerability or great ego-involvement on the TA's part" (Sprague & Nyquist, 1991, p. 309). The "self-concerns" of teaching assistants will often cause them to view their students as emotional allies/friends or, conversely, as sources of a threat to their authority. In a survey conducted in the summers of 1997 and 1998, the fear of losing control of the classroom and the fear of not being able to establish rapport dominated the worries of teaching assistants during university-wide orientations held at my institution. These apprehensions speak to a concern with basic survival in the classroom.

One strategy to help teaching assistants acquire more confidence in the classroom is initially to limit their duties to those that do not require high levels of complex interaction with students. Teaching assistants might first be asked to grade exams, set up experiments, work as tutors—literally, to assist a professor. If teaching assistants are asked to perform more extensive duties early in their graduate careers, then they need to be given very specific, even prescriptive, guidance.

Another highly effective activity at this stage is the micro-teach. A micro-teach allows the individual assistant to prepare and teach a short lesson to a small group in order to receive specific feedback from the group or facilitator in a safe, controlled environment before the teaching assistant has contact with many students. It is important that graduate students receive concrete help with their teaching duties from their home department or supervising professor in addition to an orientation that outlines more general roles and responsibilities.

A university-wide orientation can be the best place to focus on such issues as the rights and responsibilities of graduate students, on ways to establish rapport with students while keeping mutual respect alive in the classroom, and on the demographics of the student body at large. Case studies, simulations, and video clips are excellent ways to involve graduate students in these topics.

Departmental orientations build on the more general university-wide orientation, adding specificity. The department and individual supervising professor are the optimal sources for the detailed information a new teaching assistant needs in order to successfully complete the assigned tasks. Teaching assistants will learn about their specific duties, grading guidelines, as well as the resources and avenues of recourse available to them. They need to be prepared for their daily teaching assignments, whether these involve leading an effective discussion or demonstrating a lab technique. By the end of the orientation, teaching assistants should have the skills needed to be successful during the first weeks of the semester.

After gaining confidence and, indeed, "surviving" the first months, teaching assistants can begin to pay more attention to issues directly related to the craft of teaching. At this developmental stage, they become interested in acquiring and experimenting with a variety of teaching strategies. At a later point, a focus on students' learning may be added to the earlier concerns about interacting with students and instructional techniques. Changing the focus from "teaching" to "learning" produces monumental shifts in the teaching/learning enterprise—shifts that include attention to creating environments that recognize individual differences and that recognize the importance of learning outcomes (Barr & Tagg, 1995).

The supervising professor and graduate department need to be aware of and support this growth process. An optimal development plan has at least three components: knowledge and experience regarding pedagogy, data regarding performance, and feedback. Which form these components take will vary with the expertise and maturity of the teaching assistant.

Teaching strategies can be learned in a formal graduate teaching seminar or in workshops. The teaching assistant meeting, with its emphasis on the daily needs of the course, will not in and of itself provide the depth or breadth needed to gain a solid foundation in teaching. The course supervisor, departmental faculty, or outside experts can all be involved in such formal instruction. Individual consultations between peers or the supervisor and the teaching assistant augment formal instruction. Topics may range from effective presentation techniques to issues of student motivation and classroom climate.

Data regarding performance should be gathered from various sources throughout the semester. Although teaching assistants probably know to use "minute papers" to assess how well students are learning content, such techniques can also provide valuable feedback in terms of instructor behavior and classroom procedures—indeed, what is working or not working well within the classroom. In addition to the standard end of semester evaluations, student input can be gathered through a class interview called the *small group instruction diagnosis*. In this process, faculty working with teaching assistants observe instruction directly through visiting or videotaping a class. A useful format for class visits is to arrange for a preobservation meeting during which time the teaching assistant and visitor can discuss the learning goals and plans for the particular class to be visited. It is helpful if the teaching assistant gives the observer several areas in which feedback is desired—for example, the pacing of the class, inclusion of all class members in a discussion, and so on. This way, the classroom observation becomes a process in which both the observer and observed are involved. The observer should take notes on both the teaching activities and the responses of the students, being sure to look for behaviors the teaching assistant had noted.

Gathering data on the performance of the teaching assistant is the first step. These data ought to be discussed with the TA and used for formative purposes—that is, to direct growth and change. As soon after a classroom visit as possible, the supervisor should meet with the teaching assistant. Feedback that is descriptive rather than personal will set the stage for the supervisor and teaching assistant to develop a joint plan of action designed to improve on strengths and weaknesses.

Teaching assistants nearing the end of their course of studies, especially those who wish to become faculty members, are best viewed as "junior colleagues." They might be given sole responsibility for a course. Along with such increased autonomy will come a new set of concerns. They need to know how to determine learning outcomes, construct a syllabus, tailor instruction so as to allow for various learning styles, assess student work fairly, and give informative feedback. The senior faculty member might be most useful at this point by encouraging the teaching assistant to become a reflective practitioner. This can be accomplished by sharing articles on teaching and learning as well as suggesting that the teaching assistant keep a teaching journal or begin to assemble artifacts for a teaching portfolio.

Graduate students who are considering pursuing an academic career need additional mentoring. They need to be introduced to the roles and responsibilities of college and university faculty. The national Preparing Future Faculty initiative[1] is designed to assist graduate students in understanding the variety of institutions in which faculty members work and the academic expectations, institutional identities, and particular policies and procedures that characterize different types of institutions of higher learning.

A recent survey I conducted asked new faculty at a wide range of postsecondary institutions to rate aspects of faculty life as to their importance for the individual's career advancement and to rank these same items with respect to graduate training received. The items that evidenced the largest numerical gap between the perceived importance to career and graduate training were:

1. Advising students
2. Creating a teaching portfolio
3. Working on department/university committees
4. Performing community service
5. Using multimedia effectively
6. Providing feedback designed to help students improve
7. Experimenting with innovative teaching strategies
8. Constructing a thoughtful syllabus
9. Understanding student abilities and preparation

The items on this list could readily become the basis of a departmental program designed to fill in some of the gaps for their future professionals.

A truly developmental view of graduate student professionalization recognizes that graduate students must gain the values, skills, and knowledge needed to be successful in their present teaching situations and to be engaged with the teaching/learning process throughout their careers.

## REFERENCES AND RESOURCES

Abbott, A. S. (1992). Teaching at a small liberal arts college. In R. M. Sawyer, K. W. Prichard, & K. D. Hostetler (Eds.), *The art and politics of college teaching.* New York: Peter Lang.

Barr, R. B., & Tagg, J. (1995). From teaching to learning: A new paradigm for undergraduate education. *Change, 27* (6), 12–25.

Beebe, L. (1993). *Professional writing for the human services.* Washington, DC: NASW Press.

Bedient, D. (1997–1998). Teaching assistant concerns and questions: What 252 TAs wanted to know and weren't afraid to ask. *The Journal of Graduate Assistant Development, 5* (3), 127–132.

Bode, R. (1999). Mentoring and collegiality. In R. K. Menges & Associates (Eds.), *Faculty in new jobs: A guide to settling in, becoming established, and building institutional support.* San Francisco: Jossey-Bass.

Boice, R. (1987). Is released-time an effective device for faculty development? *Research in Higher Education, 26,* 311–326.

Boice, R. (1992). *The new faculty member: Supporting and fostering professional development.* San Francisco: Jossey-Bass.

Dunn, D. S., & Zaremba, S. B. (1997). Thriving at liberal arts colleges: The more compleat academic. *Teaching of Psychology, 24,* 8–14.

Fuertes, M. (1998, November). Ruling out sexual harassment. *Techniques, 42–43.*

Henson, K. T. (1995). *The art of writing for publication.* Boston: Allyn and Bacon.

Mallery, M. (1997). The answers to your questions about sexual harassment. *Workforce, 76* (11), S7–S10.

McCrumb, S. (1998, May). Of time and the writer. *Writer's Digest, 78,* 18–20ff.

Parks, B. (1998). Taking care of teachers: 7 time-management sanity savers. *Instructor, 107* (5), 46.

Punch, M. (1986). *The politics and ethics of fieldwork.* Beverly Hills, CA: Sage.

Risser, R. (1999). Sexual harassment training: Truth and consequences. *Training & Development, 53,* 21–23.

Sandler, B., & Shoop, R. J. (1997). *Sexual harassment on campus: A guide for administrators, faculty, and students.* Boston: Allyn and Bacon.

Sawyer, R. M., Prichard, K. W., & Hostetler, K. D. (1992). *The art and politics of college teaching.* New York: Peter Lang.

Schoenfeld, A. C., & Magnan, R. (1992). *Mentor in a manual.* Madison, WI: Magna Publications.

Seldin, P. (1997). *The teaching portfolio: A practical guide to improved performance and promotion/tenure decisions.* Bolton, MA: Anker Publishing.

Sorcinelli, M. D. (1992). New and junior faculty stress: Research and responses. In M. D. Sorcinelli & A. E. Austin (Eds.), *Developing new and junior faculty* (pp. 27–37). San Francisco: Jossey-Bass.

Sprague, J., & Nyquist, J. D. (1991). A developmental perspective on the TA role. In J. D. Nyquist, R. D. Abbot, D. H. Wulff, & J. Sprague (Eds.), *Preparing the professoriate of tomorrow to teach: Selected readings in TA training.* Dubuque, IA: Kendall-Hunt.

Thyer, B. (1994). *Successful publishing in scholarly journals.* Thousand Oaks, CA: Sage.

Tierney, W. G., & Bensimon, E. M. (1996). *Promotion and tenure: Community and socialization in academe.* Albany: State University of New York Press.

Weaver, R. (1992). Building a future at "The Premiere Teaching University" in the Midwest. In R. M. Sawyer, K. W. Prichard, & K. D. Hostetler (Eds.), *The art and politics of college teaching.* New York: Peter Lang.

---

## ENDNOTE

1. The Preparing Future Faculty initiative is sponsored by the American Association of Colleges and Universities and the Council of Graduate Schools funded by the PEW foundation.

# TEACHING ONLINE WITH COURSECOMPASS

### BRENDA KERR

## INTRODUCTION

Welcome to CourseCompass. This chapter will guide you through the general information you will need to know in order to take advantage of CourseCompass' integrated features.

CourseCompass is a nationally hosted learning management system available by contacting Allyn and Bacon directly by phone or by visiting our website at http://www.ablongman.com. Learning management systems provide integrated tools that facilitate the construction and management of online courses, enable synchronous and asynchronous communication between instructors and students, and provide a consistent user interface for students who take multiple online courses.

Synchronous communication refers to communication that occurs between individuals in real time. Examples include talking on the telephone or communicating in an internet-based chat session. Asynchronous communication refers to communication between individuals that is separated by time. Examples include leaving voice mail messages, sending email, or posting messages on bulletin boards. Instructors and students can use CourseCompass to easily place information on web pages, post and look up grades, and prepare and take quizzes, tests, and surveys. Assignments may even be turned in electronically. Each CourseCompass course includes state-of-the-art course material provided by the Higher Education publishers of Pearson Education.

CourseCompass is powered by Blackboard 5 and includes all the powerful Blackboard features for teaching and learning. But CourseCompass also includes feature improvements, such as streamlined registration, separate student enrollment, and course creation with ready-to-use course materials, that make it both easy to learn and easy to use. These enhancements make CourseCompass the best learning and online course content option available today.

## MINIMUM SYSTEM REQUIREMENTS

- Access to the Internet.
- A Macintosh or Windows PC with at least 32 MB of RAM
- One of the following browsers: Netscape 4.0 or higher or Internet Explorer 4.0 or higher. JavaScript and cookies must be enabled.
- Additional programs and browser plug-ins recommended. Example: Microsoft Office programs, QuickTime, Adobe PDF reader.
- Browser mail preferences configured to your preferred email program.

## WHY SHOULD I USE THE COURSECOMPASS COURSE MANAGEMENT SYSTEM?

Advantages of CourseCompass include:

- **Low tech.** CourseCompass is low tech. It does not require a great deal of technical experience from either the faculty member or the student taking the online course.
- **Common interface.** CourseCompass provides a common interface for students who are taking multiple courses.
- **Flexibility.** CourseCompass lets you add files of any type to your course, from simple text documents to complex slide presentations and animations.
- **Built-in and customizable assessment.** CourseCompass course materials include a rich selection of built-in assessments and question pools. You can use existing assessment as is, modify or remove questions to suit your needs, or create your own custom assessments.
- **Automated grading.** CourseCompass grades student assessments as students complete them and automatically posts scores to an online grade book. As a result you can spend more time teaching and less times grading.
- **Availability.** Course content (lectures, assignments, handouts) and grades are always available, 24 hours a day, 7 days a week.
- **Virtual office hours.** Office hours can be held in real time using CourseCompass' Virtual Classroom (Chat).
- **Easy-to-use communication and administrative tools.** The built-in course calendar, announcements, and email components can be used to notify students of important days and changes in coursework, etc.
- **Superior technical support.** CourseCompass provides product hosting, technical support, a printed Instructor Quick Start guide, and comprehensive online Help area tailored for you. It also comes with a Student Quick Start and online Help for students, so you can focus on teaching your course, not on teaching CourseCompass.

## HOW DOES TEACHING ONLINE DIFFER FROM TEACHING A TRADITIONAL COURSE?

An online course is not just lecture notes or textbooks cut and pasted onto a website. [Schweizer, 1999 #6][p.1] It is important that you, the instructor, take on a facilitative role and establish an interactive, student-centered, teaching and learning environment. This will include personalizing learning experiences, designing content for multiple intelligences and learning styles, and allowing students to discover learning.

As an online teacher you will need to deal with the pedagogical, social, managerial, and technical aspects of your online course. You will need to establish a collaborative and self-directed learning environment in which technical glitches are kept to a minimum and successful learning and collaboration are the norm. [Schweizer, 1999 #6]

Students who are highly self-directed, who believe that their own behaviors directly influence results or consequences, may be the most successful all-around, online students. Students who display these personality traits may do well in all types of online courses including those that are mostly text based and those that have an extensive amount of collaboration and interactivity. It is the responsibility of the online instructor to develop techniques that motivate all types of students, not only those that are highly self-directed, just as he or she would do when teaching in a traditional classroom. [Gibson, 1998 #4]

Plans for an online course, versus a course taught in a traditional classroom, need to be more complete on the first day of class. Students need to see as much of the course content as possible immediately because they need to understand what work will be expected of them to complete the course. This does not mean that you cannot change things during the class according to student and course needs. You should still be able to take advantage of the teachable moment as you would in a traditional classroom, but you will need to strike a balance between designing a highly structured class with the need to be flexible.

## ACCESSING COURSECOMPASS

Let's take a moment to log into the CourseCompass server and look around at your course shell.

### Logging In

1. Use your browser to navigate to the course URL or main CourseCompass log-in page. Go to *http://www.ablongman.com/coursecompass*
2. Type in your username and password. If this is the first time you have logged into the system you may be prompted to enter a new username

and password that only you know. You may also be asked to fill out personal information that has not been added to the course database.

3. If you logged into the CourseCompass server from the main Course-Compass page you will see your "**My CourseCompass**" area. This area contains links to all the courses you have on the CourseCompass server and to other resources.

4. Click on the course or resource link you want to follow.

## My CourseCompass

The My CourseCompass page contains a series of modules—such as My Courses, My Announcements, and Services and Support—that give you access to CourseCompass courses, features, and information. This page also displays a Tools area with links to common resources, such as your personal Tasks list and Address Book.

The CourseCompass system administrator can restrict or require certain modules to appear on all My CourseCompass pages. Beyond that, you can choose modules that you want to appear on your individual My Course Compass page.

## CourseCompass Tabs

Near the top of the CourseCompass window you will see a series of 4 tabs.

- The first tab lets you easily get back to your **My CourseCompass** area.
- The **Courses** tab displays the Course List page, which lists courses you are currently teaching or previewing. Click a course name to go to that course's Announcements page.
- The **Services** tab displays the Support and Services page, which contains information for contacting CourseCompass Customer Support if you need assistance.
- The **Academic Web Resources** tab provides direct access to the Blackboard 5 Resource Center page. You can click links on this page to visit resource sites related to your discipline.

## The Course Homepage and Content Area

When you follow a link to one of your courses its main home page will display. This page contains course announcements, located in the page content area, the course navigation bar, and the control bar. Information concerning assignment due dates, quiz and test dates, discussion topics, and other important course information will be posted there. Four display options are available for viewing your announcements. You can choose to display only the current day's announcements, announcements from the last 2 weeks, announcements from the last month, or all announcements. As you use the Navigation bar to access other parts of the course, new information will display in the content area.

## Open the Course Announcements Page and Browse through Pearson Education Course Materials

To open the course Announcements page, follow these steps:

1. From the My CourseCompass page, click the name of the course you want to open. The course announcements page will appear. The first time you open a course's Announcements page a standard announcement will appear describing the course material you selected. You can delete this announcement and add your own course information. (See Adding Course Announcements to Your CourseCompass Course)
2. To explore content that has been pre-loaded into your course, click the content area button on the navigation bar on the left side of your page.

   **Note** You *view* built-in content by clicking one of the navigation buttons on the left. You *modify* or *add to* the content using the Control Panel.

## Navigation Bar

The navigation bar is located at the top left portion of the web page. The bar consists of large, rectangular buttons that lead to the course content areas and the communication and student tools. The instructor can choose which areas are accessible only to enrolled students and which areas are available to guests. Table 1 on page 282 lists the navigation bar buttons and the functions of the areas to which they link.

## Additional Navigation Buttons

Instructors may choose to enable three additional buttons on the navigation bar. They provide quick links to the course Discussion Board, the Virtual Chat area and the Group Pages.

## Control Bar

The Control Bar is made up of lighter colored buttons located directly below the Navigation buttons. These buttons take you to Blackboard resources, and areas that are not part of a particular course, the Course Map, and the

**TABLE 1   Navigation Bar Buttons**

| NAVIGATION BUTTON | COURSE AREA FUNCTION |
| --- | --- |
| Announcements | Includes reminders about project deadlines, quizzes, tests, and other course related information. This is the first content area displayed when you enter the course. |
| Course Information | Contains general course information such as the course description, a syllabus, a list of software that is needed to complete assignments, and general course procedures. |
| Staff Information | Contains information concerning the instructor and other teaching staff involved with the course. This area usually includes staff contact information and possibly a photograph of the instructor(s). |
| Course Documents | Includes the main content of the course. Documents such as handouts, lecture materials, and readings can be found in this section, in addition to multimedia presentations or simulations. |
| Assignments | Houses quizzes, tests, assignments and surveys. Usually tests and quizzes are available only for a specific period of time and can be taken only once unless they are practice tests. |
| Communication | Groups access to all communication tools together in one area. Tools for email, chat, discussion, student and group pages, and the student roster are included here. |
| External Links | Lists URLs that the instructor has provided for a specific course. |
| Tools | Provides a place to "hand in" assignments, tools for editing student homepages and changing personal information, a student calendar, access to grades, a student manual, and a tool for taking and saving notes. |

Control Panel. More detailed explanations of each area are listed in the table below.

| Control Bar Button | Control Area Functions |
| --- | --- |
| Resources | Links to resources that can be used to enrich the learning experience such as a research center, a dictionary, a thesaurus, search engines, news, featured articles, links, products and services, and featured partners. |

| Control Bar Button | Control Area Functions |
|---|---|
| Course Map | Allows you to quickly locate content stored in your course without moving from one content area to another, click the Course Map button in the Control Bar, the lighter colored buttons located directly below the navigation bar. Clicking this button opens a small pop-up window that contains an outline of each content area; click each book image to see a list of content stored in that area. |
| Control Panel | Allows you to create and customize content and tools in your course. |

## Additional CourseCompass Buttons

| Button | Function |
|---|---|
| Home | Takes you to the CourseCompass server home page. |
| Help | Takes you to an extensive help area that provides answers to many of your CourseCompass questions. |
| Logout | Logs you out of the course. It is also wise to exit the browser, if you are working on a computer shared by others, to ensure that no one else can access your personal course area. |

## Logging Out

1. Click the Logout button.
2. Close your browser to complete the process. **Note:** Even though you have logged out of your course it may be possible for someone to gain access to your personal course information unless you completely quit your browser application.

## PEDAGOGICAL ISSUES

### Course Creation—Planning

During the initial phase of course creation you will need to analyze the course subject matter, the resources available to you and your students, course design and online learning pedagogy, the typical characteristics of students who take your course, your own teaching characteristics, and the technology available to both you and your students.

Determine the characteristics of the students who take your courses. What is their motivation for taking the course? Do they live a great distance from a university? What ages are your students? What types of backgrounds do your students have? What cultural makeup does your class have? Is English their native language? What are your students' preferred learning styles? Which of your students are highly self-directed and believe that their own behaviors directly influence results or consequences and which students need external motivation to do well in class?

It is important that you analyze your own background, age, preferred teaching style, experience, and personality and determine how you can best meet your students' needs in a manner in which you feel comfortable. As stated before in this manual, online teachers need be willing to deal with the pedagogical, social, managerial, and technical aspects of online teaching. [Schweizer, 1999 #6] It is your job to establish a positive learning environment and develop and maintain communication with the students. Students may call upon you first to help them solve technical glitches. You will need to know enough about the technologies you use in your online classroom to assure accessibility by all students and know how to provide alternative resources.

After completing the analysis phase of designing your course you will need to develop Educational Goals and Objectives, then list methods for implementing these goals and objectives, and finally, prioritize the list of methods. The next step is to develop a course structure on paper or use some type of webbing software (Inspiration or even the navigation structure of FrontPage 2000 will work) and finally make a syllabus.

The next step is to begin creating your course on the CourseCompass server. Log into your CourseCompass course and make blank web pages and navigation tools that allow for easy, intuitive navigation throughout the course using the course structure that you developed as a guide. Evaluate the course navigation and begin adding course content in the form of web pages and other media. While you are placing course content on the CourseCompass server you might also want to simultaneously develop a glossary of terms that will be useful for your students to know.

After you have finished adding content, evaluate the course navigation and the accessibility of content for people who have various physical disabilities. You may also want to prepare content for students who have lower levels of technical ability and own older versions of software on older computers. Plan alternate methods of content delivery whenever you can.

## Developing Educational Outcomes (Goals) and Objectives for Your Course

In planning any course it is important to list specific student skills and knowledge that must be attained for successful completion of the course outcomes or goals. After the ending skills and knowledge are determined, work backward to develop goals and objectives and methods for reaching these outcomes.

A performance-based curriculum design model is based on learner outcomes at three different levels: program, course, and unit. [Schweizer, 1999 #6] A curriculum committee has probably designed the program outcomes for you so we will focus on planning for the course and unit. The basic three documents you need to design are

1. the course description (a general one- or two-paragraph description of your course in narrative style);
2. the culminating course outcomes (state what the student needs to know upon completion of the course); and
3. the unit or module outcomes (a more detailed accounting of the components that make up the knowledge or skills presented in the course outcomes). This process of designing a course from general to specific knowledge is called *designing down*.

Culminating course outcomes are usually stated at the beginning of the course so that students know what will be expected from them. Unit or module outcomes are the culminating course outcomes broken down into knowledge and skill components in order to enable the learner to achieve the outcomes of the course. The next step after writing unit outcomes is to write student outcomes, or objectives, that will need to be accomplished in order to achieve the learning goals. Student outcomes use verbiage such as "explain in your own words" and "describe to the class" to indicate how the student will demonstrate knowledge or proficiency in a skill.

Keep Bloom's Taxonomy in mind when writing student outcomes. The six levels of Bloom's Taxonomy indicate an increasingly complex set of mental skills encouraging students to develop more complex understanding of the material. The six levels are

1. Knowledge (recall)
2. Comprehension (summarize, translate, predict immediate application from known data)
3. Application (use information in original form or a new form)
4. Analysis (generalize, break down an idea into its parts, or predict an outcome by recognizing new assumptions)
5. Synthesis (take learned knowledge from one or more sources and combine it to make new knowledge)
6. Evaluation (make judgments supported by facts or knowledge).

You may also find Robert M. Gagné's 5 categories or domains useful in writing student outcomes. They are

1. *Verbal information* (recall or declarative knowledge), suitable when the achievement of this outcome leads to the achievement of a more complex outcome

2. *Intellectual skills,* analogous to Bloom's levels of application, analysis, synthesis, and evaluation [Smith, 1993 #8]

3. *Cognitive strategies* (learning strategies)

4. *Attitudes* (learning is influenced by student attitude toward the course content and delivery and make learning choices accordingly)

5. *Psychomotor skills,* useful in writing outcomes. (Teach rules related to psychomotor skills in your course.)

## Listing and Prioritizing Methods for Implementing Goals and Objectives

Determine the methods you will use to implement the course goals and objectives. To determine methods for teaching course objectives construct an information-processing flowchart for each objective. (Flow-charting software may be useful for this purpose.) The flow chart should begin with the objective and then list each step that must be accomplished or each decision that must be made in order to accomplish the objective. Make another flowchart that lists the order in which each objective must be met in order to accomplish the ultimate learning goal. You may now want to apply unit headings, short titles, and due dates to each objective.

## Developing a Course Structure on Paper or on Computer Using Webbing Software (Inspiration) or a Web Site Editor (FrontPage 2000)

After listing and prioritizing methods for implementing goals and objectives, begin planning your web site. The last flowchart that you created, the one that lists the order in which each objective must be accomplished, can be used to design the structure of your online course.

1. Make a new flow chart on paper or on the computer.

2. The first web page on this flow chart should be the page that contains the syllabus and course description.

3. Next, make folder icons for each of the units of your course.

4. Make page icons for each activity (lecture, assignment, reading, group project) that will occur in each unit under the corresponding unit folder icon.

5. Continue to add to your web flowchart until you have finished designing the flowchart of your web course.

6. Gather all the unit titles, method titles (activities, readings, or assignments) and due dates into a single text file to be placed on your syllabus page in your online course.

7. Follow the directions below for accessing CourseCompass' course creation tools.

## Course Creation—Setting Up and Managing Your Online Course on the CourseCompass Server

You are now ready to start adding content to your CourseCompass course area. Most of the tasks you complete while setting up and managing your online course start from the Control Panel. You can access this area by clicking the Control Panel button on the Control Bar.

The Control Panel provides tools for

- Adding course announcements and staff information
- Adding a course syllabus by typing in its contents or linking to a file that you have created outside of CourseCompass
- Setting up course assignments
- Creating discussion board forums to solicit student feedback
- Reviewing and adding online lecture materials
- Creating and customizing course assessments from the Control Panel area
- Communicating with students and other staff members via email (can also be accessed through the Communications button on the Navigation Bar)
- Picking up and returning student work electronically
- Conducting online lectures with the Virtual Classroom (can also be accessed through the Communications button on the Navigation Bar)
- Monitoring and participating in Discussion Board forums (can also be accessed through the Communications button on the Navigation Bar)
- Tracking student performance with the online grade book.

Most of the time you spend working in CourseCompass will be spent adding content to your course. Most of the content you want to add to your course probably already exists in the form of word processing documents, PowerPoint presentations and other types of files. You may upload these files to your CourseCompass course in their original form, and, as long as your students have the programs you used to create them (or players for those programs) installed on their computers, they will be able to open these files. However, it may be helpful to the students if you use the Save As command to save each of your non-web files to a software version that will be compatible with software that may be a version or two previous to the current version of the software. As you have time you may also want to convert your course content to web pages to offer alternative viewing options.

### Adding Course Announcements to Your CourseCompass Course

When you open the course Announcements page for the first time, you will see that it includes a standard announcement describing the course material you selected when you created the course. To welcome students to your course, you can delete this standard announcement and add your own Welcome announcement. Once the class starts, you might also use announcements to send assignments, remind students of upcoming tests, or post information about course-related seminars and resources.

*To delete the standard announcement and add a course announcement.*
1. Click the Control Panel button in the Control Bar (the light colored buttons below the navigation menu).
2. Locate the Content Area of the Control Panel and click the Announcements link.
3. Click the Remove button to the right of the "Permanent—Welcome" announcement.
4. Click OK when the verification prompt window displays. The announcement will immediately vanish from the Announcements Control Panel page.
5. Click on the Announcements button in the Navigation Bar to see that the announcement is now gone from the student view, also.

*To Add an Announcement to Your CourseCompass Course.*
1. Click the Control Panel button in the Control Bar (the light colored buttons below the navigation menu).
2. Locate the Content Area of the Control Panel and click the Announcements link.
3. Click the Add Announcements button to display the Add Announcement page.
4. Type the announcement information
   a. Type in a subject for your message in the subject field.
   b. Type the text of your announcement in the message field. You may type or paste text in 3 different text formats.
      ■ **Smart Text.** Recognizes standard text, converts text URLs to links (but not email addresses) and recognizes actual HTML tags.
      ■ **Plain Text.** Displays text only. It does not link URLs that you type or recognize HTML tags.
      ■ **HTML.** Allows you to type or paste HTML documents into the message field. You may design your announcement in a web page editor view and copy its source tags and paste the tags into the message field.
5. Specify the type of text you have entered into the message field.
6. Select whether you want to have your announcements appear permanently on the course Announcements page (select Yes), or whether the announcement will appear only for set period of time (select No). Announcements that you have set to permanently appear on the course

announcements page will appear to you in the Announcements Control panel with the word "Permanent" in red, directly before the announcement subject.

7. Click the Submit button and the announcement will be created. Click the Cancel button to discard the announcement.

8. A confirmation page will appear that displays the announcement as you formatted it. CourseCompass calls this page the Announcement Receipt. Click the OK button.

9. Your announcement will appear in the Announcement Control panel. If the announcement needs to be edited, do so by clicking the Modify button next to the announcement you want to edit.

10. Check out the Announcement student view by clicking on the Announcement button in the Navigation Bar.

## Creating a Course Syllabus for a CourseCompass Course

*Typing or Pasting Text into the text box.*

1. Log into CourseCompass and click on the link to your course if you are not already there.

2. Click on the Control Panel button.

3. Click on the Course Information link in the Content Areas section.

4. Click on Add Item. A new page will open.

5. Choose the name Syllabus from the drop down menu or type in another name in the text box below the menu.

6. Choose a color for the name.

7. Type in the course syllabus information in the large text box below the color choice tool. You may type the information in plain text (just type as you usually do in a word processing document), Smart text (a combination of regular text and HTML formatting tags) or in standard HTML. You may also copy and paste HTML from a previously made web page, or browse for and upload the entire web page into CourseCompass instead of pasting in its HTML. (More information concerning uploading files can be found in the next section of this appendix.)

8. Specify whether the text box contains Smart Text (regular text with HTML formatting tags such as the Bold tag, "text"), plain text (no HTML), or standard HTML (the entire document was made with HTML tags).

9. Click the Submit button (*Note:* If you have linked to images in the HTML of the document you will be asked to locate and upload those images when you submit the document.)

10. Click on Return to Course and then Course Information to view the course syllabus as the students will see it.

## Linking to a Previously Created File

Follow steps 1 through 6 in the previous section.

7. Click the Browse button next to the File to Attach box and locate the file you want to upload.
8. Type the name that will serve as a link to the uploaded file in the Name of Link File box.
9. Click the arrow next to the Special Action box and make one of the following choices.
   - **Create a link to the file.** Choose this action if you are uploading a web page, document, or PowerPoint presentation that contains no outside links to files. You can upload files that link to other files, and CourseCompass will prompt you to find uploaded the linked files (usually images), but this may be a time-consuming process if your uploaded document contains many links. If this is the case you will want to place all files that need to be uploaded with the document into a zipped folder for uploading. Use the "unpack command" instead of the "create a link to file" command, to unpack them on the CourseCompass server. (More information can be found in the bulleted list item "Unpack a file.")
   - **Display a media file within the page.** *This action is supposed to display the contents of the file on the Course Information page itself. However, I have tried this with several file types and only see links to the media files ...as I would see if I linked to the files instead.*
   - **Unpack a file.** This feature will save you a lot of time if you want to upload a web page that contains many images. Place all the images and the web page into a folder by themselves before you link the images to the web page. When you are finished designing the web page and linking the images, Zip the folder up using a compression utility such as WinZip. Upload the zipped (compressed or packed) file up to the CourseCompass server and choose the Unpack a file action to unpack the folder. You will be asked to locate the beginning file name that the link will access.
10. In the options area make the following selections
    - Do you want to add offline content? Select "No" for now.
    - Do you want to track number of views? Either answer would be fine.
    - Do you want to add Meta-Data? Select "No" for now.
    - Do you want to make item visible? Yes, you definitely want to do this!
11. Click the Submit button to finish adding your syllabus to your course.
12. Click OK when the receipt page displays. CourseCompass will display the syllabus or syllabus link within the Course Information Control Panel. To view the Course Information from the student view click on the Course Information button in the navigation bar.

## Making Unit Folders in CourseCompass

Make a folder for each of the units you plan to teach. You will later place course content for each unit in its corresponding folders. Keeping course content in unit folders will make unit content much easier for you and your students to locate. It is wise to create folders before you create course content, as you cannot move course content into folders later.

To make a folder

1. Click on the Control Panel button.
2. Click on the Course Documents link in the Content Areas section.
3. Click on the Add Folder button. A new window will open.
4. Choose a name for your new folder from the drop-down menu or type in your own name for the folder.
5. Choose a folder color by clicking on the color swatch.
6. Type in a short description of the unit in the lower text box. You may type in regular text (plain text) adding HTML formatting if you want (Smart text) or type or paste in HTML (HTML). Make sure that you specify what type of text is in the text box.
7. Specify whether you want the folder to be visible.
8. Click the submit button.
9. Click on the Return to Course link.
10. To check to make sure your new folder has been created, click on the Course Documents link.

## Adding Course Content in the Form of Web Pages and Other Media

**Course Materials.**   Instructors can upload many different types of files into their CourseCompass courses. Web pages may display immediately upon navigating to a course area or they may display only after you have clicked on a link. Depending on your browser choice and your browser's configuration, links to multimedia files (audio, video, Flash), PDF (Adobe Portable Document Files), or Microsoft Office files may open inside your browser window or may open an external program in order to display. Typically, Office documents will open inside your browser window if you are using Internet Explorer as your browser. When links to Office documents are accessed using Netscape, the appropriate Office program will be launched and the file will display inside the program window.

*Accessing Linked Files.*   You will need to list specific plug-ins and programs that students need to access linked course materials with their browser. Course materials accessed through links may open in the main browser window, in a new browser window, in an external software program, or may open a dialogue box asking whether you want to open the file or save the file for viewing offline. How linked files open depends on the browser being used, the plug-ins and programs installed on the computer, and the manner with which the files are linked on the web page. Instruct your students to contact you if they have problems accessing a file. You may have to make modifications to your content or offer a more detailed set of directions for accessing your files.

Typical plug-ins and programs course participants need to install on their computers include QuickTime, the Adobe Acrobat Reader, Macromedia Shockwave Player, Macromedia Flash Player, Microsoft Media Player, Real Media Player, and WinZip. They may also find it helpful to install the Microsoft Office programs or some other office suite on their computers. Since assignments will be handed in digitally, students will need a word processing, and possibly spreadsheet and presentation, programs to complete assignments.

*Making Web Pages in CourseCompass Unit Folders.*
1. Go to the course Control Panel area.
2. Click on the Course Documents link in the Content Areas section.
3. Click on the folder that will contain the new web pages (documents) to open it.
4. Click on Add Item. A new page will open.
5. Choose a name from the drop down menu or type in another name in the text box below the menu.
6. Choose a color for the name.
7. Type in the document information in the large text box below the color choice tool. You may type the information in plain text (just type as you usually do in a word processing document), Smart text (a combination of regular text and HTML formatting tags) or in standard HTML. You may also copy and paste HTML from a previously made web page, or browse for and upload the entire web page into CourseCompass instead of pasting in its HTML.
8. Specify whether the text box contains Smart Text (regular text with HTML formatting tags such as the Bold tag, "text"), plain text (no HTML), or standard HTML (the entire document was made with HTML tags).
9. Click the Submit button (Note: If you have linked to images or other files in the HTML of the document you will be asked to locate and upload those files when you submit the document.)
10. Click on Return to Course, the Course Documents button and then the unit folder to view the course document you just created, as the student will see it.

**Uploading Previously Created Files to CourseCompass' Unit Folders.**    As stated previously, you may create course content in other programs and upload the files to your Course. You can upload almost any type of file. Examples include HTML (web), word processing, presentation, and spreadsheet, to name a few. If the files you are uploading are self-contained, they do not contain links to other types of media, you will only need to upload the file and link to it. If the file you are uploading contains many links to images or other media you may want to place all of the files in one folder, ZIP (or compress) the folder into one compressed file, upload the file, and tell CourseCompass to decompress the file back into the folder.

Follow steps 1 through 4 in the previous section, "Making Web Pages in CourseCompass Unit Folders" then continue with the steps listed below.

5. Scroll down the page and locate the File to Attach Box.
6. Click the Browse button next to the File to Attach box and locate the file you wish to upload.
7. Type the name that will serve as a link to the uploaded file in the Name of Link File box.
8. Click the arrow next to the Special Action box and make one of the following choices.
   - **Create a link to the file.** Choose this action if you are uploading a web page, document, or PowerPoint presentation that contains no outside links to files. You can upload files that link to other files and CourseCompass will prompt you to find upload the linked files (usually images) but this may be a time consuming process if your uploaded document contains many links. If this is the case you will want to place all files that need to be uploaded with the document into a zipped folder for uploading. Use the "unpack command" instead of the "create a link to file" command, to unpack them on the CourseCompass server. (See the bulleted list item, "Unpack a file" for more information.)
   - **Display a media file within the page.** *This action will display the contents of the file on the Course Information page itself.*
   - **Unpack a file.** This feature will save you a lot of time if you want to upload a web page that contains many images. Place all the images and the web page into a folder by themselves before you link the images to the web page. When you are finished designing the web page and linking the images, Zip the folder up using a compression utility such as WinZip. Upload the zipped (compressed or packed) file up to the CourseCompass server and choose the Unpack a file action to unpack the folder. You will be asked to locate the beginning file name that the link will access.
9. In the options area make the following selections.
   - Do you want to add offline content? Select "No" for now.
   - Do you want to track number of views? Either answer would be fine.
   - Do you want to add Meta-Data? Select "No" for now.

- Do you want to make item visible? Yes, you will probably want to do this unless you do not want your students to access this file until a specific time.
10. Click the Submit button to finish adding your syllabus to your course.
11. Click OK when the receipt page displays. CourseCompass will display the syllabus or syllabus link within the Course Information Control Panel. To view the Course Information from the student view click on the Course Information button in the navigation bar.

*Evaluating Navigation and Accessibility of Content.*   Ask a student, colleague, or friend to look at your course and assess its ease of navigation. Can they easily find content that you reference in your syllabus and other areas of your course? Do they have problems accessing any of the media you have placed in your course? Ask students to evaluate the course while it is in session and at the end of the course. Make additional changes as needed.

## Assessment

Types of assessments you may use to verify student understanding include rubrics, synchronous and asynchronous student and group presentations, group projects, quizzes, essays, assignments (hand-in via CourseCompass' drop-box), and surveys. CourseCompass has built in tools to facilitate group project work, quiz and survey design, and handing in assignments.

## Synchronous and Asynchronous Student and Group Presentations

Synchronous group presentations can be made using CourseCompass' Virtual classroom. Asynchronous students' presentations can be made using CourseCompass' File Exchange Tool in the Group Pages area. After students have finished constructing their presentations you can upload them into a course content area for all course participants to see.

## Reviewing Built-In Course Assessments

You will want to spend some time reviewing the assessments that come with the course material you select. You can decide which pre-lecture assessments, quizzes, and tests you want to use and consider whether you want to create your own assessments. To review exiting course assessments, follow these steps:

1. From the course Announcements page, click Control Panel.
2. In the Assessment module, click Assessment Manager.

3. Scroll to the assessment you want to preview.
   For example, you might want to review the Chapter 1 Readiness Assessment Quiz to see whether it fits what you expect students to understand before they start the course.
4. Click one of the following options:
   a. Click Preview to take the test yourself.
   b. Click Modify to change the assessment description, instructions, or the order in which questions appear.
   c. Click Remove to delete the assessment and all of its associated questions. CourseCompass displays a warning asking you to confirm that you want to delete the assessment. You may never have to use this option, since you don't need to delete assessment you don't plan to use in your course.
   **Note.** You can modify or delete questions in an assessment only after you make the assessment unavailable, as described in the next section.
   d. When you finish previewing assessments, click a tab at the top of the Course Compass window to continue with other course setup tasks.

You can also create your own assessments and surveys if you want to use some but not all of the questions in an assessment. For more information on creating your own assessments, see the section titled, "Customizing Assessments".

## Customizing Assessments

You can customize existing assessments by modifying, adding, or deleting assessment questions as described in this section.

**Tip:** You can also create custom assessments that include your own questions, or you can create assessments using existing questions from the Pool manager. For information on creating your own assessment, search for the keyword *creating* in the CourseCompass Instructor help index, and click *assessments*. For information on using the Pool Manager, search for the keywords *pool manager* in the CourseCompass Instructor Help index.

Modifying an assessment takes a few steps.

1. First, you make the assessment unavailable to students. By default, lecture exams and chapter exams are unavailable. If the text above the Availability button in an exam or quiz says "Unavailable," you can skip the steps in "Making assessments unavailable" and start with the steps in "Changing assessment content."

2. Then you change the content of the assessments. For example, you might add or remove questions, change the number of points associated with each questions, or switch question types.

3. When you finish modifying the assessment, you make it available again. At this point, you can also send an announcement to students so they know an assessment is ready to take.

The next sections list steps for completing the above tasks.

*Making assessments unavailable*

1. From the course Announcements page, click Control Panel.
2. In the Assessment module, click Assessment Manager.
3. Next to the assessment that contains content you want to change, click the Set Availability button, if the text above the Set Availability button says "Available."
4. On the Set Availability page that appears, click No next to "make Assessment Available?" Course Compass will display a prompt explaining the consequences of making an assessment unavailable.
5. Click OK at the prompt.
6. Review and change any assessment options you want to change.
   For example, by default, assessments allow students an unlimited amount of time to complete an assessment. You may want to set assessment time limits; for example, one hour for a chapter exam, and three hours for a final exam. You can change assessment options now, or you can change them when you make the assessment available again, as described later in this section.
7. Click Submit.
8. CourseCompass again asks you whether you want to make the assessment unavailable. You *do* want to make the assessment unavailable, click OK.

The Assessment Manager page appears. The assessment that you just made unavailable appears in alphabetical order with other unavailable assessments.

*Changing assessment content.* Now that the assessment is unavailable to students, you can begin changing its content.

1. From the Assessment Manager page, click the Modify button next to the assessment you just made unavailable. The Assessment builder page will appear.
2. Change any aspect of the assessment you want.

   For example, you can

   - Change the number of points assigned to different questions
   - Remove questions

- Add questions
- Change question types

For additional details on these and other changes you can make to assessments, search using the keyword *modifying* in the CourseCompass Instructor Help index. Click the word *assessments* when the results display.

## Quizzes

CourseCompass assessment tools allow you to easily create quizzes, surveys, tests, and practice questions. Students will access these assessments either by clicking on a link in the course announcement area or by clicking on the Quiz icon in the Assignments, the Course Documents, or the Course Information areas.

If there are multiple quizzes or surveys available students will need to carefully choose the one they want to complete and click on the corresponding Take Quiz/Test or Take Survey button.

*Answering Questions.*   CourseCompass allows instructors to create tests and quizzes using the following type of questions: multiple-choice, true/false, short answer, and essay. All question types are graded automatically and placed in the student grade book, except essay questions. Instructors or teaching assistants will grade essay questions and then assign a grade.

*Submitting Answers for Grading.*   After students finish answering all the questions in the assessment tool, they need to click on the Submit Answers button. All quizzes containing essay questions will display in their grade books as being taken. No grade will appear until the instructor or teaching assistants grade essay questions. Grades will appear immediately for quizzes and tests containing only the 3 question types gradable by CourseCompass. CourseCompass will record answers to surveys, anonymously. The grade book will show that the survey has been completed. If you have created practice tests, grades will not be computed. Instead, you may choose to display the correct answers to students after they click the submit button.

*Reviewing Assessment Results.*   Instructors control what students see after they submit their answers to assessments. You can set CourseCompass to not display any feedback after submitting answers or you may set it to display one or more of the following options: the question and your answer, the correct answer, or constructive feedback.

## BUILDING LEARNING COMMUNITIES

It is the instructor's responsibility to guide the development of the course learning community and to establish a learning environment that is conducive to learning. You as an instructor need to get to know your students, not by seeing their faces, body language and hearing their voices, but instead by reading their words and ideas. Students will not know you by personal contact but will know you instead by the comments you place on their work, by your postings in discussion boards and chat sessions, and by your email messages. [Schweizer, 1999 #6, pp. 4–5]

Dr. William Glasser, a researcher in the areas of psychology and learning, developed the "Control Theory, a research base for creating successful learning environments". [Glasser, 1986 #7; Schweizer, 1999 #6; (pp 5–7)] He stated that we have four basic psychological needs that we continually try to fulfill and that all our behavior is governed by our trying to fulfill these needs. If the instructor establishes a learning environment in which these needs are met then learning will be optimized.

Glasser listed the four needs as

1. Belonging: Our behavior is governed by our need to be accepted, to belong;
2. Freedom: We must be able to choose what we do and must make our own responsible choices;
3. Power: Personal empowerment brought about through the acquisition of knowledge—not control of others but that others value your knowledge and skills; and
4. Fun: Learning experiences that are enjoyable and fun are more likely to be repeated and remembered.

Activities must be devised that allow students to interact with other students and guest speakers in group projects and online discussions (discussion boards, chat, email). You may be surprised to find that students who do not normally speak up in class now participate because they have more time to formulate answers or they feel less shy about participating online. All voices are more likely to be heard in the online situation. To keep lines of communication open the instructor must establish standard etiquette (guidelines) and enforce rules for online course communications.

Schweizer suggests working the following activities into your course to promote the psychological need for belonging:

1. Holding an on-site (face-to-face) meeting;
2. When face-to-face meetings are not feasible, introducing yourself online using the virtual classroom (chat) with or without a live audio or video component using streaming software such as Real Video;
3. Personalizing your distance classroom;
4. Using cooperative learning;
5. Being invitational;
6. Using electronic mail;
7. Being approachable and personal.

CourseCompass provides tools for both synchronous and asynchronous communication within the course shell. Asynchronous tools include email, the discussion board, and student pages. The Virtual Classroom (chat) can be used for synchronous, real-time, communication.

Holding an onsite meeting is not always possible because of schedules and distance that would have to be traveled. Instead you may want to use the CourseCompass Virtual Classroom, possibly in combination with streaming audio or video. Students can send questions via the virtual classroom, and you can both type answers and speak to them. The streaming audio or video session will also allow you to quickly give lengthy detailed answers or explanations. Seeing or hearing a live person adds a more human quality to the course. Schweizer suggested getting together once at the beginning of the course, half way through the course and again at the end of the course. These meetings should be used to get to know each other and to answer questions about the course. They could occur before or after synchronous discussions on course material.

Send a welcoming email to each student in your course. Also add your profile and instruct any co-course designers, or graduate assistants that may be involved with the course, to create their own profile in the Staff Information area of your CourseCompass course. Ask students to fill out profile sheets that tell about themselves, their interests, and families. These sheets can be posted in a section of the course for all participants to read.

Design opportunities for students to work cooperatively in groups. CourseCompass' Group Pages feature will facilitate group work. This feature provides a discussion board, Virtual Classroom (chat), file exchange area, email, and a group member roster that is available only to group members. Instructors can choose to disable some or all communication tools except the group roster for each group.

Be supportive. Show students that you want them to succeed. Hold regular office hours using the virtual classroom tool and send prompt email responses to student questions. Encourage students to visit the online course as often as possible and become involved in discussions early on in the course.

Allowing students to choose options for completing assignments and allowing students to work at their own pace are two ways instructors can meet student's psychological need for freedom. Assignments designed to allow students to discover learning and then allowing students to share their experiences empower students. Students who are reluctant to speak up in a traditional classroom often feel less inhibited in an online classroom and thus feel more empowered.

Last, but not least, provide activities that are fun, creative, and challenging. Allow enough time for students to master the course material. Set up group projects and competitions. Post interesting outside events to the course calendar that may not tie in directly to course material but may have a connection to the subject area.

## Communication Tools

CourseCompass communication tools include email, a course calendar, a discussion board (bulletin board), a virtual classroom (chat) and student and instructor profiles.

*Email.*   The email feature allows you to send email to registered members of your course. You may choose to send mail to all course members, all course groups, all course teacher assistants or all course instructors with a single click. You can also send one message to several individual course members or several course groups. There is no need to have an external email program installed on your computer, CourseCompass will serve as the email program, however, the mail will be sent to an existing email account provided by an Internet Service Provider. The recipients will need to access their email using the email program they normally use to receive email.

To Send Email

1. Click the Communication button on the Navigation Bar.
2. Press the Send Email button in the initial communication window.
3. Click the link that best corresponds to the intended addressees of your message. A blank email form will display.
4. Check to make sure that the correct mail recipients are listed in the addressee area.
5. If the email is addressed correctly type in a subject and message in the appropriate fields.
6. Press the Send Message button when your message is ready to send.

*Student Roster.*   The Student Roster shows all users enrolled in your course. You may sort the names by first name, last name, or email address by clicking on the corresponding heading.

To View the Student Roster

1. Click the Communication button on the Navigation Bar.
2. Press the Student Roster button in the initial communication window. A list of all students currently enrolled in the course will display.
3. Sort the student names by last name, first name, or email address by clicking on the corresponding heading.

*Student Pages.*   The Student Pages have links to all enrolled student's homepages. These pages can be easily created with CourseCompass' "Edit Your Homepage" tool found in the Student Tools area. Directions for creating your own home page are included later in this document. (See the Student Tools section.)

To View Student Pages

1. Click the Communication button on the Navigation Bar.

2. Click the Roster button in the initial communication window. A list of student pages sorted by last name will display.
3. Click on the link corresponding to the student page you want view to open the student's web page.

*Group Pages.*   Registered members of groups can work on projects in these secured areas. Only registered members of a particular group are allowed access to their group page. Clicking on a group name hyperlink will access a specific group area. Once a group's page is displayed, you can view all group member names, send email, chat, and exchange files with other group members. Each group also has its own private discussion board to post messages and hold discussions.

### To View Group Pages
1. Click the Communication button on the Navigation Bar.
2. Press the Group Pages button in the initial communication window.
3. Click the link to the group area you want to enter. You will be allowed to enter only group areas in which you are an official member.
4. Choose an activity. You may send email, participate in a discussion, exchange files, or chat with other group members.

**To Send Mail to Your Group.**   Note: *Directions for using this communication tool can be found under the Email communication tool heading, page 300.*

**To Participate in a Discussion within the Group.**   Note: *Directions for using this communication tool can be found under the Discussion Board communication tool heading,* page 304.

**To Use the Virtual Classroom (Chat) with Group Members.**   Note:   *Directions for using this communication tool can be found under the Virtual Classroom communication tool heading,* page 302.

### To Share Files with Group Members
1. Click on the File Exchange button.
2. Choose to either download a file or upload a file.
   a. To download a file
      i. Locate the file you want to download. You may sort the files by the student who uploaded it, by link name, by file size, and by upload date, by clicking on the corresponding heading.
      ii. Right click on a file link and choose *Save Link As (Netscape) or Save Target As (Internet Explorer).*
      iii. Choose a location to save the file and click the Save button.
   b. To upload a file
      i. Click the Browse button in the *Add File to Drop Box* section.

    **ii.** Locate and highlight the file you wish to upload.
    **iii.** Click the Open button.
    **iv.** Type a name that will serve as the link to the uploaded file.
    **v.** Click the Submit button.

*Virtual Classroom (Chat).* Virtual Classroom (Chat) is the CourseCompass tool that most closely simulates a traditional classroom. It allows two or more people to communicate in real time by typing text messages, displaying web pages, and by drawing on a white board. There is even an area for students to type questions to the instructor. Virtual Chat can be accessed from two course areas: the communication area and from within a Group web page.

    The virtual classroom feature in the communication area is accessible to everyone enrolled in the course. The virtual classroom feature accessed from a group web page is only accessible to members of that group.

**Entering the Virtual Classroom**
1. Click on the Virtual Classroom icon in the Communications area or in a Group web page.
2. Wait for the Virtual Classroom to load. This may take a few minutes if you are using a telephone modem.

**Whiteboard Space.** The Whiteboard Space can be used to display web pages or for drawing and typing. Anything displayed in the Whiteboard Space is viewable by all others logged into the chat area. The Whiteboard Space does not support frames but many web sites that use frames have a no-frames version you may use instead.

**Menu Bar.** The Virtual Chat Menu Bars allows you to quit the chat program, navigate between slides, and set the way objects appear in the Whiteboard Space.

**Application Tool Bar.** The Application Tool Bar contains tools for moving between slides or web pages, a place for typing a web page URL, and a tool for requesting the floor.

**Drawing Toolbar.** The Drawing Toolbar has tools for drawing and typing on the Whiteboard Space.

**Status Region.** The Status Region is located at the bottom of the Virtual Classroom window. It displays information about Virtual Classroom features as well as system messages.

**Tab Panel.** The Tab Panel has four tabs. Each tab takes you to a different activity. Students can use the chat tab to participate in a discussion, the questions tab to ask the instructor questions (answers to the questions can be either public or private), and the user info tab to view user information.

*Chat panel tab.*   Use the chat panel tab to open the chat area and to talk to your students. Type your message in the small field at the bottom of the chat window. When your message is complete, press the Enter key on your keyboard to send it to the main chat window for everyone to see.

*Questions tab.*   Use the Question tab to access the question window and to answer student questions.

1. Type your questions in the panel at the right.
2. If you want the question and its answer to remain private, place a check in the Request Private box.
3. Click the Send button when you are ready to submit your question.
4. When the instructor answers a question, the question and its answer will appear in the left pane. You will see all questions and answers from all class members unless the question has been designated private.

*User info tab.*   Highlighting a student's name in the left panel of the User Info tab will display the student's full name and status in the right panel.

To learn more about the Virtual Classroom refer to the instructor help area.

**Slides.**   CourseCompass allows you to add slides or pages to your online presentations in the Virtual Classroom. Slides may be drawings, typed words, or web pages, displayed in the Whiteboard Space. Instructors may add new slides to the presentation but students can add, draw, and type in the space, in addition to calling up URLs.

*Setting up a Virtual Classroom Session.*   To set up a Virtual Classroom session, send an announcement to the class or place information in the course calendar, letting students know what the session is about and when it begins and ends. At the appointed time, enter the Virtual Classroom as follows:

1. From the course Announcements page, click Control Panel.
2. Click Virtual Classroom in the Course Tools module.
3. Click Enter Virtual Classroom.
   Text appears on your screen and status bar while the Virtual Classroom starts in a separate browser window. This process may take a few minutes, depending on the speed of your Internet connection.
4. From the Virtual Classroom window, you can
   - Participate in a group discussion with all participants
   - Receive and answer questions from any participant
   - Create and display lecture slides on the whiteboard
   - Draw on and add text to a slide displayed on the whiteboard

For more information on these and the many other ways you can interact with students using the Virtual Classroom, search for *virtual classroom* in the CourseCompass Instructor Help index.

5. When the time you allotted for the Virtual Classroom session ends, choose Quit from the Tutornet menu to leave the Virtual Classroom and close its browser window.

***Discussion Board.***   Discussion Boards can be accessible to all students enrolled in a course or to all students of a particular group. Clicking on the Discussion Board link in the Communication Center will access the course discussion board. Clicking on the Group Pages link in the Communication Center and then the link to a group to which a student belongs, will display the Group Discussion Board button.

Participants can post replies to instructor and student-led discussion topics, follow discussions, and post their own threads (discussion topics) using the Discussion Board. Unlike email lists, participants will not be notified of new postings (messages). They will have to remember to check the discussion board regularly. An advantage discussion boards offer over email lists is that all postings concerning a particular topic are grouped together. Participants can easily look through past messages to find information that may help them to understand a topic or complete an assignment. Unlike the CourseCompass' Virtual Classroom (Chat) in which communication occurs in real time, communication in the Discussion Board is asynchronous, participants can post and read messages when it is convenient for them.

**Accessing a Discussion Board.**   The Course Discussion Board can be accessed by students through the communications area of a course. The Group Discussion Board can be accessed through the Group Pages area. Instructors can set up a Discussion Board through the Discussion Board Control Panel or the link to the Discussion Board in the Communication area.

Course Discussion boards can contain several forums for major topics of discussion. Each forum can have several threads (subtopics) of discussion. Messages or posts contain the subject matter of the discussions.

**Setting up a Discussion Board**
1. From the course Announcements page, click the Control Panel.
2. Click Discussion Board in the Course Tools module.
   **Note:** You may also enter the Discussion board via the Communication button on the Navigation Bar
3. Click Add Forum.
4. Enter a title and description for the forum.
5. Click one of the options for displaying text.
6. Select one or more of the following forum settings:
   ▪ **Allow anonymous posts** lets participants add and respond to messages without identifying themselves.

- **Allow author to edit message after posting** lets participants modify their messages after adding them to the forum.
- **Allow author to remove own, posted messages** lets participants delete their messages after adding them to the forum.
- **Allow file attachments** lets participants attach a document, presentation, graphic, or multimedia file to a message.
- **Allow new threads** lets participants add a new main topic to the forum.

7. Assign forum user settings by clicking a name in the box and then clicking one of the following buttons:
   - Click the Admin button to assign administrator privileges to a forum participant.
   - Click the Normal button to revoke a participant's administrator privileges.
   - Click the Block button to prevent a participant from posting messages to a forum.
   - Click the Unblock button to return posting privileges to a participant.
        For more information on privileges and how to assign them, search for *setting forum privileges* in the CourseCompass Instructor Help.
8. Click Submit to finish creating the forum.

**Tip:** You can kick off a forum by adding a start-up message that sets your expectations for the forum. Once a forum is in regular use, you will want to check it on a regular basis to make sure that participants are staying on task. You may want to participate in some of the discussions, also. To encourage students to use the discussion forums make their participation mandatory. You may require them to post and reply to a specific number of messages each week on certain topics of discussion.

### Accessing the Course Discussion Board to Read and Post Messages (Students or Instructors)
1. Click on the Communication button in the Navigation Bar.
2. Click on the Discussion Board icon.

### Accessing a Discussion Board Associated with a Group
1. Click on the Communication button in the Navigation Bar.
2. Click on the Group Pages icon.
3. Click on the name of the group area you want to access.
4. Click on the Discussion Board icon.

**Starting a New Thread.**  Students and instructors may start new threads (discussion topics).

1. Click on the Start New Thread button.
2. Type a descriptive subject line in the subject field.

3. Type the message in the body field.
4. Attach any files that are appropriate to the posting by clicking on the Browse button, locating the file your wish to attach, and clicking the Open button.
5. Click the Post Message button when you are ready for the message to be posted to the Discussion Board.

**Reading and Replying to Messages.**   Two tools that facilitate the reading of messages appear on the main Discussion Board page. They are the Expand All and Collapse All buttons.

*Collapse All Buttons.*   When all threads are compacted, only the main thread headings display. This allows you to quickly look through thread headings to determine which threads to read.

*Expand All Button.*   If you are looking for unread replies in specific threads click the Expand All button. The replies that you have not read will appear in a different color from those you have read. **Note:** You can also see these unread replies by clicking on a main thread heading. The initial posting and all replies will display at the bottom of the new web page.

*Opening a Posted Message.*   You will have to open a posted message to read and reply to it.

1. Click on the link to the posting and the message will open.
2. Type in your reply.

*Replying to Posts*
1. Open the message to which you want to respond
2. Click the Re: Reply button.
3. Type your response.
4. Attach any files you want to include by clicking on the Browse button.
5. Post your response by clicking the Post Message button.

**Deleting Entire Forums, Posts (Messages) and Threads (Message Topics).** Only instructors are given access to this feature. Students may not delete forums, postings or threads. **Note:** You may give students permission to edit and delete their own messages. To delete a forum, message or thread

1. Enter the Discussion Board area by one of the methods listed below. The Discussion Board control area will open. The list of forums for your course will display.
   a. Click the Control Panel button in the Control Bar or click. Click the Discussion Board link in the Communications area.
   b. Click the Communications button in the navigation bar and then click the Discussion Board button.

2. Decide what you want to modify or delete.
   a. Delete or modify a forum.
      i. If you want to modify a forum title or description click on the modify button next to the corresponding forum.
      ii. If you want to delete an entire forum you can click the delete button next to the forum you want to delete.
   b. Delete a message or thread.
      i. If you want to delete a message or delete an entire thread click the link to the forum you want to enter.
      ii. Place checks in the check boxes of the messages or threads you want to remove.
      iii. Click the submit button.

### Collect (Compile) Selected Messages into One Page for Reading or Printing Purposes

1. Enter the Discussion Board area by one of the methods listed below. The Discussion Board control area will open. The list of forums for your course will display.
   a. Click the Control Panel button in the Control Bar or click. Click the Discussion Board link in the Communications area.
      or
   b. Click the Communications button in the navigation bar and then click the Discussion Board button.
2. Click the link to the forum you want to enter.
3. Place checks in the check boxes of the messages or threads you want to collect (compile) into one page.
4. Click the Collect button. The collected postings will appear on one web page. You may read the messages online or print them for reading later.

**Making and Viewing Message Archives.**  CourseCompass allows you to backup messages into archives for later reference. This removes the messages that you archive from the active forums.

1. Enter the Discussion Board area by one of the methods listed below. The Discussion Board control area will open. The list of forums for your course will display.
   a. Click the Control Panel button in the Control Bar or click. Click the Discussion Board link in the Communications area.
      or
   b. Click the Communications button in the navigation bar and then click the Discussion Board button.
2. Click the link to the forum you want to enter.
3. Click the link named "Click here for archives" The archive area will open.

4. Decide whether you want to make a new archive or read a previously created archive.
   a. Create a new archive
      i. Click on the New Archive button.
      ii. Type a name and description for your new archive and select the type of text you entered in the description area.
      iii. Choose whether the archived message will be available to students.
      iv. Click the Submit button.
   b. Read a previously created archive.
      i. Click on the link to the archive you want to read.

**Locking or Unlocking Messages.**   Course Compass allows you to lock messages.

1. Enter the Discussion Board area by one of the methods listed below. The Discussion Board control area will open. The list of forums for your course will display.
   a. Click the Control Panel button in the Control Bar or click. Click the Discussion Board link in the Communications area.
      or
   b. Click the Communications button in the navigation bar and then click the Discussion Board button.
2. Click the link to the forum you want to enter.
3. Place checks in the check boxes of the messages or threads you want to lock. Click Lock button to lock the messages. Likewise click the unlock button if you want to unlock locked messages.

## TOOLS

CourseCompass provides seven student tools to manage and enhance students' online course experience. They are the Drop Box, Edit Your Home Page, Course Calendar, Check Grade, Tasks, Electric Blackboard, and the Address book. The Drop Box, Student Homepage, Check Grade, Calendar, and Electric Blackboard will be discussed in more detail in the following paragraphs.

### Student Drop Box

Students can easily submit assignments in their personal student drop boxes using the browse button found on the Student Tools page. There is no need to use a separate program to upload files. Once a file has been uploaded to this box only instructors can remove it. Instructors may also place graded assignments with comments back into student drop boxes.

**Tip:** Files in the Digital Drop Box include information on their status.

- Files you added but have not yet sent say "Posted."
- Files both you and students have added and sent say "Submitted."
- Files you received but have not yet picked up say "Submitted."
- Files you both received and picked up say "Submitted" and "Received."

## Picking up student work

1. Click the Control Panel button on the Control Bar.
2. Click the Digital Drop Box link in the Course Tools area of the Control Panel. The Digital Drop Box control area will display.
3. Click the file you want to pick up. A prompt window will appear, giving you a choice of opening the file to view now or saving the file on your computer's hard drive.
4. Click **Open it** to launch the program used to create the file and display the file, or click **Save it to disk** to display a Save As dialog box so you can indicate where you want to save the file. CourseCompass either displays or saves the file.
5. When you finish viewing or saving, click OK to return to the Control Panel and continue with other tasks.

## Returning Student Work

1. Click the Control Panel button in the Control Bar.
2. Click the Digital Drop Box link in the Course Tools module to display the Digital Drop Box page.
3. Click Send File. **Tip:** Click the Send File button to both add the file to the Digital Drop Box and send it. Click the Add Item button to add items to the Digital Drop Box that you plan to send at another time.
4. Type a title to identify what you're returning to the student.
5. Click the Browse button and indicate the directory on your computer where you saved the file you are returning.
6. Click the file name and click Open.
7. Type additional information or instructions in the Comments box if you want.
8. Click Submit to both add the file to your Digital Drop Box and send it to the student.

## To Access the Student Drop Box (Students)

1. Click on the Student Tools button in the Navigation Bar.
2. Click on the Student Drop Box button.
3. The Drop Box window will open. The top of the window lists the files that have been uploaded to the drop box. The contents of the drop box

can be sorted by File Name, Link Name, File Size, or Status by clicking on the heading by which you want to sort. A tool for uploading files is located at the bottom of the window.

   **a.** To download a file
      **i.** Right click on the link to the file you want to download.
      **ii.** Choose Save Target As (Internet Explorer) or Save Link As (Netscape).
      **iii.** Choose a location to save the file.
      **iv.** Click on the Save button.
   **b.** To upload a file
      **i.** Click the browse button.
      **ii.** Locate and select the file you want to upload.
      **iii.** Click the Open button.
      **iv.** Type a name for the link to the file.
      **v.** Click on the Send File to Instructor button.

## Student Homepage

Each student enrolled in a course can easily create his or her own homepage to display an introductory message, a photograph, personal information, and favorite links. There is no need to know HTML to create this page, students just type their personal information in form fields and, once submitted, CourseCompass builds the page. If they do know HTML they can use it to format their text and create links.

*To build your student home page*
   **1.** Click on the Student Tools button in the Navigation Bar.
   **2.** Click on the Edit Your Home Page button.
   **3.** Type an introductory message. If you know HTML you may use it to format the text.
   **4.** Type in any personal information that you would like to share with course participants.
   **5.** Upload a photo of yourself. Use the Browse button to locate the photo. Upload the photo in the same manner files were uploaded into the Drop Box. If you want to later remove the photo place a check in the Remove This Picture box and click on the Update Homepage button at the bottom of the page.
   **6.** Add favorite URLs to the bottom of the page.
   **7.** Click the Update Homepage button at the bottom of the page when finished.

## Checking Grades

CourseCompass automatically enters the scores students have earned in quizzes and tests that do not require instructor intervention to grade. The number of times students have accessed the course will be recorded here, in addition to the average number of points they have received on quizzes and tests, their quiz average, and the total number of points that they have earned. Each course assessment title will be listed in the right window panel. The points earned and the total number of points in each assessment will display after the course title.

***Instructor Access to the Online Gradebook.*** CourseCompass comes with a built-in gradebook. As students enroll in your course, their names are automatically added to the gradebook. You don't have to do any setup work to create the gradebook.

As your course progresses, CourseCompass automatically scores and posts student grades associated with assessment questions that have defined answers. You can also manually enter scores for essay questions and for grades associated with work completed outside CourseCompass.

In addition to collecting assessment scores, you can use the online gradebook to:

- View performance statistics
- Add or change student scores
- Create reports
- Export final grades for record keeping.

For more information on these tasks, search for *online gradebook* in the Course-Compass Instructor Help index.

To view the online gradebook:

1. Click the Control Panel button in the Control Bar.
2. Click Online Gradebook in the Assessment module to display the Online Gradebook page.
3. Click the Spreadsheet View link to display the gradebook for all students enrolled in your course.
4. Click OK when you finish viewing the gradebook.

**Tip:** You use the Assessment Manager to automatically score and enter grades in the online gradebook for assessments with defined answers. For example, CourseCompass can automatically score a True/False test or a multiple-choice test. Search for the keywords *online gradebook* in the CourseCompass Instructor Help index for details on how to set up automatic grading.

You can manually enter grades for assessments that CourseCompass cannot automatically score, such as essay questions, on the Spreadsheet View page of the online gradebook. Search for *spreadsheet view* in the CourseCompass Instructor Help index for details on how to manually enter grades.

### Student Access to Gradebook
1. Click the Student Tools button in the Navigation Bar.
2. Click the Check Your Grade button.
3. The grade page will display.

## Student Calendar

The calendar includes personal information that each student or instructor has entered into his or her calendar and course information that the instructor has entered into the course calendar. A *P (personal) in a date cell indicates information that a student or instructor has entered into the calendar. A *C (class) in a date cell indicates information that has been entered by you for all students to see.

*Entering calendar events.*
1. Click on the Add New Event button.
2. Enter the information for the new event.
3. Indicate whether the information is to be public information or private information.
4. Click on the Add New Event button again.

*Viewing calendar events*
1. Click on a date to access events posted for that date.
2. The list of events for that particular day will open. The events can be sorted by time, event, and type by clicking on the corresponding category heading.

## Electric Blackboard

The Electronic Blackboard pops up in a new window allowing students to navigate to other areas of the course in the main window and take notes in the new pop-up window. Students **must remember to click the Save button** before they close the Electronic Blackboard to save the contents of the window for the next session. CourseCompass does not prompt students to save their changes if they close the window before saving.

*To access the Electric Blackboard*
1. Click on the Student Tools button on the Navigation Bar.
2. Click on the Electric Blackboard button.
3. The Electric Blackboard will display.
4. Type or paste any information you would like to save in the Electric Blackboard window.
5. Click the Save button to save the information. Blackboard will not automatically prompt you to save. If you close the window without saving all information you have entered after the last save will be lost.
6. Click the Close button to close the Electric Blackboard.

Congratulations! You've created your first course, explored the CourseCompas online learning environment, and are well on your way to customizing and managing your online course.

## WORKS CITED

Gibson, C. R. C. (1998). *Distance learners in higher education: institutional responses for quality outcomes.* Madison, Wis., Atwood Pub.

Glasser, W. (1985). *Control theory: a new explanation of how we control our lives.* New York, Harper & Row.

Schweizer, H. (1999). *Designing and teaching an on-line course: spinning your web classroom.* Boston, Allyn & Bacon.

Smith, P. L. and T. J. Ragan (1993). *Instructional design.* New York, Merrill.

# ORDER TODAY!

Yes! Please send me the titles I have selected.

❏ **Successful College Teaching**
Sharon A. Baiocco & Jamie N. DeWaters
ISBN: 0-205-26654-1 Order # T66542 $37.00

❏ **Faculty Work and Public Trust**
James S. Fairweather
ISBN: 0-205-17948-7 Order # H79486 $38.00

❏ **Writing for Professional Publication**
Kenneth T. Henson
ISBN: 0-205-28313-6 Order # T83133 $27.00

❏ **Learner-Centered Assessment on College Campuses**
Mary E. Huba & Jann E. Freed
ISBN: 0-205-28738-7 Order # T87381 $30.00

❏ **Adjunct Professor's Guide to Success**
Richard E. Lyons, Marcella L. Kysilka, & George E. Pawlas
ISBN: 0-205-28774-3 Order # T87746 $31.00

❏ **Teaching Tips for College and University Instructors**
David Royse
ISBN: 0-205-29839-7 Order # T98396 $30.95

❏ **Creating Learning-Centered Courses for the World Wide Web**
William B. Sanders
ISBN: 0-205-31513-5 Order # 1513L2 $34.00

❏ **The Online Teaching Guide**
Ken N. White & Bob H. Weight
ISBN: 0-205-29531-2 Order # T95319 $31.00

Please complete all information requested and return this entire page. The address is on the reverse of this page.

Prepay by check or money order for free shipping and handling!

❏ Payment enclosed (Make your check payable to Allyn & Bacon)

❏ I'd like to examine the title(s) FREE for 30 days. Please invoice me. My P.O. # _____

❏ Charge my:   ❏ VISA          ❏ MasterCard          ❏ American Express

Account # _____ Exp. Date _____ Signature _____

Ship to:   Name _____

Address _____

City _____ State _____ Zip _____

Phone _____ Fax _____ E-mail Address _____

Thank you for your order!

Phone **1-800-278-3525**     Fax **1-515-284-2607**     Web **www.ablongman.com**

MPG002   AB10003-8

# THANK YOU
# FOR YOUR ORDER!

Please mail to:

Allyn & Bacon
Order Processing Department
P.O. Box 10695
Des Moines, IA 50381-0695

# INDEX